Neil and Me

BOOKS BY SCOTT YOUNG

NOVELS

The Flood (1956)
Face-Off, with George Robertson (1971)
That Old Gang of Mine (1982)
Murder in a Cold Climate (1988)
The Shaman's Knife (1993)

NONFICTION

Red Shield in Action: The Salvation Army in World War Two (1949)
HMCS, text for Gilbert Milne's war photos (1960)
Scott Young Sports Stories (1965)
The Leafs I Knew (1966)
Hockey Is A Battle, with Punch Imlach (1969)
Goodbye Argos, with Leo Cahill (1972)
O'Brien, biography of M.J. O'Brien, with Astrid Young (1973)
Silent Frank Cochrane, with Astrid Young (1973)
War On Ice (1976)
The Canada Cup of Hockey (1976)
Best Talk in Town, with Margaret Hogan (1980)
If You Can't Beat 'Em in the Alley: Conn Smythe Memoirs (1981)
Heaven and Hell in the NHL, with Punch Imlach (1982)
Neil and Me (1984, reissued 1997)
Hello Canada, biography of Foster Hewitt (1985)
Gordon Sinclair, A Life and Then Some (1987)
100 Years of Dropping the Puck (1989)
The Boys of Saturday Night (1990)
Power Play, with Alan Eagleson (1991)
A Writer's Life (1994)

FOR YOUNG READERS

Scrubs On Skates (1952, reissued 1985)
Boy On Defence (1953, reissued 1985)
Boy at the Leafs' Camp (1963, reissued 1985)
Big City Office Junior, with Astrid Young (1964)
The Clue of the Dead Duck (1962, reissued 1981)
Face-Off in Moscow (1989)

SHORT STORY COLLECTIONS

We Won't Be Needing You, Al (1968)
Home For Christmas (1989)

Neil and Me

Scott Young

Original hardcover edition published in 1984
Trade paperback edition published in 1985
Mass-market paperback edition published in 1986
Updated trade paperback edition published 1997

Canadian Cataloguing in Publication Data

Young, Scott, 1918–
  Neil and me

Updated ed.
ISBN 0-7710-9099-4

1. Young, Neil, 1945–   . 2. Young, Scott, 1918–   . 3. Rock musicians –
Canada – Biography. I. Title.

ML420.Y75Y76 1997   782.42166'092   C96-932532-0

The publishers acknowledge the support of the Canada Council and the Ontario Arts
Council for their publishing program.

Every reasonable effort has been made to contact copyright holders of material used
in this book. Any information regarding errors or omissions would be welcomed.

Typesetting by M&S, Toronto
Printed and bound in Canada

McClelland & Stewart Inc.
The Canadian Publishers
481 University Avenue
Toronto, Ontario
M5G 2E9

1 2 3 4 5 6   02 01 00 99 98 97

To the next generation

Contents

Acknowledgements   *ix*

1   A Few Days at Neil's Place   1
2   Where We Came From   6
3   Polio Was a Killer – and Neil Had It   20
4   Growing Up and Breaking Up   28
5   The "Cop with Heart" and the Squires   40
6   The Mynah Birds   49
7   Over the Border, Illegally   59
8   Buffalo Springfield, and Epilepsy   67
9   The Loner and Friends   80
10 Out of the Red and into the Black   88
11 Carnegie Hall   102
12 Interlude   106
13 A Sidetracked Journey Through the Past   115
14 Tonight's The Night   124
15 Goodbye to Carrie   138
16 Travelling Music   147

17 "There's more to my life than rock 'n' roll"   156
18 Pegi – and Rust Never Sleeps   166
19 A Bright Little Boy Named Ben   175
20 A Day Off – and Human Highway
    and Other Matters   186
21 Thinking About the Road Again,
    and Getting There   197
22 A Trip to Dallas   210
23 Five Concerts in September   219
24 I Just Couldn't Leave   238

Afterword to the 1997 Edition   247
Discography   266
Musical Family Tree   272

Acknowledgements

Besides the many illustrious sources quoted in the text, many thanks for information, advice, and help to Grahame Reed, Paul Makos, Andy Cox, Comrie Smith, Jack Harper, Mary Froman, *New Musical Express* editor Neil Spencer, *Toronto Life* editor Marq de Villiers, Elliot Mazer, Joel Bernstein, Shirley Wilson, Doris Adler, Peter Goddard, Steve Babineau, all the mighty roadies, and editors Jennifer Glossop (1984 and 1986 editions), and Peter Buck (this 1997 edition).

I

A Few Days at Neil's Place

He had been on his ranch about five years the first time I went to see him there. He'd asked me a couple of times but the distances were great and he had his life and I mine, so usually I saw him only when he was on tour and came to Toronto. In the middle 1970s he asked me again. Pegi was only on the edge of his consciousness then, their marriage three years away, and he was living a bachelor life after a brief marriage to Susan Acevedo in the late 1960s and an early 1970s relationship with actress Carrie Snodgress, which was almost as brief but in 1972 did produce their son Zeke, my first grandson. Maybe I had sounded down in a letter, or maybe he just wanted to be in closer contact again, because he called and said, "Any chance you can get out here for a while?"

The evening I arrived in San Francisco he was recording, so he sent a friend to meet me. We drove south into San Mateo County then turned off on the dark and narrow forest road into Neil's property. A few miles later I could see two distant tiny lights puncturing the surrounding night and then we were pulling up at the kitchen door of Neil's modest old house. When the engine stopped I could hear a piano playing, and when I walked in and he left the piano and embraced me

1

I could feel his thinness and the thoughts flashed of the roly-poly little boy he had been and then the gangling youth and now this man.

We hadn't seen one another for more than a year, and we had a beer or two and talked while he showed me around. It didn't take long. In the tiny, and only, bedroom his bed was set on a pedestal, close enough to a big pot-bellied woodstove that he could feed it without getting out of bed. Everything was well used and comfortable. The washstand outside his bedroom door held a porcelain basin old enough that it had no drain but was on a swivel that allowed it to be flipped over for emptying into a pail below. The living room had an old dining table and chairs, two pianos, a rocking chair, other old-fashioned furniture and lamps. In an hour or two, at bedtime, he took me into a room he'd added to the original house to hold speakers, turntables, and stereo equipment. A single bed stood in the middle of the floor. "Zeke'll be here tomorrow and this is his room," he said. "But you use it tonight." At the time Zeke, then three, was living in Los Angeles with Carrie but visited Neil often.

When I wakened early, Neil was still asleep. I roamed outside in the nearly total country silence of the sunny morning. By his house, set among great oaks, was a pond dotted with mallards, geese, coots, and other water birds. When I walked down the lane towards the low-slung verandahed house of his farm manager a hundred yards away, dogs barked. Barns and other well-worn farm buildings and corrals stood beyond. Bison grazed on steep slopes nearby, and I could also see herds of shaggy Highland cattle; he'd been trying to cross-breed them to get either the world's shaggiest buffalo or humped cattle, depending on the roll of the genes. A little later, after Neil made breakfast, we got my bags and he drove me across the ranch on a narrow winding road through giant redwoods and onto a 700-acre spread he'd bought not long before because it abutted his original 140 acres. Not letting someone else buy it was privacy insurance. Soon we swung left past some small houses and into a glen of towering redwoods through which a fast stream ran. At the bottom of the glen beside the stream was a sprawling white ranch house where coffee was on and people were moving around – Ralph Molina, Billy Talbot, and Frank Sampedro of Neil's band, Crazy Horse, and a few others including a young woman who normally worked as a Playboy bunny, the friend of a friend of Neil's not there at the moment. A slim and lively Armenian girl in her early twenties, Ellen Talbot, married to roadie John Talbot, lived nearby in what was called the Little Red House and, since everyone there was expected to pull weight, cooked and cleaned and shopped for the floating population, now including me, that lived in the ranch house. When I went shopping with Ellen in an old pick-up later she asked me if I had heard of a writer named William Saroyan. I said he was one of the heroes of my boyhood. "He's my uncle Willie," she said.

The next day I began a daily ritual, often thinking how different this place was from most common conceptions of a rock star's life. I sometimes cooked. I spent a lot of time with Zeke, a cheerful fair-haired little boy who limped along in a leg brace because of the effects of cerebral palsy. Neil would feed him breakfast and bring him to the recording studio set in another redwood clearing. There, Neil also had built a large outdoor stage that he used to plan stage positions when he was preparing for the road. When the musicians were deeply into it and Zeke got restless, we'd walk up for a swim in Neil's pool on a hill behind his house. If Zeke tired of walking in his brace and said "Carry me, Grandpa," I'd take him on my shoulders. Neil said, "You two remind me of when Granddad came to stay with us in Omemee. I never let him out of my sight." I had almost forgotten that long-ago visit of my father's but it gave extra meaning to now.

At night, after dinner at the ranch house, Neil and the others often would sit in the kitchen on wooden chairs, playing and singing a little. "Try this," Neil would say, or someone else would say, and the music would go on for a few intricate or simple passages and then they'd break and discuss and go on. It was an easy and unhurried kind of life.

One morning he came along through the redwoods in his pick-up and said he was driving over to see a friend and would I like to come along. We headed off the ranch over miles of winding narrow road and were chatting idly when I happened to mention the number of times I was approached by television, radio, magazine, or newspaper people either to talk or to write about him. They couldn't get to him so they would try to do it through me. I imagine they thought of me as a proud father who would be happy to bask in reflected fame and let little tidbits of his life drop. I turned them all down because in most aspects of his life Neil stays away from media and tries to keep his offstage life private. Obviously such approaches were attempts to pierce his privacy through me. As a writer myself I know the techniques, and even invented some of them. So apart from a profoundly impressed column I wrote about his first Carnegie Hall concert and a few other newspaper mentions, I had consciously avoided exploiting our relationship. The only exploitation had been unconscious: the extra credence given my writing by some people, especially those much younger than I am, on the grounds that anyone who was Neil Young's father couldn't be all bad. Anyway, I told him that, despite my rejection of these advances, sometimes I was tempted to write about our original family relationship for my own purposes, to help me figure some things out, to come face to face with myself and my part in breaking up our home.

We were driving on a hillside road, with scrub slanting up steeply at one side and dropping off sharply on the other. He thought for a moment or two, then glanced at me sideways and said, "Well, it's your life too, you know, Daddy."

That day when I listened to him telling me what was plainly a fact – that it *was* my life too, you know – I did nothing about it. It was five years, in the summer of 1980, after his marriage to Pegi and the birth of their son Ben, before I finally decided to go ahead with my version of our earlier life and hard times. What triggered it, really, was that in letters a few days apart, *Reader's Digest* and *Toronto Life* (a big and glossy regional magazine) both asked me to write about Neil. *Toronto Life's* offer of unlimited space attracted me. It was something the *Digest*, by its very nature, was not likely to match. Anyway I thought *Toronto Life* was more suited to the kind of account I was beginning to think about (i.e., not exactly inspirational). I didn't want to be cramped for space or confined in direction while trying to beat my way through to some kind of truth about myself and the way I had affected the lives of Rassy, my first wife, and our sons, Bob and Neil.

In many ways the next few days were very painful and yet also joyous and liberating. I would write about an event, a feeling, a crisis, maybe one of the darker things I'd done, in terms I had been using for years more or less superficially whenever I felt obliged to explain this or that about my first marriage. Then I would read it and think, goddamn it, that's not true, or at least not precisely true. I would revise. I would go and walk in the woods to rest and remember, and come back and write. I sometimes drove to Omemee (population 750) to buy a paper or a bottle of rum. Passing the big red brick house on the main street where we'd lived, made love, been sick, whatever, I would remember a lot of good times and some bad. Crossing the old Mill Bridge I thought of Neil fishing there when he was only four or

five, Bob skating and playing hockey on the mill pond in winter, the
gradual dissolution of what had been love into tears (sometimes mine)
of despair. Then I would drive home and try to make each line count
for truth. I wrote from early morning to late at night for three days as
if a dam had broken.

The result was very instructive to me. In addition to showing me a
good deal about myself that I had not always faced before, the account
told me that all I really knew of Neil was his first nearly fourteen years
before his mother and I split. I knew little about his next four years
when he was in Winnipeg with his mother and I rarely saw him. There
had been a good few months in 1965 that we had spent together when
he was nineteen, turning twenty, and trying without success to make it
as a musician in Toronto. But I knew very little in a first-hand way of
his life after 1966 when he and bassist Bruce Palmer sold everything
they had and (in Neil's phrase) "some things we didn't have," and with
a few friends headed for California. In an incredibly short time after
that he was a name everywhere rock music is played. Five-dollar seats
were scalped for a hundred dollars when he sold out Carnegie Hall.
Twenty-thousand-seat arenas weren't big enough to hold the people
who wanted in. All albums sold in hundreds of thousands around the
world, some in millions. *Rolling Stone*, *Time*, *Newsweek*, *The New York
Times* at various times called him the dominant figure in pop music.
And now it was 1980 and he was known from Tokyo to Oslo and was
still my son, and Rassy's.

I sent him a copy of what I had written. He telephoned me a few
days later. He and Pegi had read it in bed the night before. He said,
"We laughed and we cried. There are so many things in there that I
never knew before." What child does know the inner life of his
parents? I began to think of *finding out* about the areas of his life I had
not been a part of, and about writing this book. I will spare you an
exact accounting of the times I went to bed thinking I would do it,
then woke in the middle of the night thinking, "Are you crazy?" Yet I
felt that even the millions of words that have been written about him
have not been able to touch what I have a particular knowledge of.

2

Where We Came From

In writing the so-called "lives" of legendary members of Neil's genre it is fairly common practice to look for roots; the how and why of Elvis Presley, Janis Joplin, Jimi Hendrix, the Beatles, the Rolling Stones, and others of that stature. Certainly Neil's mother, Rassy, put great energy and devotion into supporting his earliest attempts. I have an inkling of what fuelled Rassy besides her characteristic loyalty to those she loved. Her love of great singers, whether on the stage, in films, or on records, was by far the greatest part of her interest in any of the arts. When we were very young in our marriage, she told me once that she would give anything to sing like Amelita Galli-Curci. I don't know how many times she saw such movies as *The Great Waltz* and *The Glass Mountain*. She loved the bittersweetness of *Porgy and Bess*, *Carmen* (and *Carmen Jones*), and others I have forgotten. The song from *Porgy and Bess*, "Summertime," could bring tears to her eyes. We played the complete score often and saw it produced both on film and on the stage.

Her ambition for Neil when he began to write, play, and sing therefore came from deeply held emotions. I recognize this and yet feel that such one-on-one encouragement cannot be credited more than partially and in a preliminary way for his role in an art that reaches across barriers of nationality and language as rock music does; the tapes that Russian kids make from Polish rock stations and trade back and forth; the jukeboxes that sound the same in Milan, Tokyo, London, or Flin Flon, Manitoba. Backing up Rassy's powerful early support was a background that Neil knew nothing of until much later in his life. I sketch it here freehand in terms not only of music, and love of music, but in inherited ability to communicate through music; and sometimes in terms of unorthodox behaviour.

The traces are there in both sets of Neil's bloodlines, going back as far as both of his great-grandfathers on my side of the family. My mother's father, Robert Paterson, a better-than-average church tenor, was a tall and hawk-nosed Presbyterian spell-binder who worked his way through college theology in western Canada of the 1890s by playing semi-pro baseball. He had charisma. In the Canadian general election of 1908, he ran as a Liberal for the House of Commons and lost – but to beat him it took Arthur Meighen, a brilliant Conservative who was to become his party's leader and Canadian prime minister twelve years later. Unusually for a preacher, he bred and trained fast horses that he would race against all comers on the streets of Neepawa, Manitoba, when he had a church there. (He also had huge ears, which he could wiggle, and did so scoldingly when the choir behind his pulpit whispered or shuffled during his sermon.) In the 1920s his restiveness with the middle-of-the-road (like Neil's much later) caused him to quit a big church in Brandon, Manitoba, to hook up with an evangelistic faith healer named Dr. Price for year-long revivalist tours of the southern United States. Handicapped people flocked to the stage to be touched, and left stacks of discarded crutches and ear trumpets behind; not bad for a rock performer to have in his ancestry.

My father's father, John Young, a short and bristly pioneer who walked the last hundred miles from the Winnipeg railhead to homestead in southern Manitoba around 1878, was known as one of the great country fiddlers of his time and place. Until Neil, three-quarters of a century later, he was also the family's most arresting gleaner of the world's goods. His first home, a hundred miles from Winnipeg, was a sod shack to which he brought his seventeen-year-old bride by horse and buggy, on the final night carrying her on his shoulders through chin-deep water across the last dark slough. From there he developed an acquisitive streak which did not make him a multimillionaire like Neil, but did make him a very rich farmer with seven sons, two daughters, more than 2,500 acres of wheat land, the latest steam and oil tractors of the time, thoroughbred Clydesdale workhorses and Aberdeen Angus cattle that he raised from breeding stock he imported from Scotland, and a Pierce-Arrow automobile, which after his death in the 1920s was sold to an undertaker and converted into a hearse.

In the next generation on both sides of my family came singers and banjo-players, country fiddlers, pianists and organists (my mother), great step-dancers (my father among them), and then in the following generation (my own), more than a dozen individuals who could play anything they got their hands on – banjos, guitars, harmonicas, ukuleles, jew's-harps, mandolins, pianos, violins. My younger brother Bob (bass fiddle, piano, clarinet, banjo, uke) was one of them. Born in a later generation he certainly could have been a professional entertainer instead of finding his audiences in hard-drinking press-clubs when he was on the road as a corporate public-relations man. My sister, Dorothy, has a fine voice with tremendous range. She adjudicates local music festivals semi-professionally and has produced, directed, and acted in first-rate amateur musicals (from *The Pirates of Penzance* to *Guys and Dolls*) while bearing and raising six children.

Back in the days when I used to work summers on my uncle Herb's farm in the early dirty '30s, his family of wall-to-wall musicians gathered around the piano almost every night to play and sing. One summer they ordered from Eaton's catalogue a box of 500 pieces of sheet music – five dollars for 500 songs, one cent per song in a stupendous variety of remaindered non-hits from Tin Pan Alley. "They call the lady Louisville Lou, oh what that vampin' baby can do" – I remember nights we belted out "Louisville Lou" and other failed songs that nobody else ever heard of, four or five instruments going, including a cello that was kept under a folding couch. Everybody sang, with Aunt Beatrice in the middle hammering out a strong ragtime piano by the light of a coal-oil lamp. On those nights I was the only one who, apart from getting in a few chords on a ukulele, was not a real musician. Some of my cousins and my brother and mother were later regulars in dancebands, with occasional appearances on Manitoba television.

I simply do not know as much about Rassy's family in this regard, but she was a sharp and witty network TV panelist for years after our divorce. One sister, Lavinia (known in the family as Aunt Toots), is an excellent writer and broadcaster of humorous sketches as Vinia Hoogstraten, her married name. Another sister, Virginia Ridgway, spent much of her adult life in Texas as a writer and publicist.

As to other family characteristics, Neil's manager since 1968, Elliot Roberts, once laughed when I told him I had recently bought some land, and added more or less earnestly that if I had the money I'd become the biggest owner of cedar swamp in Ontario. "I've often wondered where Neil got his acquisitive streak from," Elliot said. He had first encountered it, he said, when he negotiated Neil's first contract for a solo album, the advance – a strange sum, I think $17,000 – being what Neil said he needed to buy a house he'd found in the Los Angeles area's Topanga Canyon. Elliot considered this an unusual kind of aim for a rock musician who at the time did not even have his first Rolls-Royce. Neil has explained buying the house, in retrospect, as being part of his need to have something solid, a core to come back to at night.

Taken at face value, that relates as well to my own early and unsettled years. My mother and father broke up when I was twelve, breaking up then being at least as hard as it is now. Mother was the musically talented and sometimes reckless daughter of the Presbyterian minister I mentioned. Dad, born on Grandpa Young's farm, was short, dark and handsome, likable, kindly, a well-loved man. When I was born in 1918 – and a few months later narrowly survived the influenza epidemic that killed tens of thousands – Dad owned a drugstore in Glenboro, Manitoba. When I was eight, he went broke – mainly, a lawyer uncle told me later, because he gave too much credit and hated dunning people for money. He moved us to Winnipeg where he had found a good job in the drug department of a big new Hudson's Bay Company store.

Early in the Depression, oppressed by pressure at work and his worsening marriage, he quit his job – a mortal sin in those out-of-work days when any job was automatically considered to be good. After that he couldn't find steady work of any kind so he headed north into Manitoba's new mining camps. Our small (it didn't seem small then) house on Parkview Street in St. James, a Winnipeg suburb, went for lack of rent money. My sister, then only five, and brother, ten, and I, twelve, were farmed out to relatives for a year.

The uncle and aunt in Prince Albert, Saskatchewan, who took me in were not geared to handling a boy, or at least a boy like me. Their only child, a daughter, had died tragically after a school accident a year or so earlier, at seventeen. I simply did not measure up to the idealized Marie of their memories, but cannot remember any feeling of being rejected – it was just that my aunt Mary was tough enough to recognize that I was complicating their lives unduly. My brother and sister did not fare much better. A year later my mother, jobless and untrained (except that she had taught school before her marriage and sometimes found part-time work as a substitute pianist in theatres showing the last of the silent movies), gathered us together again.

At first four of us lived together in a small room in downtown Winnipeg. We were on what then was called relief, now called welfare or (more genteelly) social assistance. People then on relief, though in the tens of thousands, were ashamed of it so I didn't know at the time how much relief Mother drew. Later I learned that the going rate at the time was $5.62 a week for a family of four, which was us.

However, Mother in her thirties was a bright and good-looking woman (still was, into her late eighties as this was written; her longevity is something Neil values, he has told me, as he hopes to live long himself). She was attractive to men. Sometimes she went to lively parties in a beat-up apartment not far from our single room. The apartment was shared by several bachelor bank clerks. One of them, Pete LeSeach, a dashing extrovert who had come to Canada from France as a child, had boarded with us before our home broke up. He and Mother were fond of one another and became lovers. On one of those cheerful party nights she made a deal. The bachelors were terrible housekeepers. She would find a nice, clean apartment in a good district. Pete and two of the other "bank boys," as we called them, would live with us.

They did, paying thirty-five dollars a month each for board, room, and laundry. In that two-bedroom apartment on Stradbrooke Avenue the three boarders shared one small bedroom: one double bed, one single. Their rent supported the four Youngs, three of us in an even smaller bedroom: a double bed for Mother and sister Dorothy, a cot for me. My brother Bob slept on the living-room couch, when he got home at all. He sometimes slept in a riding stable where he worked after school, and at fifteen he quit school to work in a mine. But we got by. Only the landlord, it turned out eventually, went short as Mother fell behind in the rent.

The bankers were required to wear white shirts to work. Mother ironed twenty-one white shirts in our tiny kitchen every Saturday morning. Under the stove in a big butter crock she and our lively red-haired neighbour from downstairs, Flora Britton, usually had going a popular Depression home-brew known in polite circles as potato champagne. Mother called it Drāno. My brother and I ironed sheets and other flat stuff each Saturday on a big machine called a mangle in the building's dungeon-like laundry and furnace room. My sister and I often played on the grassy boulevard after supper with a rubber ball, as she had few other playmates nearby. I don't remember being lonely, but she does. I sometimes wore the bankers' cast-off clothes, which was noted unkindly by my mainly affluent high-school classmates. I had no cash allowance. Sometimes when Mother gave me money and a grocery list, I would pack a thirty-five-cent pound of butter or other relatively costly items low in a bag of potatoes (two cents a pound) to swindle for myself a little money to take a girl named Betty McKenzie to the movies.

By then in Flin Flon, 560 miles to the north, Dad was driving a team of horses that pulled a water wagon through the rock-bound mining settlement on a regular route, selling water to housewives at ten cents a pail. Every few months he sent Mother ten dollars. Once he sent me a suit at Christmas. I couldn't believe how well it fitted. At his request, Mother had sent him my measurements. Those at school who usually saw me in hand-me-downs were amazed. "Hey, Young, where'd you get the suit?" I told them my father had sent it. Earlier I had told them he was a chemist with a big northern mining company, which they had properly treated as a lie, but now they were thrown at least slightly off-balance. Come to think of it, I also had told some of them that I was part-Indian, which they tended to believe because of my high cheekbones.

Rassy's parents had very different backgrounds. Her mother was an American of French ancestry. A beautiful dark-haired young woman, she had worked for the Grand Trunk Railway around Sault Ste. Marie. Rassy's father, Bill Ragland, was to become one of the very favourite men of my life and of Neil's. Neil's ocean-going yacht is named the *W.N. Ragland*, after him. He was born in the late 1880s on a plantation near Petersburg, Virginia, to an old southern family by then living mainly on its past. When his father died and left little but debt, Bill Ragland quit Virginia Military Institute at age seventeen to get a job on the New York Bowery. A friend of the family directed him there. He sent home almost all he earned for the next few years to keep his three sisters at Sweet Brier Academy, where southern young ladies of the time went to school. For this, his sisters – one moved to Virginia Beach after marriage, another to Richmond, Virginia – revered him for life, but he saw it simply as his duty. I loved him for different reasons forty or fifty years later as we drank rye whiskey and shot ducks together in the 1950s, criss-crossing the prairie back roads in his company Ford. His employer, Barrett Roofing, had moved him to Manitoba in 1908. Soon, still in his twenties, he was managing the company's operations in western Canada. He liked the prairies so much that he stayed for life, retaining his U.S. citizenship, but turning down dozens of offers to move up in the company. He would do anything that did not involve leaving Manitoba, and he never did. Long before I met him, when we were on relief, Bill Ragland always had a good job, a good home, played bridge and poker at his club, and doted on his three bright and attractive daughters, Lavinia, Virginia, and Edna. When Edna was a black-haired baby he used to call her Rastus, which she shortened to Rassy and kept for life. She was the youngest and the apple of his eye. Years later, when people trying to get to Neil claimed to be related to him, Neil's people would run this check: "If you're related to him, what's his mother's name?" If the answer was "Rassy," that was the accepted password.

I finished high school at sixteen, got a job as a cashier for a tobacco wholesaler at eight dollars a week, five days from eight A.M. to six P.M., Saturdays from seven to two. I paid my mother five dollars a week board and room, and after the first happy flush of having some money in my pocket wore off, I knew I had to find some way to make a living other than counting money and cigars. As a boy I had idolized my uncle, Jack Paterson, a freelance writer who led an adventurous life flying around northern Canada and writing articles and fiction, including for the *Saturday Evening Post*. There was often a fair amount of fiction technique in his colourful articles about northern trappers, railroaders, dog-team drivers, or whatever, and a good deal of fact in his short stories about hard-fisted loggers and their girls. Also, my best friend in those days was a newspaper copyboy of my own age, Jeff Hurley, who had sold to *Poetry* magazine in Chicago and soon was writing radio plays, among them one bought by CBS in New York. Once when we needed money to take some girls out, Jeff wrote four poems in one night and sold them for $1.50 each to the *Winnipeg Free Press*, where he worked. The six dollars paid for our date. He had much more talent than I but I ignored that, borrowed four dollars from the petty cash at the tobacco whole-sale, used it as down payment on a typewriter, and started to write.

For the next few years it was a bad night when I didn't finish a story or poem or sketch that would go out by mail to *Esquire* or the old "Post-scripts" section of the *Saturday Evening Post*, and promptly come back – my big thrills coming not in cheques, but when something came back with a sign that someone, a real person, had seen it. One note I kept for years was from Arnold Gingrich at *Esquire*. Never mind that the note said only "Not for us. AG." Something I wrote got as far as *Esquire's* final arbiter, Arnold Gingrich! In a couple of years, at eighteen, I sold a story for three dollars which landed me a copyboy's job on the *Winnipeg Free Press*. In a few weeks I began writing sports, and the next summer met Rassy, a good tennis player and golfer and an all-round noticeable young woman.

We were both twenty-two in June of 1940 when we married. We lived well enough (a couple could in those days) on my twenty-five dollars a week, paying $37.50 a month for a furnished bachelor apart-ment that I had shared earlier with two friends, Paris Eakins and Mark McClung, for a year or two and therefore had been rather mangy until it was transformed, totally redecorated, as a surprise for us by Rassy's mother and sister Toots when we were away for a few days on our honeymoon.

The Second World War was on then. I had tried at the outset, before my marriage, to join the navy but hadn't tried the other services. I've thought about that since and have come to certain tentative conclu-sions about my lack of an overpowering urge to follow a lot of my friends into uniform. It wasn't that I had any more than the normal dis-taste for getting bumped off on some foreign field. But for the first time in years I felt settled, secure, with a core to my life, and I didn't want to leave it just yet. Anyway, after that first attempt to enlist in the navy, which couldn't handle all those who volunteered in the first weeks of the war, I did not try again for quite a while.

In 1940 when the managing editor of the *Free Press* turned down my request for more money to support my new marriage, I sought and got a job with the Canadian Press news agency in Toronto. In 1942, our son Bob was born. When he was five months old, CP sent me to England to help cover the war for Canadian papers. From then until war's end Rassy and I were apart most of the time. I came back after a year and joined the navy as an ordinary seaman, then was gone again.

Early in 1945, by then a sub-lieutenant, I was home on leave. I know the exact time when Neil was conceived. I remember the street in Toronto, the wild February blizzard through which only the hardiest moved, on skis, sliding downtown through otherwise empty streets to otherwise empty offices. All trains were marooned or cancelled, meaning that Rassy and I and Bob, then nearly three years old, had to postpone leaving for Newfoundland, where I had just been posted by the navy. We were spending the day with close friends, Ian and Lola Munro, on a street, Soudan, that then was considered fairly far out and now is practically downtown. When the storm started, a mattress was hauled down to the dining-room floor and shoved against the wall for Rassy and me. We were just past our middle twenties and had been apart for most of the previous year while I was on corvettes, landing ships, and motor torpedo boats in England, Normandy, the invasion of southern France, Italy, Yugoslavia, and Greece. We were healthy young people, much in love, apart too much. It was a small house and when we made love that night we tried to be fairly quiet, and perhaps were. A few months later when the war in Europe ended I volunteered for the Pacific war and was in Toronto on Pacific leave when the bombs were dropped on Hiroshima and Nagasaki and it was all over. In a few weeks I was released from the service.

Then came what was in retrospect an important instruction in life; or at least I made it so. Living space was very hard to come by. Rassy and I went from place to place where apartments had been advertised. The landlord or rental agent would take a look at Bob, then a lively three, and at Rassy, pregnant with Neil, and turn us away. It seemed nobody wanted to rent to people with children. We decided we would have to buy a house. We had no money. Rassy said she was sure her father would lend us the $500 we needed for a down payment, and wrote to ask. She was shattered when he replied in a four- or five-line letter that he felt people should stand on their own feet, and were better off in the long run for doing so. I was not shattered because I had hated to have her ask him in the first place; I have always hated being obligated to anyone for anything.

When I went to a bank to arrange a loan, I was back working at Canadian Press. The general manager, Gillis Purcell, who had lost a leg early in the war, looked upon his former overseas correspondents almost as if we were his sons. He made almost daily checks on how these favourites of his were picking up their lives. When I told him that I was going to borrow the down payment for a house, without telling me he put up a savings bond that got me a low rate of interest. We bought a three-bedroom bungalow and moved in gratefully, getting our meagre furniture out of storage, buying what else we needed on the instalment plan. A week or two less than nine months after Rassy and I had spent that loving night in the February blizzard conceiving Neil, she had labour pains. We had no car but a kindly paint salesman who lived next door, Lloyd Zerbrigg, drove us downtown to Toronto General Hospital. Rassy had had a terribly long labour of forty-eight hours with Bob. It ended only when she stood on a toilet seat at another Toronto hospital on April 27, 1942, and jumped off to hurry things along, which it did. Neil came much more easily. Early in the morning of November 12, 1945, a call to me at home reported that Rassy and our new son were doing well.

I remember nothing of my first sight of Neil, except that he had a lot of black hair, as black as Rassy's, and that she, my girl, was pale but still made a joke or two while I sat by her bed and we held hands. The offices of *Maclean's* magazine, where I had started as an assistant editor two weeks earlier, were only a couple of minutes' walk away, so in the next few days before Rassy and Neil came home I could get in to see her often.

I think I was a good enough husband and father, then. From that three-bedroom bungalow at 335 (now numbered 315) Brooke Avenue in north Toronto, I took buses and streetcars to work, a trip of about an hour twice a day, including Saturdays. Bob and Neil shared a bedroom because I had taken over the smallest of the three and was trying at night to write short stories to supplement the $4,000 a year I was getting as a *Maclean's* assistant editor. We sodded the back yard to make a lawn where Bob and I played ball and, in a year or two, Neil toddled around pushing a little wheelbarrow. He was a very fat child, mostly because he ate everything he could reach. He never cried unless he was hurt. He never had nightmares or made a noise in the morning until he heard others stirring. His first word was "dombeen," which meant pudding, celery, pablum, porridge, and numerous other things he would point at while saying, encouragingly, "dombeen." In his playpen, when the record-player or radio was on, he would jig to Dixieland music even before he could stand up by himself. His whole body moved to the rhythm; it was his unconscious parlour trick.

Rassy typed my stories. They started to sell, first in Canada (for $200 each) and then the United States (eventually for up to $1,500). We got out of debt. In 1947, when that great milestone of no debts was reached, we spent what was left over, $330, on our first car, a 1931 Willys-Knight, in which Rassy drove me to work with Bob and Neil in the back seat, along for the ride. The Willys-Knight used one quart of oil for every gallon of gasoline. I had never learned to drive, and Rassy would say, "This tractor isn't the one to learn in." Rassy's general rule of thumb was that if the cloud of oil smoke behind the car thinned to the point where she could see a car following, we needed oil. A vivid woman with flashing brown eyes to go with her black hair, she usually gave back as good as she got when others made fun of our car. The only time I saw her stumped was once in downtown Toronto when a cab pulled up through our cloud of smoke and stopped alongside. The driver leaned out and said, "What do you burn in that thing, lady, soft coal?"

In the spring of 1948, when I was thirty and had sold fiction to the *Saturday Evening Post* and *Women's Home Companion* and *American Magazine* (soon *Collier's* was to become my best market), we bought a new car, which I learned to drive. I quit my job at *Maclean's* to write fiction full time. We sold our house to get capital and the four of us had a wonderful summer at a place we rented a hundred miles or so north of Toronto, a remote waterfront log house on the Lake of Bays. We fished and swam and I wrote stories that didn't sell. Neil and Bob were in the water every day, at first always in life jackets in a little sandy cove whose bottom I cleared of stones. Friends often came to visit, most of them writers and editors from Toronto. Once when a bunch of youngsters was playing tag and Neil wasn't wearing his life jacket, in the excitement he slipped off the end of a dock into deep water with no adult within shouting distance. The oldest child in the group was the young actress Beryl Braithwaite, daughter of writer Max Braithwaite and his wife Aileen. Beryl was famous in Canada then as the lead in a children's radio program called *Maggie Muggins*, and she also happened to be a good swimmer. She jumped in fully clothed and saved Neil from drowning. He was not quite three at the time.

At the end of that summer when the cottage was so cold in the morning that even roaring fires in the box stove wouldn't warm it up, we loaded the car and left the Lake of Bays. I hadn't sold a story all summer, hadn't made a nickel, but it was still a fine time, the best of my life up to then. We found a house to rent in another small Ontario town, Jackson's Point, a resort village on Lake Simcoe closer to Toronto. The house, big and frigid, had a big cook stove behind which slept our cat, Mary, and Bob's dog, Skippy, a cross between a golden Labrador and a Dalmatian which we referred to as a plainclothes police dog. At six, Bob got his first bicycle, and was in grade one at school.

That winter and spring I looked for a place to buy under a government land-settlement plan for ex-servicemen called the Veterans' Land Act, and finally found one in an Ontario village I'd never seen before but liked immediately, Omemee. A fairly good fishing river ran through the village into a nearby lake. An old mill still used water power. An old lady named Mrs. Haygarth sold us her house, a big red brick place built around the turn of the century. It had some apple trees and two privies, one outside and one in a back shed (fewer snowdrifts for the old lady to handle in winter).

I used to tell Neil about the apple trees and the nice house and the beautiful life that would await us in Omemee. I must have made the point rather strongly. That summer, before actually moving to Omemee, we drove west to stay with Rassy's parents in Manitoba on a lake at Whiteshell. It was a three-day drive. Neil sat in the back with Bob, Skippy, Mary, and Mary's four tiny kittens. At that time Neil, not quite four, could talk quite well, except that he couldn't pronounce the word "the," always rendering it as "le." On the second day, after peering hopefully out of the front window for about 800 miles, Neil finally said to me, "Hey, Daddy, where in le heck is Omemee?"

When we moved to Omemee in late August so that Bob could enrol at school, Neil for the first time had a room of his own. Each night either Rassy or I would read him a chapter from a Thornton W. Burgess book about Chatterer the Red Squirrel and Jimmy Skunk and Blacky the Crow and the Merry Little Breezes, the same books we'd read to Bob a few years earlier. Omemee life was great for kids. Neil had a sandbox always full of turtles he found, which kept escaping. He ate the apples that fell from the trees. Bigger kids pulled him in their wagons, once so fast that he crashed and lost half of one of his first permanent teeth. We went tobogganing.

The nearest city was Peterborough. Robertson Davies, the novelist and playwright, was editor of the Peterborough *Examiner* at the time. Once Neil and Robertson Davies shared a toboggan on the snowy hills nearby. On an occasional summer weekend he paddled, and sometimes piddled, in the little river, the Humber, that started around Kleinburg and ran down a gully between the homes of writer Pierre Berton and his wife Janet on one side, and writer-playwright-broadcaster Lister Sinclair, then married to the beautiful actress Alice Mather, on the other.

Neil was always known as Neiler in those days. While the adults sat and drank or flirted, or both, on the banks, the kids played in the water. Twenty years or so later when Neil was becoming famous, the only full-scale television interview he agreed to take part in at that time was on Pierre Berton's show – because long ago Neil Young was young Neiler, and Pierre Berton a young writer from the Pacific coast whose best-selling books and broadcasting fame in Canada were still years away. One question Pierre asked Neil was how he felt to be making more money than his father (which wasn't all that difficult) – not realizing that some day quite soon Neil would be making infinitely more money than even Berton, amazing as that might have seemed at the time. But anyway, playing outdoors at the Bertons, or indoors at the Davies home in Peterborough on winter nights when kids and adults alike played word games and turn-out-all-the-lights-and-hide games, with shrieks and giggles and a certain amount of wit, who knows what influences were at work on the little boy with the unruly thatch of black hair that stuck up every which way, always being too short to lie down.

In the mid-1970s, twenty-five years after those times, Neil told John Rockwell of *The New York Times* that he learned his independence from me. I was grateful for the compliment, of course, but would share it with his mother who never once said, or even hinted, that the uncertain life of a freelance writer bothered her. She was as fiercely protective of me as she was of Bob and Neil, and would verbally tear to shreds anyone who said a word against any of us, or her father, or her sisters, or anyone she loved. She was still like that for many years, with a shorter list no longer including me.

For most of Neil's childhood we lived the boom-or-bust life of trying to make a living from my fiction. Only in the direst circumstances would I give in and write a magazine article, with its sure paycheque. I remember once in Omemee when Neil was eight or nine. I was $3,000 in the hole at the Bank of Toronto branch there when I sold a story for

$3,500 that, as I remarked after walking across the street from the post office to the bank, would just cover my overdraft. Neil probably wasn't aware of such details, but must have been aware of the creed I clung to then. I said it often enough. People would say, "Doesn't it bother you when a story gets turned down by an editor?" I would reply (perhaps pompously, but never mind that), "What I do in a story is the best I can with the idea I have," an aim once echoed, about poetry, by Robert Lowell. The only way I could keep on doing that was to believe that any editor who didn't like a story of mine had to be a mental case. I could back that up with the experience of a few stories that were rejected by twenty magazines and then sold not only in North America but also in second rights and translation rights to several countries in Europe, including, eventually, the Soviet Union. I would talk about writing with Bob or Neil if they wanted to. I'm sure they often overheard me telling other adults that when I tried to write a commercial story, sometimes it would sell and sometimes not. But every time I wrote one for myself alone, it would sell – lead stories in the *Saturday Evening Post, Collier's*, almost all the big-paying U.S. magazines of the time. The stories of mine that are still to be found in anthologies are those that might have broken the so-called formula pattern of the magazines of the time, but were written from the heart. I tried to represent myself as always trying to do my best work, whether it pleased others or not. As many people do, I was thus attributing to myself the qualities I *wished* I had, in the hope that at least sometimes I would live up to them.

Did my rejection of the importance of being standardized, my insistence on being true to myself despite the many flaws my own true self might exhibit, translate into Neil's insistence on taking his own course in music and to hell with anyone who disagreed? Or is that genetic, or a mere coincidence? I do not know. His fans think of him as a great singer, performer, and composer. His music does speak clearly and poignantly to me. But the real basis of his worldwide reputation is what he says in the spare poetry of his songs. He told me once that he learned from me that the most vivid way to get an idea across was to lay oneself bare in the knowledge that others would identify with the bareness, the sometimes painful truth.

3

Polio Was a Killer – and Neil Had It

You have to be a certain age to remember the polio epidemic in the late summer of 1951, before there was Salk vaccine to control the disease. In Omemee, as elsewhere in Canada, the headlines every day gave the statistics, usually using the phrase "infantile paralysis" because the killer disease most often struck the young. News reports explained the different types. One form could kill a person in a few hours. Another could result in paralysis and leave a person crippled for life. People that August stayed away from fairs and exhibitions and were urged to avoid mingling in crowds anywhere. In cities the ultra-cautious walked instead of taking streetcars, and kept their distance from everyone else. City or country, the fearful woke in the night wondering if that back pain was the polio back pain, or that sore throat was the polio sore throat. There was, however, no polio in Omemee as the summer wore on into early September and the ducks began to flock up on the lake and partridges in farm wood lots began to feed in late afternoons under the apple and hawthorn trees.

Then Omemee did have its first case, and ten days later in September I went up to my third-floor study and wrote something, not for sale, but just so I would remember. It sat in my files for nearly thirty years, unpublished. Here it is, exactly as written in 1951:

The night that polio first made my younger son groan sleepily in his bed, I was reading. It was past one o'clock and I was the only one awake in the house. I waited for a minute or two after the first sound I heard from Neil's room. He seemed to be mumbling to himself. I got out of bed, trying not to disturb my wife, and opened his door. In the dim light that shone across the hall from my reading light I could see that he had squinched (as he called it) down to about the middle of his bed, as usual, and that he was awake.

"What's the matter, pally?" I asked.

"Nothing," he said. He's a noisy enough kid in the daytime, but at night, or when he is sleepy, he has a soft, clear voice and always is very polite. He is five years old.

"Want to go to the toilet?"

"No, thank you."

I went over to the side of his bed and started to tuck the covers around his neck and he said, with sort of a protesting whine, "Hey!"

"What's the matter?"

"My back hurts."

I touched his forehead and he seemed a little too hot. "Where?" I asked.

He reached around exploringly with his left hand and indicated the middle of his back. But when I touched him there, he said no, it was over farther. Finally we settled on his right shoulder blade. I noticed in the dim light that there were tears in the corners of his eyes. He had a round, tanned face; a crew cut, very big eyes.

"Did you fall and hurt yourself today?" I asked.

"No."

"Bang it on anything?"

"No."

I stood by his bed for a minute. As parents know, we all live with the word *polio* for months every year. I got an aspirin and some water and he moved very gingerly when he sat up to take the pill, but he took it.

"Good night, pal," I said from the doorway.

"Good night. See you in the morning," he said in his small, formal night voice.

I went along the hall for a minute and listened outside Bob's door. Bob is nine. He was sleeping peacefully. I looked out at the village street. It is very quiet in the country at night. Just seven or eight hours earlier, Neil and I had been at the village swimming hole together and he'd had a great time riding on my stomach while I swam on my back across the river. I seem to pray a lot more easily in the polio season than at other times of the year. Quite often I'd been one of God's requestmen in the middle of the night when my wife or one of our boys was sick. So I was one of His requestmen again, there at the window, before I went back to bed.

Rassy stirred and said, "What's the matter?"

"Neil's a little restless," I said. "I gave him aspirin."

He was quiet the rest of the night. I was up first in the morning, still the cook because my wife was just about three days out of hospital, where she'd had a minor operation. She said she'd come down. I went along the hall to call Bob and paused when I heard Neil's voice.

"I don't want any breakfast," he said.

I opened his door. "How's your back?"

"It hurts."

I got a thermometer and took his temperature. It was 100°F. Downstairs, while the coffee water boiled, I got some honey in a dish, and a spoon. Neil has a tendency to acidosis, which complicates every illness he has. He protested, but not too much. He took three teaspoons of honey. That, or syrup, or anything sweet, fights acidosis. Then I closed his door. Downstairs I told Rassy his symptoms and his temperature. Neither of us said the word we both were thinking, because so often before we'd been scared by false alarms.

"We'd better phone Bill," she said.

Bill Earle is our doctor, known in the village as Dr. Bill to distinguish him from his father, Dr. George. I phoned him at his summer cottage twenty miles north. He came a little before noon. I was out. When I got back I asked Rassy, "How's Neil?"

She was very pale. Her face sort of broke up when she started to cry. "Bill thinks he's got it," she said. She said a minute or two later, into my shoulder, "He's coming back about four." She told me that Neil couldn't touch his chin to his chest, and had cried out when his knees were bent and moved upward towards his chest. Dr. Bill had given him a penicillin injection, which the British found useful in polio although they are not sure why. Neil was sleeping now.

It was a grim afternoon. Even Bob, who usually spent these last days of the summer holidays swimming or swiping apples or boiling corn from farmers' fields down by the river with his pals, stayed around home. I just kept putting the thought of polio out of my mind. I thought of having a drink but we didn't, for no particular reason. When Bill came again at four, after his office hours, I went upstairs with him to Neil's room and watched.

All his reflexes seemed good. But when he got up to go to the bathroom he moved like a mechanical man, jerkily, holding his head in a tense position. And when he was back in bed he cried out when his head or neck was touched, and also when his legs were bent too far. Bill covered him up and beckoned me into the bedroom across the hall.

"He's a little worse," he said.

"What do we do?"

"One of two things. Either we can take him into Peterborough and do a lumbar puncture to confirm it, or you can take him into Toronto. If you take him to Toronto they'll do a lumbar puncture there." He explained that a lumbar puncture was the practice of taking off a small amount of spinal fluid and testing it for the presence of white cells, which would mean polio, for sure.

"Which is best, Peterborough or Toronto?" I asked.

He lit a cigarette. "I hate to say this," he said, "but you'll understand that it's better to look at the darkest side. There's only one iron lung in Peterborough and it's in use. The chances are good that he won't need one, but if you're taking him any place you may as well take him where there are a lot of iron lungs. That's better than having him go bad suddenly in Peterborough and having to be taken to Toronto in the middle of the night in an ambulance."

"When should we take him?"

"How about an hour and a half?" he asked. "Eat something, bundle him up well. I'll phone Toronto and tell them you're coming. I'll give you some disinfectant. After you get him into the hospital, whisk out your car. I'll also get him a surgical mask. Put him in the back seat."

"Do you think Rassy could stand the trip?" I asked.

"I think so. Better for her to be along and know what's going on than sitting here seven or eight hours wondering. Bob could go along, too. You won't be able to stay in Toronto overnight, though. You're quarantined."

"Okay," I said. "Let's tell them."

So we went downstairs and told Rassy and Bob.

That morning I had bought Neil a toy locomotive that gave off a clacking noise when pulled on a flat surface. He held it, but didn't clack it very much on the way into Toronto. For the ninety miles he lay on the back seat and watched the lightning of the harsh storm through which we travelled. Bob counted cars. It was the Friday night of the Labour Day weekend and we had a lot of traffic to buck. He counted 154 cars in one five-mile stretch, got the count to 1,000 in another twenty miles, and then quit. Rassy was quiet, keeping her face averted from Bob and me. Neil grumbled some about the surgical mask, but Rassy leaned over into the back seat occasionally and spoke soothingly. At 8:30 we pulled up at the admitting entrance for the Hospital for Sick Children. I went inside. A couple of women were standing by the admitting desk, talking to the nurse there.

"I have a boy in a car outside," I said. "Neil Young. Dr. William Earle of Omemee phoned about him."

The nurse looked through some notes she had, found nothing.

"What is it that's the matter?" she asked.

"Polio," I said.

The two women standing there moved swiftly, sidelong, away from me. The nurse said quickly, "Bring him in."

Writing this now, I keep asking myself, what were you thinking? I don't know what I was thinking. One of the bad things about having polio in the family is the sound of the term. There is so much dread and fear and helplessness in the word that if a man wants to do the things he has to do, the things I was doing, he has to keep it from his mind. I had kept it from mine fairly well until I had to say the word. Then when the women cringed away from me in the modern hospital in a city wet and fresh from rain, with the cars zipping over the black pavement outside and the lights of the taverns flicking on and off in promised pleasure, it was like a scene from the Middle Ages when a man spoke the name of the plague.

I carried him in. The poor little guy was stiff and it hurt him to move, but I got him comfortably into my arms, him and his toy locomotive, and I carried him through the door. A second nurse was waiting. An attendant got a wheelchair, and without any pause for paperwork at the admitting desk I pushed him along the corridor behind the nurse and into a tiny room and lifted him from the wheelchair to a high rubber-tired table. The nurse donned a mask before she went near him.

During all this time, Rassy had done well. She had broken down only once, and that time when we were alone, the two of us. But now, when the admitting doctor began to give Neil the tests for pain and stiffness, she couldn't stand it. She went back to the car. And she couldn't stand that either, and came back at the wrong time, when Neil was screaming behind a closed door while the doctor and nurse did the lumbar puncture. That time she fled and I couldn't see her face. The doctor came out in a few minutes with the sample of spinal fluid, and said, "He wouldn't take the sedative. We had to do it without."

He hurried away. I waited. I went in and talked to Neil and tried to calm him down. He said he wished Dr. Bill was here. "Dr. Bill wouldn't stick a needle in me," he said, although Dr. Bill often had given him shots in the past. "I want to go to sleep," he moaned, over and over again.

We waited.

About fifteen minutes later the doctor came back. He walked in, took a deep breath, and said, "The test is positive. That means he has the disease."

Arrangements were started immediately to have Neil admitted to the isolation ward. The doctor who wrote down Neil's medical history (a series of questions including such items as: Was he breast-fed or bottle-fed? What was his formula as a baby? Was con-densed milk used or whole milk? When did he walk? Talk? Get his first tooth?) told me that Neil would be in isolation for seven days. If paralysis or weakness developed he'd then be moved to a surgical ward for therapy. If not, he'd be sent home. He said that as long as

Neil had a temperature there was danger of paralysis, and that weaknesses had developed as long as six months after the first signs of the disease. He said we'd have to spend the next seven days waiting. By that time the temperature usually was gone.

So we waited. The waiting began immediately. Neil was wheeled off by a masked nurse from the isolation ward. On the drive home that night, we tried to reassure ourselves with the fact that the speed with which the disease had been diagnosed was a good sign, and that he had the best possible chance of coming out of this whole. After all, we argued to ourselves, some victims of polio die in a few hours. Others have paralysis almost from the beginning. I suppose the thought occurred to all of us that we had been exposed to the disease as much as anyone ever could be, if it was contagious. Only Bob mentioned it, and that briefly. "I hope Neil is all right," he said. "I hope we don't get it."

That week was hellish. Each day we phoned the hospital. The first day the nurse said he had spent a bad night, in considerable pain, and that he had a temperature. She wouldn't tell us what temperature. The next day the report was better. I can't remember much about that week. I was the only one of the family allowed out of our yard, and only to buy groceries. The white quarantine sign greeted me each time I returned to the house. We got used to it. Or rather we got so that we could keep our minds blank, or almost blank, trying to ignore the lifetimes of fear of the words on the sign, "Poliomyelitis. Infantile paralysis." We talked to the doctor on Wednesday and he assured us that Neil was coming along fairly well. That was the fifth day. On the sixth we got a phone call from the hospital.

"Mr. Young?" the nurse said. "I'm glad to say that you can come and take Neil home with you now."

I remember when I typed that last line I started to cry and couldn't go any further. By that time Neil had been home two or three days and was in his bed downstairs, very weak. All of us spent a lot of time in there with him, talking. Remember, he was only five years old then and his scope of experience was narrow. "Polio is the worst cold there is," he confided to me one day. It was years later before he told me he could still remember sitting in the hospital cot half upright, holding the sides to keep himself there because it hurt his back so much to lie down. But then he would fall asleep and let go, and when he fell back the pain would waken him again, crying.

The first thing he said when we picked him up at the hospital was "I didn't die, did I?"

4

Growing Up and Breaking Up

By his sixth birthday two months later, Neil was rather a celebrity in the village. Another boy there had died of polio, but Neil had lived. He was very weak but on nice days we would dress him warmly and let him sit on the front steps. Kids on their way home from school would stop to talk a while, but when they ran off and he tried to follow he could take only a few steps and sometimes would fall down. The heavy overshoes of early winter made things more difficult for him, which gave us an idea.

Friends of ours, writer Robert Thomas Allen and his family, had lived the previous winter in New Smyrna Beach, Florida. They were going back, but to a different house. For the price of a phone call and a promise to pay $100 a month we got the place they'd had, a two-bedroom house, fully furnished, on the beach. On December 26 we packed, including the leftover Christmas turkey, and drove south. We arrived on New Year's Day to a sunny temperature of 82°F. The kids stripped and went straight into the ocean. There's a picture around of Neil on the beach in shorts and bare feet, which is how he spent much of the next few months.

By the time we got back to Omemee in May the polio was a distant memory, and he was in shape to resume fishing in the river that ran through the town. He would bring perch and sunfish and rock bass home, but often was so tired after an exciting day on the Mill Bridge that he wouldn't carry the fish so much as drag them. His brother Bob remembers one day watching Neil wash off his catch at the town pump and then mosey on along the main street dragging his fish, while an entourage of cats leapt hungrily at the movable feast.

We had pretty good times in Omemee, it seems in retrospect. I didn't make much money, but we didn't need much. The village's operator-handled telephone office had a window that looked out on the main street. If we were ever missing a kid and he didn't come at my whistle, I would pick up the phone and say, "Gladys (or Cathy or Elzina), have you seen Neil or Bob go by?" In small communities, no one is ever far from someone who'll do a favour – a ride home for a boy tired out from skating on the river, or whatever. Our out-of-town friends who visited were almost all writers: the ones I've mentioned before, plus Farley Mowat and his first wife, Fran; Trent Frayne and his wife June Callwood; John and Lenore Clare, Ralph and Birdeen Allen, and Thomas J. Allen, an editorial writer in Peterborough. If Neil was listening, most of what he heard was about writing. There were also some musical interludes when someone would show up for a party and play the grand old foot-pedal organ Mrs. Haygarth had sold us for ten dollars along with the house. It sat in the kitchen where we spent most of our time, it being our biggest room. Neil poked away at the organ a little, but couldn't reach the pedals. And so life went on with a fairly normal boyhood for Bob and Neil until, for reasons that I don't remember very clearly now, but might have had to do with marrying young and rather impulsively, I precipitated what must have been the most serious emotional upset of that part of Neil's life. I wanted out of the marriage.

It is a cliché that sometimes a man or woman will look at what he or she has and ask that unanswerable question: is this all there is? *Sports Illustrated*, just gearing up then to start publication, paid my way to New York, and offered me a job. I considered the offer seriously but didn't accept because I still saw myself as a fiction writer. Yet the strain of never being more than one jump ahead of the bank manager was beginning to tell on me and perhaps translated into a desire for change, a way out. The short-story writer, unlike the novelist, was rarely able to hope for a big strike that would provide some breathing space.

Also, the fiction market in magazines was shrinking. I started taking article assignments from *Sports Illustrated*. On one assignment I fell for a woman I met. A few months later, in James Bay on another *Sports Illustrated* assignment, I decided. In a long letter which Bob and Neil were aware of, perhaps even read, I asked Rassy to divorce me. We had rented out our house in Omemee, on the grounds that after the James Bay assignment we would go to Florida for the winter. Instead, two weeks later, after a tearful reunion Rassy and I rented a duplex on Rose Park Drive in Toronto and stayed together, with Bob and Neil going to Whitney School. It was a terrible time, during which I wrote my first novel, *The Flood*, mainly in a twenty-five-dollar-a-month room I rented on Dundonald Street, where I could work better than at home. It sold in Canada and England but didn't make much money. The year was full of tears and recriminations and reunions and separations again.

I simply don't know what the effect on Bob and Neil was of this going away and then coming back to say, Look, I'm home now, I love you – only to go away again. They were told the name of the woman I had been seeing; one morning when they got up and I was back, Bob asked about her by name.

I said I was back and didn't want to hear anything bad said about her.

Bob (with Neil listening): "Why not?"

"Because it isn't her fault." I saw it as my flaw and still do.

But then we did have a new start. I believed in it. Maybe before that I had had something like a nervous breakdown, I don't know. A crisis of unreached expectations? I resolved that we would be happy, happier than ever. We sold the house in Omemee, bought another on two acres near Pickering, just east of Toronto, and made a new start, which worked pretty well for a while. A steady job helped. I took one in public relations for a jet engine company, Orenda Engines Ltd., and a year later, having felt very out of place at air industry conventions, moved to the Toronto *Globe and Mail* as a daily columnist. We had a small but comfortable frame bungalow with three smallish bedrooms and a big lawn. The back of the property included some old range houses that had been used for chickens when the land was a farm.

Up to that time Neil's experience as a performer had been limited but fun. His mother was great at making costumes, but on his first Hallowe'en, dressed as a witch, he stood on our front steps in Omemee so petrified by all the strange shapes around him in the dark that he bolted back into the house, until Rassy and I conducted him on a tour of our nearest neighbours.

It was not long, however, before he got some confidence. He had a zany kind of wit that gave his report cards for years one constant: his teachers always wanted an improvement in his conduct. Although his marks usually were above average, it seemed that his interjections in serious discussions caused too much hilarity in class, although I thought I could discern amusement as much as concern when one school did something about it. "Dear Mrs. Young," wrote the Omemee school principal in 1953, "This small person has been causing Miss Jones a great deal of trouble over a long period. I am sending him to you for the remainder of the day to be kept in durance – or what have you. Perhaps we could discuss with Miss Jones this afternoon and gain some ground? I am sending Bob along to see that you receive both packages. Yours, L.M. Curtis."

Bob, a good and trusted student in Mr. Curtis's own class at that time, brought Neil and the note home. Nothing much happened. He was not an easy kid to punish. Once in the Omemee kitchen when I slapped him because of something that must have seemed serious at the time, our dog growled at me menacingly. Away from the typewriter, Skippy and I were practically inseparable. He would do anything I said. So his reaction against me on Neil's behalf was rather special. Sometimes I couldn't be sure *myself* when Neil was kidding. Once in the early days of TV I was watching a football game when Neil, about nine, happened along, and watched for a minute or two during which the referees in their striped jerseys kept blowing their whistles and marching off penalties.

"Who's winning?" Neil asked.

"Ottawa," I said.

"Are they the ones in the striped sweaters?"

He was twelve years old when he was drafted to act as a shepherd with a speaking role in the Christmas concert at Brock Road School in Pickering. His mother threw herself, with a mixture of grumbles and artistic enthusiasm, into making our shepherd's costume, including baggy pantaloons, cloth slippers, a cowl-like rig not unlike those worn by his Road-Eyes in his great *Rust Never Sleeps* tour more than twenty years later. But when we got to the school we found that the other mothers had been much less active, limiting themselves to a few daubs of burnt cork to supplement the usual rubber boots and jeans. Neil really stood out among the motley throng of shepherds backstage. Knowing how some kids hate to be different, I sidled up and said, "Look, does it bother you that you're the only one in a real costume?"

"So?" he said, shrugging. "I'm a *rich* shepherd."

It was about then, or maybe the following summer, that I began to see the entrepreneurial streak in him. He and my mother, who was visiting all the way from Flin Flon, spent all one Sunday morning picking wild raspberries in the bush behind the house. Neil set up a table by the road and sold them. Our next-door neighbour, Don Scott, phoned me laughing. "Have you seen Neil's sign?" he asked.

I went out casually and had a look. He'd made it himself, of course. It just said:

Raspberries . . .
THEY'RE WILD!

And one day he came home looking rather thoughtful. He had heard of a man in the area who had about twenty-eight or thirty fertilized hens' eggs that he had no room for in his incubator. He was about to throw them out. Neil asked if he could have them. He could. Neil asked me if I knew anybody else with an incubator. I didn't. He went to Don and Alyson Scott's house next door and knocked. Don, a close friend of mine, used to tell the story of how Neil's egg business got started, with his slow-pitch opening, "Say, Mr. Scott, do you know anybody who might have an incubator they're not using?"

Don did know, and Neil was in the chicken business.

Neil's own rendition of these events is in the file where for years I have been tossing exam papers, letters, notes, the stuff of my home life, good as well as bad.

This one is headed: "Oral Composition. Neil Young." (It was written a couple of years later when we had moved to Toronto again and Neil was in grade seven at John Wanless School. He spoke only from notes, but seems to have written it out to see how it would sound.)

Miss McKay and class. The subject of my oral today is a personal experience. In July 1956, I came up the stairs of our bungalow home in Pickering and stumbled into my father.

Smiling, he asked me, "Well, what hare-brained scheme have you worked up in your head now?"

"Well, Dad," I said, "I was thinking about that old range shelter in the back field and, well, I'm going into the chicken business."

"Okay," he said. "Good luck."

It was a simple, plain answer showing he thought nothing would ever come of my "just another idea." I set out to prove that I really could go into business for myself. This is the story of what I did to prove my sincerity.

In less than one week I had furnished a shelter for the chicks. I received the chicks from a friend a few doors down the road who had an incubator. Maybe you can imagine the thrill of watching young chicks grow into healthy, husky chickens. They have more body than feathers, more feet than body, and more pep and energy than their odd bodies are capable of. It is very easy to become attached to these abnormal birds. I did.

Every morning I would go out to our back field, feed, water, and set free my chickens, and return home for breakfast. One morning I went ambling out to do the work and spotted some feathers on the path. At least one of my chickens had escaped the shelter. I rather anxiously ran to the pen to find out how many chickens were left, if any. Around the pen were nine dead chickens, apparently dead from shock. The rest seemed all gone. I found no more chickens that morning, but there seemed to be traces of a fox or raccoon.

In the afternoon I went out to the pen, I don't know why, and just looked with not a hope for ever trying to raise chickens again. Then a dirty white chicken popped its head out from under a clump of weeds. Everything seemed to change and I knew I wasn't finished yet. I called that one surviving chicken Petunia and then everything seemed to go well. I sold the dead chickens for seventy-five cents each and with $6.75 purchased twenty-six female chicks from a hatchery and raised them the same way as before. On December 27, 1956, I got my first egg. From then to summer I made around ten dollars clearance per week. In mid-summer I got more chickens and doubled my profits.

My father had told me not to be surprised if we moved. I didn't really think we ever would move, anyway, so I thought nothing of it then. But one day it happened. We were forced to move to Toronto because of my father's work. I was asked to sell my chickens to my neighbours.

When I finish school I plan to go to Ontario Agricultural College and perhaps learn to be a scientific farmer.

I remember something about that chicken business myself, not as a partner but as co-advisor (with Don Scott). I worked nights and I used to leave a shirt card where Neil would see it before bed, crayoned in large black letters: LOCK UP CHICKENS. I still have it. Underneath, in Neil's writing, is a mild, "Neil is a good boy."

In summer he would sleep in a tent out by his new chicken house made from wooden crates used to ship plate glass from Europe. The panels were eight feet by twelve feet. Don Scott, who was in the glass business, brought them out by truck when Neil made his comeback as a chicken farmer. I would whistle shrilly through my fingers from the back door and I can still see Neil's bare arm appear through the tent flap and wave to show that he heard. Then he'd feed the chickens and come in. When he was getting four or five dozen eggs a day I began to deliver some in my VW bug on my way to work. At that time I was also the intermission host on Canadian television's most popular show, *Hockey Night in Canada*. During one egg delivery that autumn the lady told me about her little boy, three or four, running into the kitchen from the living room on the previous Saturday night and yelling, "Mommy, come quick! Our egg man's on television!"

We seemed happy. Bob was playing hockey and golf, both well. Neil and his small fair-haired buddy Reggie Taylor would disappear across the fields in the morning of any day off from school and limp home at night ravenously hungry, tired, and dirty, having been God knows where. I would run a bath for him, and once remember delivering to him in his bath a scrambled-egg sandwich and some milk. Some mornings later, when he began doing a Saturday paper route, we would do it together and then have a breakfast of pancakes at home. Bob, being older, seemed to have a much more organized life – mainly involved with sports and his school friends. He has always had a special, more than brotherly, feeling for Neil; Bob, compact, strong, and athletic; Neil, gangly as a young colt. One time I happened along to find Bob had backed two bigger kids up against the store where the Pickering

High School bus let him off after school. He was hammering hell out of both of them. I got them stopped. It turned out that when Bob got off the bus that day the two other boys had been hammering Neil. He took them both on, furiously, and nobody around there picked on Neil much from then on.

Apart from that foot-pedal organ in Omemee, we had no musical instruments of any kind for much of Neil's childhood. He never asked for any until one day (which he remembers but I do not) when he saw plastic ukuleles in a Pickering store and allowed that he'd like one. We did have a barely passable Seabreeze portable record-player, but our records ran heavily to Slavonic dances, an old set of Tchaikovsky's Fifth cut by Willem Mengelburg and the Amsterdam Symphony in 1911(!), Gershwin's *Porgy and Bess*, Benny Goodman playing Mozart, Fats Waller, Louis Armstrong, Paul Whiteman, Goodman's "Sing Sing Sing," Artie Shaw, Clyde McCoy's "Sugar Blues," and others of that ilk. Still, Neil found something to like because he told me much later, "When you guys used to go out and leave me alone in the house I used to turn that old Seabreeze record-player up to full volume. I had bought a couple of records the day I got the uke – I'd throw myself around, dancing, and I would have fantasies about winning dance contests. I'd always win them. The place where I won the most dance contests in these fantasies was the old legion hall in Omemee." Which was probably the only hall he knew at that time.

But he got the more current stuff on the radio, going to sleep with his radio tuned to 1050-CHUM, the big Toronto rock station. He told Cameron Crowe in an interview much later, "That's when I really became aware of what was going on in music. I knew that I wanted to play, that I was into it. 'Maybe' by the Chantels, 'Short Fat Fannie,' Elvis Presley, Larry Williams, Chuck Berry, those were the first people I heard. I used to just fall asleep listening to music. I was a real swinger, those weekends I'd stay up late listening to the radio."

When we rented our house in Pickering and bought another in Toronto, the nice two-storey place on Old Orchard, Neil took up his personal financial slack with a full-time *Globe and Mail* route. He did that on his own. I would hear his alarm each morning at six. Once, hearing sleet driving against the window, I got up to offer to drive him, only to hear the door slam down below and see him hunched over on his bike, head bent against the storm as he struck off to do his papers. Once, only once, was he sick; Rassy and I did them together that day.

Neil said he liked the early morning streets. "There are other paper boys I don't even know, but we wave at each other from a block or two away, and it's company," he said. On Christmas morning 1958, when he was thirteen, delivering his papers along a dark, quiet street a little after six A.M., he came up on a verandah quietly and saw inside a little boy in sleepers coming into the room where the Christmas tree was. The little boy obviously was just awake, with no one else in the house up. As he hunkered down in front of the pile of presents, Neil put the paper down quietly, tiptoed off the verandah, cupped his hands and boomed in his deepest voice Santa's traditional "Ho! Ho! Ho!" He then ducked almost out of sight to see the little boy run to the front window and peer goggle-eyed into the starry sky. "There was this one place this morning, and a little kid," he began, telling us about it when he got home.

That Christmas is the first time I can remember Neil playing any instrument – the plastic ukulele Rassy and I had bought him. I thought we bought it for Christmas but Neil insists we picked it up a few months earlier, in Pickering. A couple of sheets of cowboy songs came with it and he remembers (I do not) me playing the few simple chords I knew. I do remember that he would close the door of his room at the top of the stairs and we would hear *plunk*, pause while he moved his fingers to the next chord, *plunk*, pause while he moved again, *plunk* . . .

I am trying to tell you that apparently we had a normal, happy home. Rassy and I jabbed at each other some, maybe even a lot; we had very different views on many things, from life and love to bringing up children, and sometimes we were rude to each other in public. Anyway, the nineteen years of pinpricks were coming close to adding up to a mortal wound. For myself, I was frankly looking elsewhere, again. A friend of mine once told me that if his wife did not give him what he wanted, either in tenderness or sex or whatever, he felt justified in going elsewhere. I didn't ever think of it that way. I have no talent for the quiet affair that, in some marriages, may remove pressure temporarily and, when over, leave things as before, or better. I was sent on a long royal-tour assignment by *The Globe and Mail* and met a quiet blonde, Astrid Mead, who attracted me a great deal. She worked in public relations, was divorced, had an eight-year-old daughter, drove a blue TR-3, was twenty-nine (to my forty-one), and seemed to like me, too. Her maiden name was Carlson and she was Canadian-born of Swedish parents. For six days while the tour moved around British Columbia, we saw one another at work and sometimes at lunch or dinner, but both of us were working and we didn't go to bed or even come close. Did we fall in love then or later? I don't know. But a few weeks after I returned home, Rassy and I had a major, name-calling fight and I left with two bags for a hotel. What can be the worst time of any person's life had begun, for both of us.

A day or two later I took Bob and Neil to dinner at a restaurant we'd often gone to as a family, Ciccone's on King Street West. I tried to explain to them that I loved them but that I didn't want to live with their mother any more. I'm not sure that I made much sense. After dinner the three of us walked back east along King Street to where the Globe and Mail building was then, at King and York. When we parted there Neil reached over and patted me on the shoulder as if he was sorry for me, which perhaps he was. By most lights, I had treated Rassy unfairly. She had been with me all the way, never complaining about my quitting a job, selling house after house, moving from places she had painted and decorated (and, boy, could she paint, as she herself used to say). We were kids together and she understood my ambitions perhaps better than I understood them myself, and if she ever had less than total faith in me up until the first time we separated briefly in 1954, she never showed it. After that she couldn't have trusted me as fully, and in the end I didn't deserve trust. And the kids were caught in the fallout.

Anyway, I know that I made a hell of a mistake then. I did not state clearly to both of them that if they wished to come with me, I wanted them. Somehow I couldn't bear to think of Rassy without any of us; I thought I was going to be all right, that the kids would not stop loving me, but I did not know about her. That was the mistake. Oh, all ye men who leave your families, don't forget to tell each and every child that you love them now and forever, and want them to love you, too, and come with you. Then nobody ever can say, "Your dad left you. That means he doesn't want to be with you."

The theories about what happens to kids in such situations do not always take into account individual natures. As far as I can determine, there was no time when Bob or Neil reached the conclusion "I prefer

Dad." Or, "I prefer Mummy." At the time I did not know that Bob would soon be coming to live with me. If I had I would have chosen something larger than the downtown bachelor apartment I rented. All I knew was that I had to get my life together again in a hurry.

I did, at least on the surface. I had my work and a growing long-distance relationship, in letters and occasional visits, with Astrid in Victoria. Bob stayed with me part time while going to school in Pickering. But part of every sleepless night I had was spent turning over and over in my mind the self-accusation that I had failed not only their mother but our two sons. Only another parent suffering long withdrawal pains from a broken family understands fully that there are virtually no holds, fair or foul, that guilt will not employ against a sleepless quarry. Rassy divorced me two years after our separation and soon Astrid and I married, but years later I used to see myself in every miserable bastard who showed up in Neil's songs. Like in "Ambulance Blues":

> I never knew a man
> Could tell so many lies
> He had a different story
> For every set of eyes . . .

Jesus, I'd think, is that me?

In another song: Who is "the great pretender" in "Yonder Stands the Sinner"? Me?

"I Am a Child" reminded me of when he was a child and I used to look at him and be afraid that he was too good to be true, that some disaster would happen to him, that God would make me pay for my sins by taking him away. My early upbringing was Presbyterian, which I suppose conditioned me to expect a bill for everything.

"Don't Be Denied" begins,

> When I was a young boy
> My mama said to me
> Your daddy's leavin' home today
> I think he's gone to stay
> We packed up all our bags
> And drove out to Winnipeg . . .

Thus saying in six lines what took his mother and me a year or more to live, in bitter acrimony.

It was only later that I began to wonder what Neil would have become if he had grown up in a happy home, continuing to get fairly good marks in school and playing a lot of golf. At that time he wanted to finish school, go to the Ontario Agricultural College in Guelph, Ontario, and learn to be a farmer.

5

The "Cop with Heart" and the Squires

Many years later, curious I guess as to where Neil felt the influences in his music had come from, I asked if there was a book he could recommend to me on the early history of rock 'n' roll. He said, "Maybe there is one but I haven't read any books like that at all, good or bad, that I can remember." This tells us, among other things, the truth of the conviction expressed in most books about the rise of rock music that adolescents in the middle and late 1950s and through the 1960s took in the music (you might say, romantically) through their pores.

Neil remembers us all sitting ("it was a family thing") fascinated by Elvis Presley's first TV appearance. But he was only about ten or eleven, and even Presley was only the sharp end of something that had been around for a few years. It wasn't seen then in clear focus that growing audiences for a new kind of popular music, played and sung mostly by blacks, had provided the climate that made it possible for Presley to be heard. By preferring the vitality of these many black singers and groups, hunting down their records, twiddling the dials of their radios to pick up the few small radio stations that played the new music, these fans, as consumers, were beginning the long process of forcing the majors in the recording industry to provide something other than Benny Goodman and Artie Shaw and Tommy Dorsey and June-and-moon-and-spoon on which previous generations of music fans had been raised. Often at first, when a black musician's bouncy, alive, sex- or drug-oriented record was a hit, a white singer or group would "cover" it with a more-or-less laundered version that would become a bigger hit. Presley served to cut out the middle man. He opened the way for a flood of rough, exciting music in which life was more real and not so goddamn earnest, with thumping and shouting and tales of real life and real sex sung in language not learned out of a rhyming dictionary. The new music was about to sweep the world, make the tame old hit parade obsolete, with (years later) Neil Young as one of rock 'n' roll's principal prophets and practitioners. Bill Haley, Fats Domino, Chuck Berry, Little Richard, and other pioneers had not yet made their first records when Neil was dragging his rock bass, perch, and sunfish one jump ahead of the village cats through the streets of Omemee.

The wave began to hit Neil hard only after he and his mother drove to their new home in Winnipeg in the late summer of 1960. At the time he'd never owned an electric guitar, just that first ukulele, then a banjo uke, then an acoustic guitar that his brother Bob called "rather uncertain in tone." But when he went to my old Winnipeg high school, Kelvin, even to the class of my old teacher, Clarence Kerr, the music began. "There was a kid in my class who had an electric guitar," Neil told me much later. "There was another kid who didn't have a guitar, but he *wanted* to. The first one had a good guitar and also an amp. So I got a guitar and would plug into his amp. Then my other friend, Ken Koblun, got a guitar, a bass. And we started playing, you know . . . we just started."

In a broader sense, he said in a Cameron Crowe interview years later about this period in his life, he felt he'd had a "pretty good upbringing. . . . I remember good things about both my parents." But the transition from school to school bothered him. He always seemed to be breaking in. In Winnipeg the break-in was violent, a series of attacks by bullies in his room. "Once I looked up and three guys were staring at me, mouthing, 'You low-life prick.' Then the guy who sat in front of me turned around and hit my books off my desk with his elbow. He did this a few times. I guess I wore the wrong colour of clothes or something, looked like too much of a mama's boy. Anyway, I went up to the teacher and asked if I could have the dictionary. This

was the first time I'd broken the ice and put my hand up to ask for anything since I got to the fucking place. Everybody thought I didn't
speak. So I got this dictionary, this big Webster's with the little inden-
tations for your thumb under every letter. I took it back to my desk and
thumbed through a little bit. Then I just sort of stood up in my seat,
raised it above my head as far as I could, and hit the guy in front of me
over the head with it. Knocked him out. I got expelled for a day and a
half, but I let those people know just where I was at. That's the way I
fight. If you're going to *fight*, you may as well fight to wipe who or
whatever it is *out*. Or don't fight at all." Of course, as he well knows,
some of those tormentors would grow up to remark on occasion, when
it might be a help socially, "Yeah, well, Neil Young and I were in the
same room at school, y'know."

I saw Neil sometimes when I was going through Winnipeg on a
newspaper assignment, or for other reasons. One such occasion was on
my trip west for my marriage in Victoria, British Columbia, to my
second wife, Astrid, in May of 1961. At lunch in a dim restaurant that
day Neil told me a lot about his music. I couldn't fully comprehend it; I
wasn't with him all the time, hadn't been there to see and hear. He was
fifteen then and had taken the afternoon off school to meet me. Later,
when I dropped him by taxi near his mother's apartment I got out with
him on the curb and told him that I was going to Victoria to be married
and that as a result he would soon have a ten-year-old stepsister,
Deirdre. In our family we had had a family word, half-mocking: corn-
grad-ulations. He smiled at me a little bleakly but self-possessed, and
said, "Corn-grad-ulations."

Neil visited us for a week in Toronto a year later, in the summer of
1962 just before his half-sister, Astrid, was born. That first morning at
our home on Inglewood Drive, Neil stood at the kitchen sink with a
glass of juice and looked out across the sunny, flower-filled back garden
and said, "Is that all ours?" The word *ours* gave me a happy pang. I said
it was.

Neil got along fine with Astrid – which was not the case with his
brother, Bob. Bob and Astrid had had hot words very early in our marriage. He was not living with us, but visited from time to time. He had
been an excellent amateur golfer, an alternate on Ontario's team in the
annual Canadian team championship for the Willingdon Cup, and
once the victor over Nick Weslock, one of Canada's greatest amateurs

ever, in a play-off in the Kawartha Open at Peterborough. Then he took a job as an assistant pro, his aim being to make a living as a tournament player. This decision was taken only after he'd had a full golf scholarship offer from Florida State University which he missed narrowly because his score on his College Entrance Board examinations had been a fraction of a point too low. The problem between Bob and Astrid was that when he visited he treated our home as his own, where he had the freedom to act as he wished without consulting Astrid. She felt that he owed her some deference, which Bob refused to give. They never more than tolerated each other, and in one-on-one situations there was not even tolerance.

So Bob was living elsewhere that first week Neil visited us. I spent every spare minute with him, fervently eager to resume the relationship we'd had. We talked about school, where he was doing badly, and music, where he was doing well – already, at sixteen, playing out-of-town dates in smaller centres, Selkirk, Brandon, and Portage la Prairie. One day when we were driving along in Astrid's TR-3 sports car, heading for a golf game, I said to him, "Maybe you should quit school and go to a music school, the conservatory (!) or something."

"But it says in the agreement between you and Mother that you pay so much for my upkeep as long as I'm in school."

"If you're taking instruction in music, I'd count that as school and keep on paying," I said. "Tell her that."

"Well," he said, "I did take some guitar lessons, but I found the guy didn't know as much as I did, so I quit."

I saw him briefly a few months later when my father died of a stroke and I went to Manitoba for the funeral. By that time he was playing rhythm guitar with a group called the Esquires. He gave me its business card: *The Esquires. Instrumental and Vocal Styling. Fine Music and Entertainment.* With a phone number for eager bookers to call. (But not many did.) Then came a group called Stardust, which played some shows, before he and Ken Koblun moved on to the Squires, with Neil on lead guitar and calling the shots. Others in the group were more or less a parade. "We'd get different people, and we'd change," he told me years later. "It was quite a way to grow up, you know, learning how to let people go and then get different people. . . . It's hard, still is, when you have to go to somebody and say, 'We're going to get somebody else.' Usually when you have to do that, it seems it happens to somebody who's had the same thing happen before. The thing repeats itself. You always feel the rejection of all the other times, like a compounded domino effect."

By that time he and his mother had moved from their first apartment to the top of an old house in a good residential district, 1123 Grosvenor Avenue, closer to Kelvin school. "We'd come home after school and do a little playing. Sometimes at noon even, we'd come home and play from twenty minutes to an hour. We played loud, for sure, and some of the neighbours complained, but we did it mainly in the daytime, not at all hours of the night." When neighbours became rancorous enough to call police, the landlord would help pacify the policemen who came around apologetically to tell the group to keep it down. Rassy informed Bob later that the landlord always told the policemen, "Pay no attention to the complaints," and after a few visits this constable sometimes would sit in on the drums. "A cop with heart," Rassy told Bob, "fondly remembered by us all."

As the Squires became popular in Winnipeg, Rassy was their booking agent and troubleshooter. Once a school official tried to cancel a concert on the grounds that a mention which had been made on a local radio station would bring rowdy Squires' fans flooding in from other schools. Rassy, according to an article Bob wrote about Neil in 1971 for *Maclean's* magazine, explained it this way: "The goddamn fool told me all about camp followers right back to the War of the Roses. So I told this idiot that if he wanted to cancel the dance that was fine with me. The contract read that the Squires got paid regardless, and I'd be right over to pick up the cheque. He soon backed down."

Some time in there, the group's amplifier blew up, an event that will strike a responsive chord (pardon me) among people familiar with the earliest Neil Young folklore. Years later I was asked if I'd been disappointed that Neil chose music as a career. I was astonished at the question until I found that it went right back to that blown amplifier. Neil had written to me and asked for $600 to buy a replacement – "an advance on my college education" was the way he put it. At the time I hadn't been getting copies of his school report cards so before I replied I called his vice-principal. The word was grim: bad marks and worse attendance. Remember, I'd suggested he quit school and study music; but if he was in school, I figured he should be working at it. I wrote to him and said I would co-sign a bank loan for the $600 (he was playing lots of gigs by then) if he did a lot better on his June report. I heard nothing back, and Rassy got him the amplifier; but to some who learned about that incident, which was written about and talked about at the time, it made me a hard-hat. Either that or a cruel and unfeeling parent. So be it. I'd do the same thing again. It's one of the ways I operate; value for value. Perhaps not surprisingly, Neil does too. Many years later a couple of musicians he'd played with in the 1960s wanted to get back together with him to play and record. Neither was working. The word he sent was that when they had some gigs of their own under their belts, had demonstrated that they were serious, to call him again. When he told me that I laughed, and remembered the amplifier.

It seems to me now that during the years from 1960 to 1964 the relationship between Neil and me proceeded on two levels. One was the sound and fury of embattled parents, one on the spot, the other far removed, with Neil caught between. The other must have been the residual warm feeling, love, from all the years before.

"Dear Scott," Rassy wrote to me acidly from Winnipeg in September 1964 when Neil was eighteen, "Neil has decided to follow your advice and become a dropout."

Two or three weeks later, on the letterhead of the Victoria Hotel in Fort William where Neil and his group were playing, Neil addressed a letter, "Dear Daddy, Astrid, Deirdre and other Astrid: We leave for the Town and Country in Winnipeg on Sunday and we're coming back here in two weeks. I will try to get us lined up in the East so that the chances of dropping in on you will be better."

A few weeks later, back at the Victoria, a three-page letter, early in November, 1964, just before his nineteenth birthday: "Here I am in the scenic lakehead at the Flamingo again. We've been here a week and I haven't found time to write anyone. However, it's three A.M. and I've found time. This is a good booking, $350 a week plus food, a $25 raise from the last time." He wasn't sure where they were going from there, but "I'm not particularly worried about where we go right now, as long as we get paid and improve ourselves." He hoped to save enough money to buy a good second-hand car. "I'm learning more about the entertainment business every day. I have a feeling I'll be seeing you soon but no concrete reason for having that feeling. However, here's hoping! Love, Neil. P.S.: Thursday will be my first birthday away from home. When was yours?" And a second P.S.: "One of the guys just said all he wants is a Corvette with a telephone in it. Good grief! I look around and I haven't even a phone in my room!"

I have often thought of the contrast between the jaunty tone of that letter and the wistfulness of one of his classic songs, "Sugar Mountain," which he wrote on that nineteenth birthday. Nearly twenty years later on a gravel road near my farm I picked up a woman whose car had broken down. She knew I was Neil's father. "'Sugar Mountain' is my all-time favourite," she said. Maybe she was nineteen when she heard it first. Here, printing the words, I rather wish that singing books were at a higher stage of development, because trying to project the feeling of a song *only* through the words, without the music and the art the singer brings to it, is like describing the Mona Lisa as "a woman smiling." However,

Oh, to live on Sugar Mountain
With the barkers and the coloured balloons,
You can't be twenty on Sugar Mountain,
Though you're thinkin' that you're leavin' there too soon,
    You're leavin' there too soon.

It's so noisy at the fair
But all your friends are there
And the candy floss you had
And your mother and your dad.
(Oh, to live on Sugar Mountain, etc.)

There's a girl just down the aisle,
Oh, to turn and see her smile.
You can hear the words she wrote
As you read the hidden note.
(Chorus)

Now you're underneath the stairs
And you're givin' back some glares
To the people who you met
And it's your first cigarette.
(Chorus)

Now you say you're leavin' home
'Cause you want to be alone.
Ain't it funny how you feel
When you're findin' out it's real?
(Final chorus twice)

It was another seven months, June 1965, before I heard from him again, and that indirectly: a letter from the Toronto-Dominion Bank in Fort William saying that "we find ourselves involved in the temporary loss of $150." A cheque for that amount had been made out a couple of weeks earlier to Neil by Circle-Inn Limited, where Neil's group had been playing. "The young lady teller knew the boys as performers at the Circle Inn, so cashed it for another of the boys, Ken Koblun, without checking the other bank, but a few days later the cheque was returned marked, 'Payment Stopped.'" It seemed one member of the group had failed to turn up, the second week of a contract had been cancelled, and could I tell the bank where Neil was?

I couldn't, but in another week or two I had a phone call from Neil. He was at Sudbury in northern Ontario. By then he had his first car, an old Buick hearse. "It broke down at Blind River on the way east," he said. "We were coming to take Toronto by storm, but it looks now as if we're going to have to walk." He laughed. "Anyway, what I wanted to say is that now we're hitchhiking. I've given the other guys your address and phone number. So if you see strange-looking half-starved guys turning up at your door. . . ."

A young drummer named Bob turned up first. Then Terry Erickson and Ken Koblun. Finally, Neil. Hitchhiking out of Sudbury at night, long-haired and broke, he'd been picked up by a group of teenagers who drove him down the highway a few miles, then along a country road, where they hit him a few times, pushed him out into the ditch, and drove off laughing and yelling, "Hippie!" Maybe unreasonably, that incident has been Sudbury to me ever since. He walked all night before finding the highway again. Two days later, arriving at our place tired and hungry, he ate and fell into bed.

In the next few weeks I saw Neil as commander, leader of the band. For a few days the group stayed with us on cots and mattresses on the floor. Downtown Toronto's Yorkville district was teeming with youth and music, booming its allure to wandering minstrels clear across the land. Still he imposed a one A.M. curfew on his group. "Don't want them coming in all night and disturbing the household," he told me. One was late one night and rang the bell. Neil was the one who rushed silently downstairs and opened the door. Not knowing that I could hear through our open bedroom window just above, he laid down the law like a sergeant major.

They were all dead broke except Terry Erickson, the only one out of his teens. His father, a policeman in Sudbury, had given him some money. Soon they moved out of our place. I found eighteen-year-old Bob, the drummer, a room downtown on Church Street. The others bedded down wherever they found themselves at night; a lot of Yorkville kids did the same. But they still came often to eat. A turkey Astrid cooked on the back-yard barbecue one sunny Sunday afternoon was cleaned up entirely, ravenously. Neil insisted that he and the group would do the dishes. They all were very kind, playing like temporarily displaced big brothers with our youngest, Astrid, then not quite three. Neil had been hunting for a place to rehearse. I found him a studio in a downtown lane off Yonge just south of Bloor, but it was fifteen dollars a day. I think I paid for one day, maybe, not more. After a week or so I made a deal with Neil. We went to a trust company and arranged a loan of $400, to be paid to Neil at forty dollars a week for ten weeks. That was to tide him over the summer. Then, if he could start paying it off at about twenty-five dollars a month, fine. If not, I would pay it. This has become enshrined in newspaper clippings, copied time and again by people writing about him, as a quote from Neil saying that when he went to California about six months later it was on a loan of $400 from me, which was not the case at all.

By the end of summer, he broke up the group. "It just isn't good enough," he told me. He and Ken Koblun stuck together and were regulars around Yorkville through the next little while, living God knows how.

ld get a fill-in job, a single night for twenty-five dollars, he phoned to me know.

He would come occasionally for dinner or would drop in for an evening with boyhood friends Bunny Stewart or Comrie Smith. I remember one night when he and I were standing in my basement study he told me, "I wrote five songs today, Dad," and showed me a couple that he hadn't yet written the music for. But I don't remember him showing me his later hit "Nowadays Clancy Can't Even Sing," written about that time.

One night that autumn Neil and I went for a walk after dinner through the wet fallen leaves from the big oaks and maples that lined the quiet streets near my home. Even after six years and another marriage I was still obsessed by my break-up with his mother. We couldn't help allusions to the past when we were together. Then I would be off like a bloody Lady Macbeth doing a million encores of "Out, damned spot!" It was all very tiresome and we both knew it. This night when we scuffed through the leaves past a streetlight and I was running on lugubriously he said, "That isn't a factor any more, Dad. I accept what has happened. We don't have to talk about it again." I guess I was a little crazy where he was concerned. I felt tears in my eyes when I heard him say that.

Another night the loan I'd co-signed for him was bothering him. "I'm supposed to start paying it back now but I'm just not making enough. I'm going to get a job. I can still play at nights." He didn't sound down. He has always been good at dealing with what needed dealing with. He'd never been so long without money before, from his egg business and paper route on. We talked about what he might do. Going on welfare, which other kids were doing, was never mentioned. First thing, he said, he'd register at the government's Manpower office where many employers listed open jobs. At that, he laughed, "Guess I'd better get my hair cut."

He was very straightforward about it. The way of the world in 1965 was that it was a lot easier to get a job without long hair.

"Where do you get yours cut?" he asked. "They don't seem to hack it all off, like some places do."

I took him to the place I used, Mister Ivan's on Yonge Street. The owner, an imposingly handsome and bearded English immigrant named Stan (I guess he figured Mister Stan did not have the *je ne sais quoi* required to charge four dollars, a high price then, for a haircut), was an artist in his own way. I told him the problem: to make Neil's hair neat enough to help get a job, but not so short as to cause withdrawal traumas among his friends. Stan did the job himself. I paid him the four dollars. Neil wound up with lots of thick black hair, styled neatly. First place he applied, a few doors from Mister Ivan's, he got a job: fifty dollars a week as a stockroom boy at Coles bookstore at Yonge and Charles. That week he paid the first twenty-five dollars due on his $400 loan.

The only way to tell what happened next is just to say that it happened. As I tell it, some events might be narrowly out of sync, but the facts are there. Instead of looking for that job, he could have retreated west again to Winnipeg, Fort William, Brandon, Selkirk, Churchill, the places he'd played when he was sixteen or seventeen. Once the state of being a good minor-leaguer has been accepted, it is not an ignoble way of life. He'd have been known, and could have gotten his jollies as a local somebody. Instead, even as he began spending his days carrying cases of books at Coles, the other door he'd been leaning against for months began to give a little.

Martin Onrot, his agent, kept telling him that if he could get a group together there'd be some work. Neil and Ken Koblun were trying. They needed a drummer and practised in the lobby of an old Toronto theatre, the Victoria, trying out different drummers until they settled on Geordie McDonald. He had a flat at 88 Isabella in a big old house. He was moving out and said Neil could move in. This was right down the street from Coles, making getting to work easier on bleary mornings. But the flat was pretty bare, Neil told me. "Do you happen to have a spare cot or something, a few old blankets? Maybe some pots and pans you aren't using?"

Astrid and I rounded up and delivered what we could find: a two-burner plate, cot, sleeping bag, dishes, pots and pans, some worn cutlery, none of which we ever saw again. I don't know who shared the place with him. Bruce Palmer says he and Rick James (then going by the name Ricky James Matthews) were in it from time to time. Maybe Ken was there, too. In those days when Neil worked at Coles and played the nights away trying to get the group into shape, sometimes he would be roaming the streets at three or four in the morning, unable to sleep, getting by on the odd joint, the odd meal, experimenting with speed, pushing himself to the limit.

Five weeks after Neil started work at Coles, I was out of the city when he phoned my home one morning. In a voice so weak Astrid could hardly hear, he said he was sick. She immediately got into the blue TR-3 she'd brought into our marriage, drove to 88 Isabella and brought him back. She put him to bed in the room of our fourteen-year-old daughter, Deirdre (Astrid's by birth, by then mine by adoption). Astrid phoned Coles to book him off sick. Coles was not pleased. "He's been late a lot lately," the man said morosely.

For the next few days Deirdre slept elsewhere in the house. Neil used her bed. He slept eighteen or twenty hours out of twenty four, waking only to eat ravenously or go to the bathroom. In a few days he was better. His job was gone, but the group was still there. Soon after that Martin Onrot found them a booking: a ski lodge in Vermont. Neil and the others needed help to get their baggage, instruments, and a big amplifier to the bus depot. We loaded my Chrysler. I drove them and saw them off on the bus.

The gig went well. At the end, Neil and Ken Koblun figured they would detour to New York on their way back to Canada. There were at least two good reasons.

When they'd been playing in Fort William earlier, a five-man folk group called the Company was playing there at the Fourth Dimension. They were an offshoot of a group of ten or twelve that had been put together a year or so earlier in New York, the Au Go Go Singers. The originals included two folkies who had moved to New York as teenagers to sing and play wherever they could find an audience – Stephen Stills, born in Dallas and schooled in Florida, where he'd worked with young groups in Tampa and Gainesville before moving north, and Richie Furay from Dayton, Ohio. They sang together from time to time in New York and their group was supposed to be an east coast answer to folk groups that were doing well on the west coast, the New Christy Minstrels and the Serendipity Singers. Very upbeat, smiling, neatly dressed, controlled.

Stephen was with the smaller Company in Fort William. Richie was not. That's where Neil and Stephen Stills first met. Neil and his group had gone to hear the Company play and sing folk music. Stephen and some of the others had come to hear Neil's rock group. The admiration was mutual. Stephen kept saying he wished he could play with Neil, he really wanted to do rock 'n' roll. At the same time Neil was beginning to lean towards folk. Ken Koblun fell in love with the girlfriend of the bass player in Stephen's group. "He was really gone on her," Neil said. "So when our gig ended in Vermont after a few days, we thought we could just swing a bus trip to New York as a detour on our way back to Toronto. I wanted to see Stephen, and Ken wanted to see the girl. We hardly had enough money to make it work. I can remember lugging that big amplifier through the bus station in New York, trying to get somebody to give me a hand. They just said, 'Hey, you're in the Big Apple now, kid. Lug your own!' When we hunted around Greenwich Village for the people who'd been with the Au Go Go Singers, Stephen was gone. Somebody said he'd gone to L.A. to try to put together a rock 'n' roll group. That was funny, because at exactly the same time I was getting more and more into folk. Anyway, Ken found the girl and we hung out there for a few days. That's when I met Richie Furay. We got along well. I taught him a song I'd written a little earlier in Toronto, 'Nowadays Clancy Can't Even Sing.'"

The matter of folk-versus-rock, as those with long memories will recall, was a dichotomy in pop music at the time. Pete Frame, in his remarkable book *Rock Family Trees*, summed it up: "The Au Go Go Singers . . . didn't last long, because along came the most influential and seminal [music] film of the mid-sixties, *A Hard Day's Night*, which fired the Byrds and the Spoonful into rock and had the same effect on Stephen Stills. You have to understand that in America electric music was considered base and unworthy until the Beatles arrived in 1964. Up until then, folk was the only possible pursuit for a kid with brains." Stephen, a kid with brains, was thus in a way in the vanguard of change, while Neil, another kid with brains, was going temporarily the other way.

Nobody can tell what might have happened if Neil had found Stephen in New York that time, but as it was Ken and Neil hauled themselves and their equipment back to Toronto to find something else waiting.

At the time, Bruce Palmer, who had just turned nineteen about when Neil had turned twenty, was in what soon was to be seen as a permanent state of financial stress, basically because he liked to enjoy instantly any money he made. His wife was gone, his apartment was gone, his lead guitarist was gone. A little earlier Colin Kerr, then owner of a coffee house called the Mynah Bird, decided that if a group were named after his place the word would get around. Bruce did the recruiting, but later lost his first lead guitar, Tom Morgan. Bruce brought in Neil although Neil by then didn't even have an electric guitar. He had sold (at a Yonge Street music store) his original orange Gretsch, the one his mother had helped him buy in Winnipeg, the one with a white case autographed with little personal notes and signatures by everybody he'd played with until then, including Stephen Stills.

The people he was listening to that summer and autumn – Bert Jansch, Hamilton Camp, Bob Dylan, Phil Ochs – had given him the big push into folk, causing him to sell the Gretsch and buy a used twelve-string acoustic. Bruce Palmer laughs when he talks about the first blossoming of the Mynah Birds as a big-beat rock 'n' roll band with the country sound of Neil's twelve-string coming through loud and clear. But the Mynah Birds could play, no doubt about that, and also lucked into what they needed most right then, an angel. In the nick of time.

John Craig Eaton was then and is now a very large wheel indeed among Canada's business and social elite. The family's wholly owned national chain of department stores would see to that even if the Eaton brothers were not as bright and effective as they are in their own rights. At the time, 1965, they were being groomed and tested rigorously, the family custom, to see if they were good enough for the Big Store's big jobs, but John must have had some entrepreneurial energies left over. For a man acting on a tip from a friend and his own instincts to jump in and back Neil Young, Rick James, and Bruce Palmer before they had proved themselves was either bloody smart or bloody lucky. He put up expense money and, in what turned out to be a much rasher move, arranged a substantial line of credit for the group's musical equipment through Eaton's downtown store. He helped the group get dates, including some at private parties, and was there every night they played. "He'd come into our dressing room in his trench coat and stride up and down like Knute Rockne, telling us to go out there and knock 'em dead," Bruce Palmer said. Eaton also saved a little on his outlay by sometimes having the group rehearse in his living room in the quiet and stately downtown area where he and his wife Kitty lived. Once, Bruce says, Kitty couldn't stand the noise and stormed in to order them out, but John placated her.

Which brings me to an unimportant but still rather incredible coincidence which I only now notice, and perhaps should keep to myself (but what the hell). Lady Flora Eaton, John's grandmother, was born in Omemee, daughter of a carpenter and cabinet-maker named John McCrea. While I'm in the longbow-drawing line, it is also true that Lady Eaton pioneered the family's musical patronage nearly fifty years earlier, on a vastly different scale. She befriended in the 1920s a young Canadian tenor named Edward Johnson, who eventually was to sing with and then become general manager of the Metropolitan Opera House in New York. The Edward Johnson Building at Toronto's Royal Conservatory of Music is named after him. The public school in Omemee is named Lady Eaton Memorial. Perhaps for balance I should give some thought to naming something after Neil.

I expect I would have known more about the Mynah Birds at the time if I had spent that winter entirely in Toronto. Instead, I spent much of it in Florida and missed the most important event. The Mynah Birds quickly (in a matter of weeks) became so hot that they were given a chance to record an album for Motown Records in Detroit.

Part of that story was detailed in *Musician* magazine late in 1982, when Neil was interviewed by Cameron Crowe: "Ricky [James] was really into the fact that we were going down to Motown, and I thought that was great, too. I knew the music. But when we got there – these guys would just come in, like Berry Gordy, or one of the other heavies, Holland-Dozier-Holland . . . they'd be around. We went in and recorded five or six nights, and if we needed something, or if they thought we weren't strong enough, a couple of Motown singers would just walk right in. And they'd Motown us! A couple of 'em would be right there, and they'd sing the part. They'd just appear and we'd all do it together. If somebody wasn't confident or didn't have it, they didn't say, 'Well, let's work on this.' Some guy would just come in who *had* it. Then everybody was grooving. And an amazing thing happened – we sounded hot. And all of a sudden it was Motown. That's why all those records sounded like that.

"Probably 90 per cent of the acts there were better groups than the Mynah Birds. But we were weird, we were really different. We were the only group with a twelve-string guitar on Motown. Playing a country twelve-string with this rock beat. And actually they kind of liked the sound of it."

John Eaton had put them up at a Detroit motel while the recording sessions went on. Motown's enthusiasm for the result was indicated by the long-term contract the group signed, described by Neil as gargantuan – tying him up, among other things, for seven years to Motown for everything the Mynah Birds recorded in that time. "Another thing," said Bruce Palmer in 1983, "a really big thing was that we were the first white group Motown ever signed."

"But you did have one black, Rick James," I reminded him. Palmer, laughing: "He's getting blacker all the time but as far as we knew he was white then."

Then came disaster. It came out for the first time that Ricky was absent without leave from the U.S. Navy, a fact that had sent him fleeing across the border to Canada in the first place. Considering the U.S. attitude to their war in Vietnam then (Muhammad Ali later was stripped of his world heavyweight boxing championship for refusing the draft on the grounds that "I got nothin' against them Viet Congs"), Motown decided to put the album on hold. Nothing from it was ever released. It may still exist somewhere, filed and forgotten, and in 1983 Motown was trying to trace it. One Motown executive thinks it might have been lost a little later when the company's operations were moved from Detroit to the west coast. Rick was persuaded (Bruce thinks by someone at Motown) that he had no future in U.S. music until he had settled his service status, so gave himself up and was imprisoned for a short time.

Ricky James became one of rock's millionaires, his big move to the top coming in the late 1970s after more than ten years of not getting the breaks he deserved around Toronto.

But at the time his imprisonment broke up the Mynah Birds and, as Neil told Cameron Crowe in the 1982 interview, left them broke – "Our manager never gave us the money, and then two weeks later ODed . . . ODed on our advance, ran right through twenty-five Gs (laughs). What a guy!"

About that time I came back from Florida. I was driving downtown one frigid day when I saw ahead of me on the sidewalk a familiar, gaunt figure in jeans and a jean jacket. I was in traffic and it was just a glimpse, but I was sure. I turned off and went back to hunt through nearby streets until I found him. "Hey!" I said. "Want a lift?"

Neil got in. He wasn't wearing gloves. The temperature was near zero Fahrenheit. He had been at the Eaton home, a few blocks from mine. I asked him about the group. "We've got problems." He told me no details.

Actually, I was more concerned about his bare hands. Where were his gloves? He said he'd left them somewhere. He was shivering in his light clothes. I said, "Let me buy you some gloves." He said no, he knew where he'd left them, he was all right. I dropped him downtown on Yonge Street.

"Keep in touch," I said.

"I will," he said.

That was, my memory assures me, perhaps erroneously, February 20, 1966. That date sticks in my mind. Maybe I made a note somewhere. When a couple of weeks went by and I hadn't heard from him again I went to the rooming house at 88 Isabella and climbed the stairs to the door of the room where he'd been living. The man who opened to my knock was someone I'd never seen before.

"Is Neil here?"

"Who?"

The man had moved in just a few days before. The place had been empty awhile when he took it. "I think the landlord is looking for his rent," the man said.

I went away disappointed but not especially worried. It was a good deal later (years, before details were filled in) that I found out what had happened. The Motown experience and the Rick James disaster had been preceded by Ken Koblun having a kind of breakdown. Rock groups form and break up every day. Neil, twenty, and Bruce Palmer, nineteen, could have found other musicians, gone on, but. . . .

7

Over the Border, Illegally

Bruce Palmer: "One day about then Neil and I were sitting in a place called the Cellar along Yorkville, a place where people met to play chess. We were talking over various things we could do next when suddenly Neil decided it. 'Let's get the hell out of here,' he said.

"'What do you mean?'

"'Sell everything we can and get a car and go to L.A.'"

In a day or two of lugging instruments and equipment around the frigid, icy streets, they sold most of the stuff that John Eaton had got for them on credit. It wasn't theirs to sell – they hadn't paid for it. But now they had a stake. Neil hunted through the used-car lots for something that might last out a long trip south, and when he found a 1953 black Pontiac hearse he saw it as an omen. The other time he'd made his big move, to Toronto, just ahead of the Toronto-Dominion Bank in Fort William trying to get its $150 back, it had been in his first hearse, the Buick. It had broken down but never mind that. The Pontiac seemed solid. Old hearses are not a hot item on used-car markets so it was cheap. He bought it. Now that the big adventure had wheels, some friends said they'd like to come along, too. Neil thinks they were six in all, Bruce thinks five. One girl was a good friend of Neil's, a pianist and

59

folk singer named Tannis. Another was Tannis's friend Jeannine. There was also a youth called Mike and a girl whose name Neil can't remember and Bruce can't remember being with them at all. They had several more volunteers, but these six (or five) were the chosen ones because, Bruce said, "We were all considerate of one another." They threw their scanty belongings into the back of the hearse, turned the heater up full (it was late in February), and set out.

As registered owner of this latter-day covered wagon, Neil was the one who decided where to cross the U.S. border. He and Bruce had been back and forth across the border at Detroit during the Motown experience. Too often it had been difficult. Once Neil had had to enlist some backing from his uncle Bob (my brother) and aunt Merle, who lived across the river from Detroit, in Windsor, Ontario. Hassles, searches for drugs, and questions could be expected of any border crossing in southern Ontario. Immigration people then and now are extra hard on long-haired young travellers with no visible means. "We just don't want to blow it before we even get started," Neil told his little band of pilgrims, no doubt influenced as well by the fact that some were carrying marijuana. (Bruce, laughing: "Those little plastic bags were hanging out of every pocket!")

"So where do we go across, Neil?"

"Sault Ste. Marie."

"Sault Ste. Marie! You're not serious!"

Neil was. He drove more than 200 miles north to Sudbury, another hundred or so west to Sault Ste. Marie, Ontario, and late one night was facing border officials at Sault Ste. Marie, Michigan.

"Where were you born?"

"Toronto," said Neil, and from the depths of the hearse came other avowals of Canadian birth.

"Where are you going?"

"To Winnipeg, where my mother lives. We're just driving through the U.S. to western Canada because the roads are better." Many Canadian travellers take that route, a day or so in the United States before surfacing into Canada again at Emerson, Manitoba, south of Winnipeg.

There were a few other questions about whether they had anything to declare or had any plans to overthrow the U.S. government, standards of that time, but there was no search.

"Okay," the border official said, and soon they were rolling south along the flat straight road through northern Michigan.

It wouldn't make a bad movie, you know. Six kids in an old hearse, at that time in history. Naturally, the smoke trailing behind the hearse was not all from petroleum products. But they were considerate of one another, Bruce Palmer says, no matter what the mood. It was the way of the time. You comfort the one who is down, you sing, you talk. You stop for gas and the toilet, or hamburgers and the toilet, and sometimes the hearse would be singing and strumming, and sometimes it would be quiet. Neil sometimes tapped the steering wheel to a rhythm in his head while he drove, and sometimes he was sombre, coming out of it only to answer a question or laugh at a joke.

He was going through a change. When he'd sold, as he said later, "everything we had and some things we didn't have" to shake free of Toronto it was not only because the ass was just about out of his pants and he'd been working hard and not getting anywhere. It was all only in his head as the hearse rolled south, but he spoke of it to me later, his feeling that in Toronto at that time it didn't matter if he did something good, "You were just doing it for nobody. That's not to put down the people who were there. There just weren't enough of them in one place, enough people who knew what was going on or who made a reaction big enough to warrant doing it again. Even when the reaction did say Yes, all it meant to me was, 'If these few people like it, I've got to find a place where there are more people like that.' I meant people with social style, social awareness. I saw those people as being like a species, an advanced species. I knew that the species was spreading, thriving, in England and the United States – or, rather, *parts* of the United States. Not, for instance, in the Midwest. So I felt there was an audience somewhere, must be, that could support what I was doing. It wasn't in Toronto, so I just had to go for it. The two places I could go were the United States or England, and there was no way I could get to England."

The trip proceeded on various levels. One was deep and individual, hopes and fears mixed in with love and smoke and laughter at the very idea of what they were doing. "Jeez, wait'll we tell so-and-so about this!" But another level was Neil's immediate worry, the hearse. When his group hitchhiked away from the old Buick in Blind River eight months before, it had been summer and the livin' fairly easy. They were in their own country, with help a phone call away. Now they were in the dirty end of winter, in the U.S. illegally, nearly broke, strangers in parts where a lot of people treated anyone with long hair and no money as hippies, like dirt. The old Buick's breakdown had been unexpected, but final. This was a longer trip, and the Pontiac was showing signs of weakness. Neil felt that when he drove it was all right, he could baby it along. But they didn't have the money to stop overnight anywhere, and even with the good heater keeping the back of the hearse fairly comfortable for sitting or sleeping, everyone wanted to get south, and warm, as soon as possible. This meant going day and night. But when Neil had to sleep and turned the wheel over to Jeannine, Tannis's friend, he felt too uneasy to sleep. She didn't know how to baby the car. She was used to cars that worked. So Neil couldn't sleep long enough even to calm down before he'd get up and drive again.

As they headed south towards St. Louis to pick up Route 66 they lived on French fries and hamburgers. For gas, Bruce thought Neil had an Esso credit card belonging to me, but I don't remember that. After three days the hearse pulled into Albuquerque, New Mexico, and Neil passed out. He lay in the back of the hearse while Jeannine drove to the nearest hospital's emergency entrance. The doctor on duty checked Neil over and said, "You're okay, just exhausted. But you've got to rest before you go any farther."

Luckily, an alternative was found to convalescing in the back of the hearse. Some college kids they met on the street had some extra floor space. It was the sharing instinct of the time. A mattress was put on a floor. Neil lay there, Bruce thinks, for a day or two. "I hardly left his side, and I was scared for him. He hardly moved. Even when his eyes were open, he just seemed right out of it. I'd bring him food and water and he'd take some of it and then be gone again, almost as if he was unconscious. I sometimes think that was the first warning of the trouble he had later, with epilepsy."

When Neil was ready to go, there were complications. Tannis had found a café or coffee house where she could play and sing. Jeannine wanted to stay with her. There was talk of all of them staying awhile, then moving on. Neil dismissed that and told them all, "We're leaving here at nine tomorrow morning. Anybody who wants to come better be here. We won't be going looking for you."

At leaving time, Tannis, Jeannine, and Mike weren't there. So Bruce and Neil and the girl whose name is lost (Neil), or didn't exist in the first place (Bruce), drove off and left them. They headed west across the desert through Needles, San Bernardino, and into Los Angeles. Driving along Sunset Boulevard for the first time they were like Hollywood-struck kids in hundreds of old movies, full of more hope than food, their eyes wider than their prospects. They had no papers allowing them to be there, no visas, no work permits, no place to stay, no friends to bunk in with. Nobody waved hello. The homesick girl whose name no one can remember had had enough. She phoned home for money and caught a bus back to safety.

Neil believed Stephen Stills was in L.A. somewhere, but didn't know where to start looking. Stephen wasn't a name in music then. He was a kid like the rest. Even in places where groups were playing or young musicians crashing for the night, "Anybody here seen Stephen Stills?" drew blanks. Neil and Bruce lugged their instruments from place to place looking for someone to play with, and striking out. Money was so low that even a place to sleep was unaffordable. Sometimes they found a meal or a bed, even an off-street parking place, provided by people who didn't have much more than they did. When they tried to park on the street to grab some sleep in the back of the hearse, police told them to move along. They hadn't been expecting a brass-band welcome but (hope springing eternal) they hadn't been expecting this, either.

After a week, Neil said, "Maybe we'd do better in San Francisco." Couldn't do worse. That day they drove down Sunset Boulevard looking for the way out of town. Sunset was one huge traffic jam, both ways, inching along, when the throng ahead of Neil stopped for a light. He checked his rear-view mirror but nothing registered except the line of cars stretching back for blocks. He didn't give the car immediately behind a second glance; it was just another car to him, not looking fateful at all. But it was.

For months, Stephen Stills had been in L.A. doggedly trying to put together a rock group. A record producer named Barry Friedman, who knew Stephen's work with the Au Go Go Singers, had told him there'd be work if he could get together a group that could play. When he couldn't find the right people on the loose locally and had been unable to induce people already working to break off and join him, he'd enticed Richie Furay to fly out, painting a rosy enough picture to make Furay think that Stephen had a group ready to go. Instead, the reality was that there were just the two of them. But they began to work up some songs. Richie told Stephen about Neil hunting for him in New York. Stephen, remembering Fort William, tried to locate Neil but didn't have any Toronto connections who might have had a clue.

This day he and Richie were caught in the same big traffic jam as Neil, on Sunset. It is hard to get the next few minutes straight. Neil thought that Stephen yelled at him from the street, and that only Richie was with him. Bruce thought Stephen's car was coming the other way, and that Barry Friedman was with Stephen and Richie. Richie's account is the one that has been accepted as official: that as he and Stephen sat in the traffic jam Stephen suddenly focused on the car immediately in front. An old hearse. Bearing Ontario plates. "Stephen, knowing that Neil used to drive around in an old hearse, shouted, 'That has just got to be Neil!' We rushed out into the traffic [which could have caused Neil later to think they came from the curb] and up to their open window and sure enough there sat Neil and Bruce Palmer."

They yelled back and forth through the hearse's windows. Traffic moved again. Neil found a shopping-centre lot. Stephen followed the hearse in. Their reunion took place with a lot of laughs as they leaned against the hearse and Stephen told them the same story he'd told Furay, that Barry Friedman would get them work, and all he and Richie needed were a guitar player, a bass player, and a drummer. Neil played guitar, Bruce played bass. Cars pulled in and out past them and crowds walked by, not aware that they were in the presence of what rock music journalists later were to call an historic moment. Furay (quoted by Pete Frame): "I'd taught Stephen 'Nowadays Clancy Can't Even Sing' which Neil had taught me in New York a few months earlier. And so we went home and played it for Neil. He liked it and that was it! We started a rock 'n' roll band."

Neil: "That same day Barry Friedman put us in a house on Fountain Street and told us to start working. All we needed was a drummer, and I think it was in two or three days that he sent Dewey Martin along. The whole thing was great, a tremendous relief. We had a place to sleep and could take a shower. We had a house and weren't on the street. Barry gave us a dollar a day each for food. All we had to do was keep practising. Barry did it all, you know. He basically put it together and kept it together. The people were good from the start. There was no down time. Everybody was ready. These were people who had come to Los Angeles for the same reason, identical, all finding each other.

Three days were enough, you know, even a day and a half, it didn't take any time before we all knew we had the right combination. Time meant nothing; we were ready."

At first, they didn't even bother to think up a name. One day they were outside for a break and saw a big piece of road equipment with the name Buffalo Springfield on it. They decided that was their name, *Buffalo Springfield.*

I asked Neil, some years later: "How long before you had your first job?"

"About a week and a half." Neil laughed. "It takes a little time to get established, you know."

Barry Friedman, their hard-bitten angel, had talked to his friend, the road manager for the Byrds: "These kids are good." The Byrds had a concert tour scheduled at sites within driving distance, the first at Pasadena, and were looking for a group to do the opening act. Buffalo Springfield couldn't have started under better auspices. The Byrds were the hottest group in the United States right then. Their 1965 recording of Bob Dylan's "Mr. Tambourine Man" had made them nationally famous. The crowds that came to hear them went away talking also about Buffalo Springfield. The Byrds themselves started showing up early to listen to Buffalo Springfield.

Which brings us back to the old Pontiac hearse. At Barry Friedman's house they would load themselves and their equipment into the hearse. Neil would drive it to the parking lot beside an office building on Sunset Boulevard where the Byrds had their business headquarters. They would leave the hearse, pile into a Lincoln rented by the Byrds' road manager, drive out and do the show, return, get into the hearse, go back to the house again. "One time when we got back into the hearse and started home, the drive shaft fell out into the street," Neil said. "We just left it there and unloaded our equipment and walked away."

About three weeks later a call came for me at my home in Toronto.

"Mr. Young?"

"Yes."

"This is the Ontario Provincial Police. We have an enquiry here from the California State Troopers about a Pontiac hearse with Ontario plates that has been found abandoned in Los Angeles. It is registered to Neil Young at your address. Can you tell us anything about it?"

"Well, he's my son, that's about all I can tell you," I said. "I haven't seen him for a few weeks."

At the time of the police phone call, I still didn't know for sure whether Neil was in Los Angeles, whether he owned the hearse when it was abandoned, or *anything.* Nobody I knew knew. His brother Bob, working that spring at a golf course on the northern outskirts of Toronto, took a long bus ride into the city to look for Neil around Yorkville. No trace. All this time the new group Buffalo Springfield was knocking them dead in California and we didn't know a thing. Finally the call did come, I think late in April. "Didn't want to call until I was sure this is real, but it's looking good, Dad. Got a group and the managers have a place for us to live and cars for us to drive around in. (Laugh.) No money to spend, but everything else is great. Best of all, we're doing our own material."

8

Buffalo Springfield, and Epilepsy

Around the time I've just described, Neil began having epileptic seizures. When he and Rassy told me about this, I wondered about other times when I'd known he was ill but hadn't been close enough to learn details. It had crossed my mind earlier that an illness in Fort William and the time when he crashed for a few days in Toronto while working at Coles might have been drug-related in some way; my knowledge of drugs at that time being pretty well limited to the phrase "bad trips," which I sometimes heard or read, but never had experienced even second-hand. But Neil, being the only expert in his own case, says that his first "big one," grand mal seizure, came in Los Angeles just when things started happening to Buffalo Springfield. Bruce Palmer suspected in retrospect that the collapse a few weeks earlier in Albuquerque "was at the very least a neurological warning" but he was on hand also on the day when all guesswork ended. "We were standing together in a crowd around somebody demonstrating a Vegematic or some other kind of gadget for chopping vegetables, and when I turned to say something to Neil he wasn't beside me. Then I saw him on the floor having tremors that led to convulsions. I was scared as hell."

So was Neil. The turmoil in his mind in the next few weeks, months, even years, was such that until he came to terms with the condition he rarely could forget that a seizure was always a possibility, every day of his life. When he seemed erratic then, in relations with others, male and female, he had good reason.

I suggested to Neil one time that the course of his life up to his first seizure might have been leading to that point. He had driven himself hard, from his middle teens on, expressing hopes and fears and even nightmares through his music. When he reached the point of success or near success, of being recognized, of finding his goal in some degree reached, the sudden *getting there* might have caused some sort of readjustment of energies that showed up as epilepsy, no? He kindly resisted the temptation to laugh and say, "You could be right, doc," but he did say, "Maybe."

At the time, he went on daily medication to control the epilepsy – and grew to dislike the medication's effect on him so much that a few years later he stopped using it, feeling that in his case control had more to do with personal stability than with medication. Not that he feels he's left epilepsy behind. "It's part of me. But it's only part of me once in a while."

At first I knew little except the bare bones of what he was going through, or the life he was leading. After the house Barry Friedman provided, there was an apartment where they lived after Charlie Greene and Brian Stone became their managers. But to me the wider milieu was a blank. Even the Springfield had to learn to understand it in terms of every day's new excitements, as they went along. Bruce Palmer since has made an important point: that the 1960s were an innocent time by the standards of the 1980s. Perhaps their ages had something to do with it: Neil and Stephen were twenty, Bruce nineteen, Richie twenty-one, Dewey Martin twenty-three. As Bruce saw it, Hollywood, the milieu, was a fertile central focus point, "a community, a family. Everything else seemed distant. When people came to Hollywood, played the Whiskey [au Go Go], that was the real action. Albums were being sold, people were touring, but in L.A. the family got together. Day in day out we would jam together, be at each other's houses, just using society to make a rock 'n' roll family. You got to know everybody, Janis, Jimi Hendrix, hell, once we even got together with the Beatles, sans McCartney, at Stephen's house. We had to take things, in those days, not as seriously as they were, just as an outlet. All those people in music who were important and made statements that can't be compared to today's music had a common bond and a common paranoia and they were there."

Buffalo Springfield became very big in that world very fast. When the word about them got around they were hired to be the house band at the Whiskey au Go Go, the prestigious drinking, eating, and music place everybody called the Whiskey. It may even be that they were at their very best, that early, that the original five in their first excited regard for one another had a kind of magic that one could relate to lines in a song Neil wrote later:

I am a child. I last awhile
You can't conceive of the pleasure in my smile . . .

They were young, innocent of the stresses and competitions between them that would come with time. The pop-music world is a place of sweeping enthusiasms. The individualistic personas of the youthful Springfield complemented their startling musicianship. Neil in fringed jackets and Comanche shirts became the Hollywood Indian. He and Steve Stills took opposite sides of the stage to wage guitar duels. (Neil sang very little in those days, unsure of his voice.) Richie Furay had a remarkable voice and a strange custom of tiptoeing across the stage with his toes turned inward (teeny-boppers loved him). Dewey Martin dressed in Carnaby Street style, flamboyant shirts and neckerchiefs, and Bruce Palmer was the foil for all; his very stillness, back usually turned towards the audience, projected its own mystique. But most of all it was their music that within a week had the Whiskey overflowing not only with off-the-street fans but with famous musicians and entertainers, Sonny and Cher, Barry Maguire, the Mamas & the Papas, David Crosby and Chris Hillman of the Byrds, and every hungry agent and manager in town. Yet it all happened so fast that nobody even had the sense to tape what they were doing. They were being paid a little more than $100 a week each.

It seems plain now that none of them knew how to handle what was happening. They didn't really see, except in retrospect, that their troubles began then. Women in waves – "these dumb chicks," Neil called them later – began to come at them with no purpose except to get in bed with somebody; actually, anybody. The groupies, the agents, the promoters, the hangers-on, each would pick out someone they wanted to make it with, for business or sex, and tell him he was the greatest, the others were just riding his back. It was a scramble. None of the group looked upon what was happening to them off the stage as a college education in pop-group sociology of the time, but it was definitely a learning experience. Before their very eyes egos were being blown up to the size of Goodyear blimps.

It was more or less inevitable that the first single the group released would add to the friction. Stills, seen by himself and some others as the musical director of the group, had written a song called "Go and Say Goodbye," counselling any guy about to split with his girl to tell her to her face, the honest way. It had a lively tune and was seen as a good commercial theme. The flip side was to be Neil's "Nowadays Clancy Can't Even Sing," a longish song (more than three minutes) with lyrics mysterious enough that critics had been discussing them at length in print, theorizing as to what the hell they *meant:*

Hey, who's that stompin' all over my face
Where's that silhouette I'm tryin' to trace
Who's puttin' sponge in the bells I once rung
And takin' my gypsy before she's begun? . . .
Who's sayin' baby that don't mean a thing
'Cause nowadays Clancy can't even sing.

The song was also a main request at concerts. In July before the single was released, distributors began besieging Atlantic Records (Steve's company originally) to make Neil's "Clancy" the A side of the single, Steve's song the B side. This eventually was done. It was the first time that Neil's work and Stills' work had met head to head in the market-place, and the way it was decided – in effect demoting Stills – was bound to hurt. The contest was on. The single got into the Top 30 nationally, but that meant it was only a semi-hit (except in Los Angeles, where "Clancy" was on top or close to it). Six months later the group's greatest-ever hit single reversed the process, with Steve's "For What It's Worth" on the A side and Neil's "Do I Have To Come Right Out and Say It" on the B side. That one reached number seven nationally. Neil and Steve were becoming household names.

Yet Neil, partly because of his struggles with epilepsy and its medica-tion, was in trouble, much less able than the others to ride carefree on the wave of suddenly being the hottest new group in west coast music.

They were so innocent it was laughable. Charlie Greene and Brian Stone were their first real managers, having bought out Barry Friedman; but they had somehow worded the deal so that the Springfield wound up paying for the switch. They really needed somebody to fight with their own managers to see that they got a square deal. They had a place to live and a car to drive but real cash money was an elusive commodity. Charlie and Brian were the company store. "We always owed," Neil said. "We never got out of hock. They'd give us an advance and then when an advance came in from somewhere they got it. A lot of things didn't add up right or at least we couldn't follow the addition." In his song "The Last Trip to Tulsa" there's a line, "*Well, I used to be a folk singer, keeping managers alive.*"

That's the way he saw it then. Later he modified his views. "I saw eventually that they had done things the way they were done in Hollywood back then. If we had made it a lot bigger, they would have been heroes – same as they were when they did Sonny and Cher, which worked." But at the time Neil's emotional stress, not only with the business side of the music industry but with his own sense of himself and his life as well, was easily discernible in many of the songs he wrote during the time the Springfield survived. Try 1966's "Out of My Mind":

Out of my mind
And I just can't take it any more
Left behind,
By myself and what I'm living for.
All I hear are screams
From outside the limousines
That are taking me
Out of my mind.

Or, the first verse of "Flying On the Ground Is Wrong":

Is my world not fallin' down?
I'm in pieces on the ground
And my eyes aren't open
And I'm standin' on my knees.

Or, the first verse of the classic "Broken Arrow":

The lights turned on and the curtain fell down,
And when it was over it felt like a dream,
They stood at the stage door and begged for a scream,
The agents had paid for the black limousine
That waited outside in the rain.

Short of reproducing almost all the songs Neil recorded about then (among the several notable exceptions being the wistful "Sugar Mountain" and "I Am a Child") I can't convey all of what seemed to be disillusionment and frustration with the kind of life his new fame had brought. Sometimes it showed as a kind of irony, or cynicism, which really is what he was growing into – as in the first three lines of the 1967 song, "Mr. Soul," which he was to turn eventually into a hard-driving standard of his concerts fifteen years later, with synthesizer and vocoder and computerized drums:

Oh, hello, Mr. Soul, I dropped by to pick up a reason
For the thought that I caught that my head is the event of the season
Why in crowds just a trace of my face could seem so pleasin'.

What he seems to be doing here is mocking not only the fans who were raising him so high, but also mocking himself – the fact that he *accommodated* these public reactions, waving back to the crowds, acknowledging the screams while thinking (last verse, first line, "Mr. Soul"): "*In a while will the smile on my face turn to plaster?*"

Yet there was still some trace of innocence. When they began to travel, at first it was just out and back, but then on longer trips they began to stay in Holiday Inns. "We thought we were on top of the world when we started to stay in Holiday Inns!" Neil said. They had a good time, liked one another, fought without seeing any one battle as something that would break up the group. Their first album (*Buffalo Springfield*, February 1967) and singles were drawing praise and good sales, and there was still the conviction that they would make it big – a sense I got very strongly from thousands of miles away one day in Toronto when *The Globe and Mail* copy-boys whom I'd often overheard saying, "There goes Scott Young," turned (in one electrifying instant) to "There goes Neil Young's father."

After Neil had been away a year, Bob went to Carmel, California, to see him and get his own golf game into shape. In April of 1967 he and Neil sent me a birthday card from a nightclub, the Rock Garden, in San Francisco where the Springfield were playing. A year into their first burst of fame, they'd been on TV's *Hollywood Palace* the previous Saturday night, and Bob wrote, "It's not definite yet but they should be on the *Tonight Show* soon if all goes well. Love, Bob and Neil. Enjoy your birthday!"

If Neil had been writing the note on that card, and levelling, it would have been a very different message. While Bob must have picked up on the excitement everybody else in the group felt about the possibility of playing Johnny Carson's *Tonight Show*, Neil was fighting it. When Charlie Greene and Brian Stone had taken on the group their reputations were as specialists in creating stars by shrewd use of the media. The *Tonight Show* would have been a major publicity coup. To their amazement, Neil was against it and they knew they couldn't do it without him.

His reasons were simple, even idealistic, but that didn't mean they were understood by Charlie and Brian. Basically, Neil didn't want to start chipping away at his sense of what Buffalo Springfield was all about. To Charlie and Brian, this band was business. They handled it as they would anything – grab the ball and run with it. To them, it was a rock 'n' roll group, people said the best on the coast, with a new album out that was doing well, everybody clamouring for the group, and Neil was fighting progress. Johnny Carson's *Tonight Show* would give Springfield national exposure, a great leap forward . . . *and Neil was against it!*

And for the stupidest reasons . . . if we imagine Charlie and Brian telling it: one mimics Neil's measured, unhurried tones: "I don't want to do the Carson show. Not that I have anything against Carson, I watch him quite a bit, but the thing is he, ah, our music is not *entertainment on television*. It's something else and I think it would be degrading to our music and to our fans and to what they thought they were part of, for us to be on that show."

Charlie and Brian, decibels rising: "For Chrissake, *degrading* to our *fans* and what they thought they were part of! To be on Carson! Which every other group in the world would bust their own grandmother's ass for a chance to do! And when I ask if he would have the same objections to Ed Sullivan, like, going on Sullivan, what he said to that, I just can't believe it: 'Ed Sullivan would be cool because the Beatles were on Ed Sullivan, the Rolling Stones, Elvis, Buddy Holly. So that would have historic proportions to it. Sullivan broke major acts. He had the courage to do something different. He did that for rock 'n' roll, did a hell of a lot for rock 'n' roll, he brought rock 'n' roll to the living rooms of middle America. . . . I remember sitting in our living room when I was little, a family thing, all of us watching Elvis on Ed Sullivan's *Toast of the Town*, singing "Tutti Frutti," I think. I can remember the whole family was going, "Gosh!" Without Ed Sullivan we wouldn't have seen Elvis for a long, long time.'"

Charlie and Brian lean back at that point, speechless at the perfidy of this guy they'd rescued from a fucking hearse, for Chrissake, and after a long sigh one says, "And after all that about Elvis and Sullivan and the family sitting around their goddamn crystal-set TV in the snowbanks up there, he adds, 'Carson never did that for rock 'n' roll.'"

When that came into the open, soon after Bob wrote that birthday card in the spring of 1967, the battle was such that Neil left the group for the first time. But leaving the group, it turned out, was somewhat like a divorce with visiting rights, or, as the English put it when a divorced couple keeps winding up in bed, going back for afters. When he left, the group tried to continue as a quartet, then pulled in Doug Hastings on guitar for a couple of months. Ken Koblun had been brought in earlier on a rescue mission from Canada to replace Bruce Palmer (who had been deported after a drug bust) on bass until Jim Fielder (later with Blood, Sweat and Tears) sat in for a while. Neil came and went, whiling away the time, mainly with a musician friend, Jack Nitzsche, who had a house in the Hollywood hills, writing songs, trying to pull himself together.

A year or so earlier, not long after the Springfield started, he'd met some musicians he liked, a group called the Rockets. Billy Talbot was one of them. Neil used to go to Billy's place in Laurel Canyon and they'd sing in Billy's garage – Neil, Billy, Danny Whitten, Ralph Molina, and others including singer Robin Lane. When Neil first met the Rockets they had just moved from being a straight singing group to playing instruments. A longtime roadie called BJ, or Baby John, recalls that these musicians, who were to become such a strong part of Neil's life as Crazy Horse, had started out as Danny and the Memories, street-corner singers. "Then acid rock came along and they decided they'd better learn how to play. At first Ralph was playing boxes [drums] and everybody else had these five-dollar guitars." Ralph remembers starting as a singer in New York, his birthplace, "singing mainly in hallways to get the echo." He was living in Florida later when a cousin called to say he should go to L.A. and join this singing group. Ralph: "We all lived together in an apartment complex called Mark Manor, managed by Billy Talbot's mother, Verna, a wonderful lady. She used to let us be late on the rent and was very kind – Billy got a lot of his character and personality from her."

When they changed their name to the Rockets and played at Whiskey au Go Go, Neil sometimes would sit in with them. But all that summer he was in touch on and off with the Springfield and in September rejoined the group – having missed, among other things, appearing with Springfield at the Monterey Pop Festival; he had simply objected to playing a pop festival ("I was very picky about things around that time").

For a while during the next eight or nine months the five originals were together again, Bruce Palmer managing to sneak back from Canada for a few months. They made an album called *Stampede*, which was not released, but when *Buffalo Springfield Again*, their second album, came out late in 1967, Tom Phillips in the Sunday edition of *The New York Times* called it "varied and weird and beautiful," and, as it is not easy to finger new talent unerringly, he might feel some satisfaction these many years later in rereading his last paragraph in that piece: "The lyrics on this album are to be listened to, especially the ones by Steve Stills and Neil Young. Stills' 'Hung Upside Down' tells in two verses of simple language exactly how it is to be young, stoned and hung upside down. And Young's 'Broken Arrow' has a real mythic quality – not too clear, maybe, but mysterious rather than just obscure."

That Christmas, 1967, Neil managed to visit Rassy and Bob in Ormond Beach, Florida. Rassy was renting a place and Bob was staying with her while he played golf. Neil was back in Florida a few months later when the Springfield was the opening act in a Beach Boys tour. Rassy later wrote to say, "You didn't miss much by not seeing him here. He had mislaid his pills two or three days previously, and due to some trouble on my line, no one could get me on the phone and no one would fill his prescription. Anyhow, he collapsed in the middle of their set. Fortunately I always carry the kids' pills when we go anywhere." She described him "lying ashen-faced" on the ground until he was well enough to be lifted into her car, which Bob had brought into the infield. "We brought him home here and he slept for several hours, ate, walked a bit on the beach and then we drove him to Gainesville where they did a fabulous show. . . . I'm glad I was there because no one else knew what to do. I would have sworn I couldn't run that fast under any circumstances – even with the police clearing a path for me as they were. Bob was a great help . . . Rassy."

It seemed possible later that, given his dislike of this medication's side effects, Neil's "mislaying" his pills that time might have been an early experiment in trying to do without them – as he managed to do some years later. At the very least, the incident hinted at emotional stress that soon led to a major change in his life.

That letter was dated April 19, 1968. Buffalo Springfield had been together one way or another for twenty-five months since their chance meeting on Sunset Boulevard. Buffalo Springfield were back on the west coast about three weeks later when the end came.

Earlier that winter, Elliot Roberts was with Joni Mitchell one day in an L.A. recording studio. She and Neil had kept in touch sporadically since Christmas 1963, when she and her first husband, Chuck, had been playing in a tiny club on Winnipeg's Main Street. Neil, then just turned eighteen, met them there and found they had no place to spend Christmas, so the three of them had walked south through the snow and across the Norwood Bridge to visit Neil's aunt Vinia (Toots) and her husband Neil, the tall, calm artist after whom Neil had been named. Toots made them a big dinner. Two years later Joni was a name in Yorkville while Neil was carrying the top of that amplifier down the street. Now in L.A. Elliot, already showing strong signs of knowing the difference between natural sevens and snake-eyes, was managing her and they heard a group recording in the studio next door.

"Who is it?" Elliot asked.

"Buffalo Springfield."

Joni: "Hey, I have a friend with Buffalo Springfield. Neil Young from Winnipeg."

Elliot and Joni went in. This was the first time Elliot met Neil. He had admired the Springfield from a distance. They were tied up to Brian and Charlie but Elliot found that to a greater or lesser extent, all musicians in the group were dissatisfied with that arrangement.

Getting across to them the idea that it didn't have to be that way took some time, but Elliot was a new breed of Hollywoodian; a far cry from what Neil calls the weasels in the woodwork. Elliot has the clear idea that what is valuable about his clients is their talent; which thus must be protected from harm in all its forms, including overwork and over-exposure to the media. This attitude puzzles and infuriates the media, but his idea is that talent, with his shrewd judgement of when and where to offer it, really needs very little between it and the audience except the distance between a stage and the front row of seats, or the distance between a record rack and the cash register.

A couple of weeks after the Beach Boys' tour ended, Elliot thought he had reached agreement in principle to manage Buffalo Springfield, beginning with buying out Charlie and Brian. He worked the points into a contract, took it to where the Springfield was playing, and showed it to them. Four wanted to sign. Neil said no, told Elliot to get lost; he wouldn't even stop playing to talk. Nobody knew that he had decided once again to quit the Springfield, or was close enough to that decision that he wouldn't commit himself to a new deal and then con-tinue to go through the screwed-up quitting and coming back, quitting and coming back, that had been happening. Elliot didn't understand it at all until a few days later there was a knock at his door. Neil was standing there. He said, "Look, I've split with Buffalo Springfield. Will you handle me as a single?"

Springfield's final gig as a group was on May 5, 1968. The laments began immediately, and have continued. Their audience had been rel-atively small compared to the Beatles' or Rolling Stones' of that time, but it was totally devoted. Springfield albums have sold steadily ever since. Listeners, both originals and latecomers, have never stopped stoking the fires. In every extensive interview with any member of the group, even this many years later, the question almost always is asked: how could a group that good break up? There are usually more clues than answers. Stephen said later he was a large part of the problem, impossible to live with because he tended to drive everybody, "like they were a team of horses, or something." Neil acknowledged that there were battles centring on him and Steve, but said they weren't impor-tant enough to break up the group. "We were good, even great – I thought when we started we'd be together forever. We were just too young to be patient, and I was the worst. I was having these seizures and I was sure, I'm sure now, knowing more about it, that the way I felt and acted was mostly because of nerves, the seizures. It got that I didn't care. I didn't *want* to make it with them. I didn't want to be a slave to the medication I was taking for epilepsy. I couldn't stand the way I was feeling. My thing, I figured, was to keep on going, doing something else. I know I should have been happy, but in some ways it was the worst time of my life. . . .

"The tremendous reputation the Springfield has now tells you something, but I'm not sure what. The fact that we weren't completely successful at the time makes it a stronger kind of story now, in retrospect. You know: the line that we were *really great*, and yet didn't make it."

Really great? In Lillian Roxon's authoritative *Rock Encyclopedia*, her assessment is, "The story of the Buffalo Springfield is a sad one because they had all the makings of being *the* rock group of the sixties." That is saying something, considering that among the big groups of the sixties were the Beatles, The Band, and the Rolling Stones. In *Rock Family Trees* Pete Frame wrote: "One of the best rock in' roll bands there ever was!" *The New York Times* of Sunday, October 6, 1968, reviewing the post-break-up album *Last Time Around* noted that "in the war of sound that the pop revolution has become, the quietly beautiful Buffalo Springfield albums have been consistently overlooked and underrated," underscoring the truth of Neil's remark that Springfield seemed stronger in retrospect than it had at the time of its demise.

A thoughtful assessment came recently from Neil's brother Bob, who said: "Buffalo Springfield was the beginning of something that couldn't be seen as clearly at the time as it could be seen later, especially because the kind of life lived by Buffalo Springfield supported what was said in its music. They were young, they were troubled, they experimented with drugs but were not terminal victims, they didn't understand their own talents or their own times. In other words, they were so much *like* the people who listened to them. Lyndon Johnson was president, Americans were dying in Vietnam, the Kennedys were being assassinated, and the young were not puzzled as much as stupefied by where the world was going; so when someone seemed to make sense of it, the feeling was one of enlightenment. Buffalo Springfield was part of the beginning of something which soon was to get a boost from Woodstock, and which contains, or perhaps signifies, an expression of social significance relevant to our society today. Sometimes people come to me who say, 'Your brother, Neil, was part of my growing up – he said things.' Neil's poetry and music combine some kind of wisdom and native perception. From what I hear and what I feel, it hits home often enough that he must be seen as part of the balance between what we are day to day, and the Utopia we seek."

Throw nuclear weapons into that social mix, along with the CIA, Richard Nixon, Jimmy Carter, Ronald Reagan, the Hiroshima anniversary photos, Cruise missiles, and the rest. When you think of the young of any generation being faced with all that on one side and terrorists on the other, much of humanity is in the vast middle ground between the two adversaries, listening eagerly for people who seem to understand their lives, and live to tell the tale.

9

The Loner and Friends

A little after six one morning early in June 1968, a month after the Springfield broke up, my bedside phone rang. R.J. (Dic) Doyle, editor of *The Globe and Mail*, was on the line.

"Have you been listening to the radio?" he asked.

I hadn't.

"They shot Bobby Kennedy in Los Angeles late last night," he said. "He's unconscious."

I was writing a daily column for the *Globe* and also was sent to cover some major news events as a reporter. Doyle did not ever phone me just to pass the time of day.

"The next flight out is about nine this morning," he said.

A few hours later I was in Los Angeles going by cab directly from the airport to the hospital. Thousands thronged the streets outside waiting for word. I phoned a story back to the *Globe* quickly from a pay phone across from the hospital and then finished a longer piece, working elbow to elbow with everyone else in the gymnasium of the hospital's nurses' residence. This had become instant headquarters for about 600 reporters of all shapes, sizes, sexes, and media. Phone and other cables littered the floor. By around six P.M. desk space was non-existent. The man at the next typewriter agreed to guard my place against squatters while I got a cup of coffee, if I'd bring him one, too. When I returned I told him, "I have a son around here somewhere but I haven't an address or phone number. He might even be on the road."

"On the road?"

"He's a musician."

"What's his name?"

I told him.

"Buffalo Springfield!" he said. "Christ, he's the one who wrote 'Nowadays Clancy Can't Even Sing'!"

"That's the one."

He was a reporter for the *Los Angeles Free Press*, one of the better underground papers of the time. "Let me see what I can do," he said. "Our music people should know where he is, or be able to find out." He picked up the phone. Two hours later the public-address system set up for medical bulletins and other news or announcements said, "Call for Scott Young."

I yelled out the number of the phone extension closest to me, picked up the receiver, and said, "Hello?"

"Daddy!" Neil said.

I told him I had to stay there until the *Globe*'s two A.M. EDT deadline, eleven P.M. in L.A. We arranged to meet at a place nearby if he couldn't get through the police barriers. About eleven I was called to the entrance. The police had let him through when he said his father was in there. We embraced and I could feel his thinness but he looked and sounded lively and exceptionally well; dressed in an easy-going way, classy, but unostentatious. We walked back downhill through the crowd to where he'd parked his boxlike British Mini, a hell of a change from an old hearse.

"Better acoustics, too," he said. "Listen." He pushed a cassette into the tape deck. For a minute the stereo speakers surrounded us with music, then he switched it off. "You feel like a beer and some food?" he asked.

He drove a few miles and parked I don't know where. The place was dimly lighted, with old-fashioned lamps hanging over big plank tables set in booths between comfortable benches, sort of country in its atmosphere.

"What'll it be, Neil?" the waiter asked.

We had cheeseburgers and beer. Yeah, the Springfield had broken up, he said, but what he really wanted to talk about was his next move – to record an album of his own. It all flooded out, with enthusiasm. He was working on some of his earlier songs and writing new ones. Elliot Roberts had negotiated a contract with Warner Brothers/Reprise Records, and with the advance Neil had put a down payment on a house. "The deal hasn't closed yet but it's a great house. I'd like you to see it if you have time tomorrow. It's in one of the canyons, Topanga, where the prices haven't gone out of sight yet. I love it there." While he waited to take possession he'd stayed a while in Topanga with his friend David Briggs, "sleeping on his couch, sleeping on other people's couches." That night we ranged a long way into his life, catching up. I can't remember exactly how we got talking about his relationships with women, but this is the earliest time I remember him talking about the way his obsession with music didn't help such relationships. "I lived for a while with a girl that I liked very much, but she left," he said. He thought for a while, staring at the beer label, then said with some regret, "I think when I was with her, too often when I got home I picked up the guitar instead of the girl." He didn't have a steady girl-friend right then, meaning that he either didn't know, or didn't know well, Susan Acevedo, who managed a restaurant in Topanga. They were married less than six months later.

He drove me back to my hotel around two or three in the morning and gave me the phone number where he was staying. He'd be in and out the next day but if I'd call when I was free he'd pick me up. I left an early call so that I could check on Bobby Kennedy's condition. When the wake-up call came I turned on the radio. Kennedy was dead. I reached the hospital pressroom half an hour later. A posted notice said that the body would be flown immediately to New York. That meant the media had to move, too, and fast. It was mid-morning when I called the number Neil had left me. He was out. I could only leave a message. Yet when I flew east later that day I felt as if a great gift had been given me, those unexpected easy hours that were good for *us*, but came about through terrible tragedy.

I was an admirer of Bobby Kennedy. I stared from the window at the clouds thinking of another early afternoon, nearly five years before, when I'd driven through a downpour in Toronto to catch an aircraft on ninety minutes' notice. That was the day President John Kennedy was shot in Dallas. Mixed in with that sadness for a country that kept assas-sinating its best, I thought from time to time of Neil, the look of him, the sound of him – not the sound of his music at all, but the sound of us in that booth last night, the father and son from the polio year, the chicken business, the Saturday morning paper route followed by pancakes in the quiet bungalow on the Brock Road in Pickering, the pat on the shoulder on the night I tried to tell Bob and Neil why our family, which had been so good a lot of the time, was breaking up. Those thoughts were in the background, but there, for much of the next two days. When I stood in Arlington National Cemetery on the final night watching in the misty glow of floodlights as the Kennedy family slowly followed the coffin to its final resting place, I wept, and not all for Bobby Kennedy.

As it turned out, I never was to see the Topanga house. (Nobody else of widespread international interest was assassinated out that way in the next few months.) But one way or another I have come to understand its ambience, a good deal of which persists in Neil's life to this day. Which brings us to David Briggs.

Neil's introduction to Topanga Canyon had been through the Springfield. The group had lived a while in a rented house there. When they left, it was rented by a young record producer who had run away from his Wyoming birthplace when he was fifteen, worked in a mine for a while, and had various other odd jobs that eventually led him into music. David Briggs. He was about Neil's age. One day after the Springfield breakup, David was driving a friend's war-surplus army personnel carrier in Topanga Canyon when he passed a lanky longhair, Neil, walking along the side of the road. They didn't know one another even by sight, but David pulled up and said, "Hey! Want a lift?"

Neil, an aficionado of strange vehicles (not only hearses), stood and gazed at the car, the metal benches in the back for troops to sit on. "Nice car!" he said. "Nice car!" Then he got in. As has happened several times with Neil when he meets people who are going to stay in his life, he and David got along immediately, spent the next week or two walking the area and holed up in David's house talking about the solo album Neil had told me he was planning, his first as a solo, and trying out some of the music on the spot. They were both young, both relatively inexperienced – with a lot more ideas than know-how.

They worked over some of Neil's songs one word at a time, used every guitar that Neil had, every amplifier he had, Neil doing all the guitar work himself and bringing in people he knew on other instruments – drummer George Grantham, who had joined Jim Messina and Richie Furay in a band called Poco; Jim Messina on bass, and some others. There were even violins. When Neil had ideas, for instance, for the string parts on "The Loner," since he didn't write music David called in a friend, David Blumberg. Neil would sing his tune and Blumberg would translate it into notes. Jack Nitzsche did some piano work and arranging, including on "The Old Laughing Lady." For recording, Neil and David Briggs blazed trails to a lot of different studios, picking rooms for their particular sounds. They cut tracks in one place and went somewhere else to record acoustic guitars and somewhere else to do the electrics. And then after all that work, something right outside of their control almost blew it.

Even before the first release, Neil – by autumn living in his own house along the canyon – was extremely concerned about what he saw as an album that might make or break him. A Los Angeles newspaper piece by Pete Johnson describes him sitting on his Topanga verandah late that summer. "He is nervous about the album, as nervous as if it were the first time he'd been in a studio. During the interview he worries about a single, about the sequence of the songs on the album, and about the mix – the relationship of instruments and vocals. He plays it and is alternately proud and fretful, wanting it to be the best he could possibly do, thinking first that it is, then that it isn't, then that it is, and so on."

As it turned out, his nervousness was justified, but for a reason he couldn't foresee. Someone had just devised a process by which a stereo record could be made to sound like a mono record on radio. David: "It was one of my first impressions of Neil, and it has continued: give him something new and he's there! He's going to be the first guy knocking on the door to try it! Sometimes it works and sometimes it doesn't. This was just one that didn't work." The process sounded okay on radio, which was what it was designed for, but the album sound itself was so disappointing to Neil that he went back to Warners and fought for not only a remix, but also for a deal whereby anyone with the first pressing could return it in exchange for the second version. It was a tough battle. He didn't have much clout at the time. He told the company he wouldn't record for it again if his wishes were not met this time. Warners reluctantly said okay. Several critics since have said there wasn't a great deal of difference between the two mixes, but to Neil there was a difference – and that's what counted. He didn't have the confidence in his voice then that he did later, but it was developing – and one of the principal functions of the remix was to bring his voice up more.

The critical reception was excellent for a first album, a warm-up for what was to come. The songs on that album, released simply as *Neil Young*, were "The Emperor of Wyoming," "The Loner," "If I Could Have Her Tonight," "I've Been Waiting for You," "The Old Laughing Lady," "String Quartet from Whiskey Boot Hill," "Here We Are in the Years," "What Did You Do to My Life," "I've Loved Her So Long," and a nine-and-a-half-minute run at an epic, "The Last Trip to Tulsa." Several have been among his standards ever since. Fourteen years later he opened one concert with "The Old Laughing Lady."

The autumn before the album's release, Bob visited Neil again. His recollections of Neil at Topanga have fun in them. That June night with me in L.A., Neil had been enthusiastic about life at Topanga, and the interesting neighbours he would have – people in the entertainment business, in films, in music. He'd mentioned to me that one of his neighbours, um, ah, owned a goat. "I don't know what the guy does," he said, then laughed, "I guess that's what he does – owns a goat."

It turned out that Neil now had goats of his own. To keep the weeds down because of fire regulations, he had them staked on the slopes around his house. Bob laughed, "It was like a comedy turn when Neil moved them to some other part of the yard. One was okay, but this other, Neil would have to turn the hose on it to keep it at bay while he took the stake out of the ground and moved it. Then he'd run and the goat would run, trying to ram him."

By then, besides the Mini, Neil had a 1940 Lincoln. Bob had an indication of Neil's finances at the time, when he and Elliot Roberts rode into L.A. with Neil. On the way he pulled in to see a mechanic who specialized in antique and foreign cars. When Neil was out of the car, Elliot – who also was staying with Neil at the time – sighed to Bob, "God forbid anything should go wrong with this car. To fix it probably would cost a million dollars. Which nobody has." At the time Bob describes Neil as just working on his songs, scraping along, living from day to day.

That September I was in Moscow as part of an advance party from the Canadian Broadcasting Corporation to negotiate filming a TV documentary about Soviet hockey, which through the 1960s had dominated the Olympic and world championships. I had written a skeleton shooting script. The main event of our four days in Moscow that first trip was a meeting with the deputy minister of culture to hammer out ground rules for our shooting a few weeks later. It was my first experience of the profound difference between the social status of a TV writer in the Soviet Union and in North America. The Russians treated the writer as *the* important person in the equation, the one who had to be listened to, and influenced, if possible. Wowie! Our producer, director, and budget manager languished uneasily at the far end of the table. The writer, S. Young, sat in the middle. Directly opposite the deputy minister.

He wanted to know what I had in mind. Amazing! I told him. I spoke eloquently and won everything but one point: I stressed the importance of visiting a Russian village to see how kids' hockey there compared with ours in Canada; not to compare the skills developed as much as where the game stood in the social fabric of a community. The deputy minister took that point under advisement (and later didn't give us a village after all, but did give us a place normally closed to visitors, a small steel-mill city named Tcherepovetz).

All else was business, negotiated by one of the CBC's top negotiators, then or ever, Thom Benson. Our crew would be mixed fifty-fifty between Russians and Canadians. We could take film out raw. We had all broadcast rights on our side of the Iron Curtain; they all rights on their side. The agreement was put in final form by telex after we returned to Canada. Our shooting began in November in Moscow, with moves to Kiev and Tcherepovetz to follow. All of which is intended to impart that I was busy as hell eleven time zones east of Topanga Canyon when a message came to me on CBC Moscow's telex. Neil and Susan Acevedo, someone I was hearing of for the first time, would be married December 1. Astrid and I were invited. I wrestled with that (among wistful congratulations from the three young Russian women who were our interpreters). And it did turn out that I left the shoot late in November, my work pretty well done, with a day or two to make the wedding – if I hadn't been exhausted. Still, I hadn't made up my mind when I landed in Toronto and read Susan's handwritten invitation on a plain folded white card:

> Susan Acevedo and Neil Young
> invite you to attend their
> wedding reception

Med., 1944: I sent this along with a letter to tell Rassy I'd soon be home.

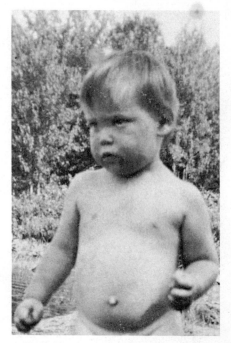

September 1947: Neil at twenty-two months on our first family holiday.

March 1948: Rassy and I at my sister's wedding.

June 1948: Neil and Bob at the Lake of Bays. My best summer ever.

As a family we were pretty good in that summer of 1948 (opposite). Rassy made pies of wild strawberries and I wrote every day and friends visited. When the cottage became too cold in the mornings we moved to Jackson's Point and then bought a house at Omemee where Neil spent his days fishing and later, after surviving polio, became the resident mischief in Miss Jones's room at school. The years then started to skim by. Rassy and I had our first serious rift in 1954 when Neil was about nine (above, right) but we stayed together and moved to Pickering. When I started writing a daily column for the *Globe and Mail*, Neil, nearing his teens (at right), was the hero of some columns. A friend of ours once warned me that if I didn't stop mentioning him so much I'd ruin his life; he would come to expect to be the centre of attention all the time, would have trouble in later years, and so on. If that's a rule, I guess Neil is the exception.

When our family broke up, Neil went with Rassy to Winnipeg where music took over his life. Soon he was leading groups, hiring and firing, ready for bigger things: in California (in an old hearse), where he and his friend Bruce Palmer became charter members of the best new rock band on the coast, Buffalo Springfield (below with Bruce in foreground and Dewey Martin, Richie Furay, Neil, and Stephen Stills; and opposite, same people, different order). Two years later they broke up. Neil toured alone, including to the Riverboat in Toronto (left). Next came the group called Crazy Horse (inset, opposite). I almost forgot – in Toronto I got him a passport so he'd no longer be an illegal in the United States.

(Joel Bernstein)

Opposite page: By then Neil's persona was firmly established as a moody, tortured singer and songwriter who spoke directly to young people puzzled and scared by Vietnam, Richard Nixon, and the killings at Kent State, about which he'd written his searing song "Ohio," banned from air play in many states.

Above: Neil, beside Elliot Roberts, his longtime manager and friend, with fans on the *Time Fades Away* tour, 1973.

Right: One Christmas I gave Neil a subscription to the *Globe and Mail*. The guy who is always looking for a piece of paper to write a song on wrote "Yonder Stands the Sinner" on the first piece of paper that came to hand, a *Globe and Mail* wrapper.

The *Tonight's The Night* tour, left, with Nils Lofgren (straw hat), Billy Talbot (front), Ben Keith (head turned), and Ralph Molina (No. 32), came after two of Neil's friends died of heroin overdoses. The music's tortured roughness was a needed antidote to his smoothly professional work with supergroup Crosby, Stills, Nash and Young (below).

on Sunday, December 1, 1968
at 2 o'clock P.M.
611 Skyline Trail
Topanga, California

I should have made the effort: landed in Toronto, changed clothes, picked up Astrid, flown to Los Angeles. My fatigue is a reason I don't accept any more. I phoned Neil. He told me they would book a room for us in a Malibu motel they had checked out. "It's thirty-five minutes away but it's the closest one," he said. When I told him I couldn't come, he sounded sad. "I really would like someone from our family to be here," he said.

I called him on the day of the wedding, but apparently the reception had got out of hand. When the phone rang, someone simply took the receiver off the hook. I could hear loud music and voices in the background, and then someone came on and said Neil and Susan weren't there. Neil told me later that it got so wild he and Susan decided to get out and go off by themselves.

I wrote with a suggestion. In January Neil was going on a small tour to promote his new album – the Bitter End in New York, the Riverboat in Toronto, Le Hibou in Ottawa, and some others. I proposed that as a wedding present we would fly Susan and her seven-year-old daughter Tia to Toronto, to be there when Neil was.

I was delighted when Susan accepted. I intended to make sure that it was the right kind of welcome for my first daughter-in-law. The trip seemed definite even the day before New Year's when Susan wrote to tell us about their Christmas, adding as a sidelight that "Neil has become a maniac about the house, has torn down a wall, panelled the kitchen with redwood and built closets in our room. I'm afraid to leave the house. All he needs is some idle time and he's off. We're looking forward to our trip." She sounded warm and easy-going.

But a few days later she wrote to say the trip was off. Tia's teacher felt she was not doing well enough in school to miss the time and "then I was going to come alone but Tia felt so badly about being left that I decided to stay." She hoped to see us in the summer instead, but that didn't happen either, and as it turned out, we never met.

10

Out of the Red
and into the Black

Sometimes I am tempted to write my part of this account as comedy. Maybe I'm doing that without even trying. I never really knew what the hell was going on, even when I was more or less in the middle of it. I didn't know which girl left Neil because when he got home he picked up his guitar instead of picking up the girl. I don't know if the main reason he used to go to Billy Talbot's house in Laurel Canyon was to sing and jam with Billy, Danny Whitten, and Ralph Molina, the musicians who later were to be known as Crazy Horse, but then were part of the Rockets, or to see singer Robin Lane, one of whose close friends was Danny Whitten. Also, some might think it ludicrous that I and my bank overdraft would make the grand gesture of offering *economy* airfare to Susan and Tia so I could meet my new daughter-in-law, when even incipient rock stars are known to be rolling in money. But I was innocent of such things, as you might have gathered, and I happened to know that Neil didn't have money to spare then, no matter what he had later. (That year he was buying himself out of his pre-Elliot contract.)

In 1969, the year that Neil's career really took off, he told me his dates at the Riverboat and I asked him by phone to stay with us, but was not especially surprised when he said that because of his working hours and other things he'd stay at a hotel and would let us know where when he arrived.

But late on the night he flew in, he phoned from the airport.

"I wonder if I could stay with you tonight," he said.

"Sure."

"I'll explain when I get there."

He'd been hassled by customs. Long hair was regarded very suspiciously at borders in those days. His luggage and instruments and body were searched, which took a couple of hours. Then he was allowed to put his clothes back on and phone me. He was shaken and wanted to be somewhere easy, like in a bed at our place. When his airline cab pulled up outside and I helped him in with his stuff we talked for a while and then went to bed.

In the morning we ate and drank coffee and he told me the details of his battle with the record company over the remix, but he also had more immediate things on his mind. First he wanted to buy a leather jacket. I drove him to a place on Yonge Street just below Bloor. On the way downtown we were stopped at the Inglewood Drive traffic light when he said, "I guess I owe you some money."

He'd made the one payment on that $400 loan in 1966, the month he worked at Coles. I'd paid the rest, one month at a time.

I said, "You remember the deal?"

He thought a moment. "You mean, that if I paid it back I could always borrow from you again if I needed it?"

"Yeah."

"I remember."

"Well, I don't think you're going to need money from me again, so I'd like to leave it as one time when you needed help and I gave it."

He glanced across at me and smiled. "Okay. Thanks."

We were driving south on Mount Pleasant when he said, "How long does it take to get a passport?"

I'd wondered from time to time about his original illegal entry into the United States, but assumed it had been fixed up somehow. It hadn't. "I haven't been out of the U.S. since then, so it didn't matter so much, but now I'll probably be doing more travelling, so I'd better get it cleared up."

Getting a Canadian passport in those days was usually about a two-week affair. He wouldn't be in Canada that long – a few days at the

Riverboat and another few in Ottawa at Le Hibou. I told him that there were ways to do it faster, but I'd have to check around. At the leather shop, I left him trying on jackets and phoned a friend, Thomas B. O'Neill, a lawyer who as the low-scoring but hard-hitting Windy O'Neill had been a professional hockey player back when he weighed 100 pounds less. He had run for office occasionally, supported by us on one occasion when we had a coffee party in our home for him to meet prospective voters in our neighbourhood. By nature he would do anything for a friend even without such campaigning on his behalf.

"I think I can get it through in a day," he said.

"How, for God's sake?"

A powerful cabinet minister in the fairly new Liberal government of the time, Pierre Trudeau's first, was Donald S. Macdonald. Windy had worked in his election campaigns. Windy would have liked to make it in politics as a Member of Parliament, a member of the Ontario legislature, a Toronto alderman. He also would have liked an appointment as a judge. He never was any of those things, but political parties don't forget people who work for them. "I'll call Don Macdonald's office," he said.

Neil had the necessary photos taken that day. He and I went to Windy's office to fill out the forms. Windy signed all the places where someone respectable (postmaster, police chief, ordained minister, or whatever) was supposed to vouch for the applicant. The next day Neil had his passport. He was impressed.

The Riverboat that night was the first place I had heard Neil play and sing as a professional. I can see it still: a dim little place with a small stage a few inches off the floor, nearby booths holding the offspring of friends who used to visit us twenty years earlier at the Lake of Bays. Some had known Neil since they were babies. Some were a little hostile to me. The story had got around that he and I were at odds because I hadn't rushed to help with the $600 for that bleeping amplifier of long ago. And he had this amazing presence. When he spoke, played, and sang, there wasn't another sound in the place. After his first set someone came to me and said, "Neil wants you to come up to his dressing room." I followed up a narrow flight of stairs and onto a sort of outdoor walkway. A teenage girl was waiting there in the half-dark.

"I knew Neil in Fort William," she said earnestly. "Will you tell him I'm out here?"

Inside, the room was about six by eight, with one or two straight chairs. A news photographer took a picture of us, Neil's arm around my shoulder, both smiling straight into the camera, the first photo taken of us together for ten years. The girl came in and Neil did remember her, and after a minute or two she left.

We saw one another only a couple of times more before he left for Ottawa. He was busy catching up with old friends and I was busy as well, but also didn't want to be a constant figure hanging around in the background like a faithful old retainer. Because of my part in breaking up our family I found it difficult to push myself forward uninvited. Perhaps because of that, I missed early opportunities to bring my relationship with Neil back fully to what it was as a memory, in my mind. For whatever reason, I was not at the Riverboat *every* night. I was not always hanging around when he surfaced at his hotel in the morning. Scarcely an hour went by that I wasn't thinking about him, but also I was helping to edit my Soviet hockey documentary, great haste being dictated by the fact that at the time a Soviet team was in Canada for exhibition games in Winnipeg. We had agreed to show a Soviet representative a rough cut of the show, to check our facts. I flew out with the rough cut and screened it in a Winnipeg motel room for my Moscow connection, Andrei Starovoitov of the USSR hockey committee, and the big and affable V. Kaluzhny of the Soviet embassy in Ottawa, who acted as interpreter. They liked it, so that was that. Meanwhile, Neil had left for Ottawa.

Soon after, I decided to make a drastic change in my life. I had become tired after twelve years of writing columns, usually six a week, for *The Globe and Mail* and *Globe Magazine*. The editor, Dic Doyle, knew my feeling. Many of my columns in the previous few years had been engaged with both federal and provincial politics. When there was an opening in the *Globe's* Ottawa bureau I asked for it and was accepted. I moved to Ottawa almost immediately. Astrid stayed to rent our house in Toronto. She would follow me in a few months with young Astrid and Deirdre, at the end of the school year. We met each weekend at our then recently bought country place near Omemee, a hundred acres with our new house finished just enough to be livable. So at a time when I might have been on the phone to Neil once a week or so, I was living in a furnished apartment in Ottawa, having a bad bout of influenza, and at the same time writing the first of two books I was to do (thirteen years apart) with Punch Imlach, then recently fired (for the first of two times) as coach and general manager of Toronto

Maple Leafs. That spring also the Queen's Canadian representative, Governor General Roland Michener, undertook a major tour of the Canadian Arctic. I was sent along to cover it, flying usually in small aircraft, from one Inuit settlement to another, landing on the ice at Rankin Inlet, Eskimo Point, and dozens of other outposts until eventually we reached the northern community of Resolute, and flew from there to Alert, the world's most northerly permanent settlement, about 500 miles from the North Pole.

A few weeks after I got back from the Arctic there was another crisis. I had offered the Imlach book, a hot item in hockey-obsessed Canada, to the Globe for excerpting. It had not been picked up. But two other Toronto newspapers, the Telegram and the Star, bid for it. The Telegram with the better offer got first serial rights. The Globe then invoked a clause in the American Newspaper Guild contract that said an employee could not work for any publication in direct competition. I was torn. The money involved for serial rights and syndication was $9,200 – normally not enough to change one's life over, but half was Imlach's and I felt there was a principle involved. Only a week or two after the Globe had moved my furniture into the four-bedroom house I had rented in Ottawa, this dispute came to a head. John Bassett, the Telegram's publisher, sometimes a go-for-the-jugular man but not in this case, phoned to say that he would let me out of our agreement if I wished; "You've been at the Globe a long time. I wouldn't want to be responsible for you ending your association there." But I felt that the Globe was being unfair, because it had had first refusal. When I said that, he asked me to join the Telegram. Those are the facts, although later it was put about that I had simply succumbed to a rich offer to move to the Telegram along with the book excerpts. Bassett did give me $12,000 a year more than the Globe had been paying, but the basic dispute was my feeling that the Globe had blown it and was trying to recover at my expense. Anyway, a month after the Globe had paid to move my family and furniture to Ottawa, the Telegram paid the same movers to bring us back. Our Toronto house had been rented; we had to rent another – ah, it was all very tiresome, but it was done, and with a couple of weeks to go before starting at the Telegram we packed the family Chrysler and drove west to visit relations on the prairies.

All this had taken place six months or so after Neil had played those coffee houses in Toronto and Ottawa. We didn't see one another or talk much, beyond bare-bones details. During that time, Neil was making some of the most important moves of his life. But it was September before I began to catch up.

Once a few years later Neil told an interviewer that when he said one thing today, he meant it today, but the answer might be quite different tomorrow. "Okay, we'll interview you tomorrow," the interviewer said. In the summer of 1968 when he was in Topanga writing songs and working towards his first album, he'd spoken strongly on behalf of going it alone, not being part of a group. Obviously, that couldn't be taken quite literally – he meant he didn't want to be *tied* to any one group any more. Working with other musicians in a looser arrangement was part of his life. On his first album, he was joined in this song or that by five other musicians, George Grantham, Jim Messina, Jack Nitzsche, Dr. John, and Ry Cooder. The album was well reviewed, but no blockbuster. His coffee-house crowds in Toronto and Ottawa were good, but he and Elliot still joke about the poster for Neil's appearance at the Bitter End in New York. Neil: "*Super* poster! Bigger than the crowd." Elliot had sold Neil to doubting engagers with a one-two punch; he'd had to promise that if they would take Neil, he would send the then better-known Joni Mitchell on the same route soon after. Like a sports deal, for future considerations.

After Neil returned home from Canada, he sat in from time to time with the Rockets at the Whiskey au Go Go on Sunset Boulevard. One day when he was home with a bad cold he wrote three songs, "Cinnamon Girl," "Down by the River," and "Cowgirl in the Sand" – and thought they'd go great with Whitten, Talbot, and Molina from the Rockets, who also included at that time Leon Whitsell on guitar and vocals, George Whitsell the same, and Bobby Notkoff on violin. The Rockets were no green hands. They had released an album in March 1968, on the White Whale label, featuring all their own compositions, including four songs by Danny Whitten, one by Talbot/Molina, four by Leon Whitsell, and one by George Whitsell. Nevertheless, Whitten, Talbot, and Molina agreed to record with Neil and then go back to the Rockets. But things didn't turn out as they had planned. The recording session was so good that the three Rockets became Crazy Horse, and the remaining three musicians went on to other things.

Neil and Crazy Horse liked one another. They fitted. In the instant way of the rock world then and now, when something seems to work you don't wait around – you go out and use it while it's hot. They went on a nationwide tour of small halls as Neil Young and Crazy Horse. There was incipient difficulty because Danny Whitten was using heroin, but it hadn't yet got him as badly as it was going to. By the time Neil and Crazy Horse came back from the tour, Neil's songs (and some by the others) were well honed. They rang up David Briggs and talked about a recording session. But this one was different. David: "I think all the thought and work that Neil and I put into his first album, going from studio to studio, just made him tired to think about. I mean, for *him* it had really dragged on – he's a really immediate guy, as we all know. I remember after that, he said, 'Boy, I don't want to do that again, I want to get a band together and make band music and go in and *do* it.'"

So this time, with Crazy Horse, they tried a couple of studios and found one that really worked. Except for a couple of things at one other studio, the whole album *Everybody Knows This Is Nowhere* was recorded in one place. That also was when Neil first started experimenting with singing live to tracks (recording words and music simultaneously) – which back in the old days was the way records were made; it was the way Ray Charles made records and Little Richard and people of that generation, people of Neil's earliest musical roots. By then Neil had developed confidence in his voice, his ability to sing, to the point that he wanted to go in and play his guitar and sing his music and record both at the same time. They did some songs that way, but not all at this first try. Some background vocals were recorded separately and some of his vocals were also recut, but it was no longer a matter of course that he would lay down music tracks first and later do the vocals.

David and Neil were getting to know one another very well. The long friendship and recording relationship that lasted through many more albums had its foundation then, at least partly because Neil likes an edge in people and David was not the world's easiest person to get along with. Another of David's close friends once told me, "David and I have a friendship that ranges from him being so tough on me once that I had tears in my eyes, right from that to hugging each other like brothers when something went well." But with Neil, David had made up his mind: "The thing that really struck me the most about him during that time and subsequently was like this – he was such a great writer of moody ballads that everyone's perception of him as a person was totally different from what the guy is really like. You analyze his songs and everybody thinks, here's this brooding, melancholy guy, this tortured, inner-looking person. But from the first minute I knew him, I saw him as a prankster and a joker, a happy-go-lucky guy who loved to hang out and have fun; really a brilliant *writer* who could sit down and put himself in a context and write about a subject that has nothing to do with his real personality. I mean, he's got his share of torments but they certainly never apply to his dealings one on one with normal people. In my life of working with artists, I've never met anybody like him. He'll sit down and talk, he doesn't care if you're a bartender or a mechanic, he'll talk to you straight up, no condescending, just be a really open guy. It's always a shock to people."

Everybody Knows This Is Nowhere was released in May 1969. If anybody had been counting, that made three albums in less than a year that Neil had out working for him – *Last Time Around* with Buffalo Springfield, put together by Jim Messina with some help from Richie Furay after the group broke up; *Neil Young*, his first solo album; and what was seen later as his big breakthrough album, *Everybody Knows This Is Nowhere*.

But, and it is a big but, at the time when he first recorded with Crazy Horse Neil had been married to Susan for only a few months but hadn't been home much. When he *was* home, anyone visiting was charmed by the atmosphere. A good writer, Marci McDonald, described his home atmosphere glowingly for a *Toronto Star* piece in February 1969:

> He's created a world of his own in this incredible house on stilts high on the side of the canyon, a world filled with the things that make him happy: Spanish-American antiques and exotic skin rugs that glow rich with age in the candlelight, art made by a friend, a recording studio sound system, a half-husky dog named Winnipeg and a half-dozen Persian pedigree cats. There is, too, a sunny blonde named Susan with hair that flows down to her waist, and an equally sunny seven-year-old daughter, Tia.
>
> When the interview is over, friends drop by, including David Briggs (who lives down the hill). Neil perches on a chair with a cat. Susan lights more candles, then spreads a fantastic table, mountains of ham and sweet potatoes and small sweet peas, washed down by mugs of cider and warm talk and easy laughter, with a sort of glow over everything as she curls at his feet, her hair shining in the candlelight, Tia playing in pyjamas with her doll.

There's a good feeling in Neil Young's mountainside refuge, and it's broken only by the occasional howl from a coyote prowling the rocks outside after one of his cats. Even in the shelter of Topanga Canyon, there are the coyotes.

Bob spent a little time with Neil at the house in Topanga Canyon early that summer. He didn't know Susan well enough to make any judgement as to how they were getting on, but found Neil in good shape, writing songs, "and just being Neil as I knew him, fun, witty, full of ideas, really good to be with." Neil enjoyed his stepdaughter Tia; he's always been good with kids. He really liked his house but he'd been so long calling his own shots that if he wanted to go out, he went out for a day or a week or whatever. This caused friction.

Meanwhile, the old Buffalo Springfield had scattered – and the one landing most squarely on his feet was Stephen Stills. David Crosby had been kicked out of the Byrds in 1967 because he'd done some playing with other groups. Stills spent a few months in the summer of 1968, supported by his income from the three Springfield albums put out by Atlantic Records, looking for something else. He and Crosby were fooling around on some songs one day at a friend's house when Graham Nash of the Hollies dropped in to sing with them. "Willie [Nash's nickname] tried to join in a couple of songs," Stills said later. "When he did, David and I just looked at each other; it was one of those moments." That's how Crosby, Stills and Nash was born. Nash gave the Hollies a month's notice and the new trio rehearsed in London, then flew to L.A. and recorded their phenomenally successful first album called *Crosby, Stills & Nash*, released a few weeks before *Everybody Knows This Is Nowhere*. But they hadn't toured together, and cutting an album in a studio calls for much different elements than touring. Stills explained to the other two that for touring they'd need a lead guitar, somebody who could make the show come alive on stage in the format he had planned: first set acoustic and second set rock 'n' roll.

Stephen, a recollection:

"They said, 'Far out! But who do you want on lead?'

"'Neil Young.'

"'What? We've got enough problems deciding whose songs we're going to do already!'"

They were against it all the way, argued long and hard, but Stephen is a very difficult man to deny.

Neil: "It was that June of 1969 when their album was just out and going like hell, that Stephen came to the house one day and tapped on the door. He wanted me to play with them, not as a member of the group, but to be introduced as sort of a walk-on guest, in other words, a backup. Maybe that's something he'd used as a compromise with the other two. I told him if I was going to play with them, I wanted my name on it."

Steve: "Aw, c'mon, everybody'll know who you are, man."

Neil: "Nothing doing, man."

That's how the "and Young" was added to Crosby, Stills, Nash. Within a month they were in Chicago (not in New York, as some accounts have it) to begin their first long and successful tour. Their second stop was Woodstock. That mighty festival pulled half a million fans from across North America to a tent-strewn, trampled field in upstate New York. The event stands, and always will, as an historic moment in rock history. Every group that was anybody was there. To the musicians, it was a fantastic blur – the announcements about bad acid, warnings, instructions, medical tents where doctors looked after people on bad trips, nudity, loving, fighting, listening to group after group boom forth from the raised stand while it all was recorded and filmed.

One of Neil's memories of Woodstock is of the helicopter flight in to a small, nearly deserted airfield near the site. A few other musicians were waiting around there as well. That is where Neil first met Jimi Hendrix, whom he later called the greatest electric guitar player who ever lived. For a while that afternoon Neil and Jimi liberated a pick-up truck and drove around together in it.

Crosby, Stills, Nash and Young appeared as thirteenth group on the Woodstock bill, and in some accounts were rated the top act of that remarkable gathering of rock stars. The first Crosby, Stills and Nash album was well on its way to winning a Grammy award for best new group of that year. Neil's *Everybody Knows This Is Nowhere* was a national hit. Putting the two elements together was the most crowd-catching event of that autumn. The fact that Neil was staying with his Crazy Horse association, recording with them, keeping that road open, sometimes didn't sit well with Crosby, Stills and Nash, but actually set the tone for what the group soon was to become – a loose federation that would come together and fall apart several times in the next few years. In interviews, Neil tended to differentiate between the two groups on his own terms: with CSNY, he felt he didn't have a big load to carry; he played an instrument, sang a few songs, but didn't feel any heavy responsibility. About Crazy Horse he had a different idea: "With Crazy Horse I'm trying to make records that are not necessarily hits, but which people will listen to for a long time." Which has been true; some of his lifetime standards date from that period, never high on the charts and sometimes not on the charts at all, but he still plays them more than a decade later. A sampling of these includes "Cinnamon Girl," "Cowgirl in the Sand," "Dance Dance Dance," "Down by the River," "Expecting To Fly," "Here We Are in the Years," "I Am a Child," "The Last Trip to Tulsa," "Mr. Soul," "The Old Laughing Lady," "Sugar Mountain," "Wonderin'," "Helpless," "Tell Me Why" (*"Is it hard to make arrangements with yourself, when you're old enough to repay but young enough to sell"*), "After the Gold Rush," "Only Love Can Break Your Heart," "Southern Man," "Don't Let It Bring You Down," "Birds," "Ohio." All those songs had been written by the end of 1970.

There is no doubt on earth that the fifteen months or so after Woodstock in the summer of 1969 transformed Neil's career. His marriage was one of the casualties. From this distance it seems plain that neither Susan nor Neil was to blame. He was twenty-three and she about thirty when they married. To oversimplify drastically, Neil obviously was not ready to handle both that marriage and the demands his career forced on him (and which he accepted willingly, with enthusiasm, headlong). Susan was strong in her own right. She probably believed more in Neil than she did that he would suddenly be snatched from her by his work. Anyway, their troubles began that early, and grew.

When Neil was away so much, Susan filled part of her time with *her* friends. The Topanga house that he had wanted so much as a refuge was not that. Nobody's fault, really, but solitude had always been part of his nature. For a brief time it had seemed not as important as the warmth and support of marriage, but I had from Neil later some kind of terse explanation. "It got so that every time I came home to Topanga, the house was full of people I didn't even know." That may be as much of an explanation as anyone is likely to get.

After going on from Woodstock to finish that tour with CSNY, he was on the coast again for a short time. In November he and Crazy Horse played at the Santa Monica Civic Auditorium. He changed gears and went with CSNY later that month into a short U.S. tour that ended late in December and then moved to Europe in January 1970, playing Royal Albert Hall in London and dates in Denmark and Sweden. Neil flew back for a tour with Crazy Horse and Jack Nitzsche starting in February. That one included widely hailed dates at Fillmore East in New York and the Music Hall Theatre in Boston. Susan travelled with Neil on that tour in what must be seen, in retrospect, as something like a last try to make the marriage work. Newspaper reporters are not privy to everything that goes on, of course, but when she was mentioned it was as the background of an interview, or coming in from shopping, getting about equal billing with his D'Angelico guitar, or his sheepskin coat. Treating beautiful young women as a mere part of the scenery is not uncharacteristic of the rock world and many other parts of the entertainment industry. The chroniclers are used to beautiful women or handsome men as the consorts of the stars. It takes someone of great character (I think now of Neil's wife, Pegi) to deal with the culture shock of being treated like a picture on the wall once the two people of the marriage step outside of their home circle of friends.

From time to time as all this went on, CSNY spent many long hours in studios putting together the album *Déjà vu*. One, perhaps mythical, statistic is that the group spent 800 hours in the studio recording that album. Neil's sardonic comment later: "Ten eighty-hour days." When it was released in April, *Déjà vu* had a staggering $2,000,000 in advance orders before the first copy was passed across a record-store counter. Someone noted at the time that within eight or nine months after Woodstock, CSNY was now playing more music, making more records and more money, than any of the twelve groups that had appeared before them on the Woodstock bill. The high being ridden was not only as a group. On May 4, student demonstrations at Kent State University ended with the tragic shooting of four students by U.S. National Guardsmen. When Neil's angry song about the incident, "Ohio," was released a matter of days later the song had a vast national protest appeal – and met an immediate angry official response. Many radio stations banned it from air play. Vice President Spiro Agnew, not naming Neil but obviously aiming at him, denounced rock music as being anti-U.S.

All this time, settled into my new job as sports editor of the *Telegram*, we were in touch, if at all, in sporadic letters (by me) and phone calls (by him), as Neil was finishing his tour with Crazy Horse and trying to cope with Danny Whitten's deepening involvement with heroin. Neil and the others were back in L.A. recording his most important album yet, *After The Gold Rush*, when Neil decided Whitten's addiction was intolerable. Neil's sudden announcement on May 24, with the album partly completed, that he was not going to record again with Crazy Horse caught a lot of people, including, quite possibly, Neil himself, by surprise. There is some possibility that he fired the whole band in an attempt to shock Whitten off his road to disaster. Then unable to find full replacements, Neil hired Molina back to handle the drums, and made a phone call that deserves at least a footnote in rock history. In the previous year in Washington, D.C., a youngster named Nils Lofgren, who was sixteen at the time, appeared in the Crazy Horse dressing room to give an impassioned account of how good he was, and if they ever needed anybody, etc. At which time Neil handed him a guitar. He could play. He also could sing, and had a lot of skill as an accordionist. During the hiatus after firing Crazy Horse and hiring Molina back, Lofgren got a telephone call from Neil, which after the opening routine went like this:

Neil: "I want you to come out here to L.A. and play on the sessions for this album I'm doing, *After The Gold Rush*. Can you do it?"

Lofgren: "Well, sure, but why not Whitten?"

Neil: "I don't want you to play guitar. I want you to play piano."

Lofgren, laughing: "Look! I don't play piano!"

As Lofgren related the story, at this point Neil just said, "You can play piano," and hung up the phone.

David Briggs remembers Lofgren arriving at Neil's Topanga house, where the album was being recorded right on the premises. "I'll never forget this brash kid, I think he hitchhiked at least from the airport, walking up Neil's drive with his guitar under his arm and knocking on the door. He comes in and sits right down and starts playing." A keyboard player for the group called Spirit let him go to his house and practise piano for a couple of days and nights. Then he was ready. "Neil was right about the piano," Lofgren said later. "He knew I played accordion and the right hand work is the same, so all I had to do was get my left hand together. He wanted a plain, simple style – and it worked."

But maybe the most remarkable feature of those final days of Neil and Susan's marriage was the way that soon-to-be-famous album was put together in their home. David Briggs: "It was a very inspired record done under the worst possible conditions. You can hear dogs barking outside if you listen real close. When you do something that fast, under those conditions, you know, you think – it's the old value system – how can it be so good if rehearsing and recording and even some of the writing only took a few days? A lot of those songs were written right on the spot. Neil would sit upstairs in the living room working on a song and then we'd all go downstairs to the basement and turn on the tapes and away we'd go."

When the album came out with the entire back cover a photo of the seat of Neil's artistically patched jeans, one of the credits read: "PATCHES: *Susan Young*."

All this happened in May and early June of 1970. *Déjà vu* was topping the charts. CSNY was heading out on tour. The other three had had a three-month lay-off while Neil was touring with Crazy Horse, battling Whitten's heroin addiction, doing *After The Gold Rush*. Only a few days later Neil was on the road again, CSNY billed as "the highest paid group in the world." Their live double album called *4 Way Street* was recorded on that tour for autumn release.

Somewhere in there, while with CSNY in San Francisco, a road manager named Leo Mikoda told Neil enthusiastically about a ranch for sale in nearby San Mateo County, a few dozen miles past the San Francisco airport. He took Neil out to look at the hilly, remote property. It was smallish, 140 acres. Neil loved it. Back in Topanga, he told Susan about the ranch. They drove up there together in an old car a couple of times and looked around the ranch and talked about it. Neil decided he would buy. But a short time later, home again in Topanga, he and Susan had their final parting. Neil moved into the Chateau Marmont Hotel while he waited for the ranch purchase papers to be made final. It was a measure of another side of his life at the time that he paid cash for the ranch, $340,000. "I know now that I was crazy to pay cash," he told me a few years later. "I could have paid the down payment and invested the rest. But I just poured all my money into it so that I knew it could never be taken away from me. I was going good right then but I didn't know how long that would last, didn't feel secure, so I just went for it." The Topanga house had doubled or tripled in value by then but eventually he sold it to a friend for what he had paid for it.

11

Carnegie Hall

When I'm with people, I usually have trouble showing my emotions in situations that plainly call for emotions to be shown. When I am alone, I walk out to my deck on a summer morning when the sky and trees and birds and the long green valley stretching southeastward are glitteringly perfect and shout, "You've done it again, God!" and the echo comes back from McCamus's sugar bush a mile across the valley, ". . . done it again, God!" But in public moments of life's high dramas, I'm different, like the Friday night of December 4, 1970, when Neil played Carnegie Hall for the first time. Just when everyone was expecting to see tears as big as light bulbs rolling down my cheeks, all my rockets were going off inside, unseen. To the innocent bystander I looked as if I was auditioning for a role as a graven image, or a cigar-store white man.

Jack Nicholson (whose most recent movie at that ancient time was *Five Easy Pieces*) rushed backstage after the concert and up to Neil exclaiming, "You sold out Carnegie Hall, man. You sold out!" Then, introduced to me and seeing me apparently calm, he clasped my upper arms and expostulated, "You don't seem to understand what an achievement this is for your son!"

"I do!" I exclaimed. (How does an habitually poker-faced guy defend himself against such an accusation?) "I do!"

"People work their whole lives to get to Carnegie Hall. Neil comes here and, boom!"

"I know! I know!"

But people whose art depends on their emotions being in full view do not understand. I could not tell Nicholson of a walk I'd taken on that cold and raw afternoon. (I would have had to yell and, in the confusion, maybe not finish.) Neil had called a few weeks earlier to tell me about the Carnegie Hall booking and say, "I thought maybe you'd like to come. I can't tell you what a big deal this is for me." He called his mother in Florida with the same message. He told his brother Bob, "You have to be good at Carnegie Hall. The money you make there isn't important. I'd do it for nothing – it's playing Carnegie Hall, that's the important thing." When Astrid and I flew in a few hours before the concert it was my first experience of one part of the rock world: being met at the airport by a limousine hired by Neil, and taken to the hotel suite he'd booked for us. Around four or five that afternoon I left Astrid in the hotel and said I was going to walk around a little. Back in the happy days when our family was unfractured, safe and sound in Omemee, Rassy and I used to go to New York fairly often when I would be seeing editors who bought my short stories. We would stay at Jack Dempsey's old Great Northern Hotel, not far from Carnegie Hall, so I knew the district. Carnegie Hall had a magic for me. In the late 1930s I had read everything I could find in *Down Beat* magazine, *Variety*, and the New York papers on the first Benny Goodman concert there, the historic breakthrough of swing music into that sanctum sanctorum of great musicians. While I was thinking of that and trying to match it with Neil playing there I came to a full stop in front of a tall poster that read: TONIGHT. NEIL YOUNG, FOLK SINGER. Across it was a sticker: SOLD OUT. I walked past slowly and turned and walked past again. I couldn't get enough of it. My mind was full of images of years ago. As I walked away I wiped at tears and muttered to myself aloud, "What the hell happened?"

There was one other element of those moments. I knew Rassy was in the city, too, up from her home in Florida. I would have liked to see her then, just for the moments when we might have touched, and remembered what the best part of our marriage had been. In my heightened state of emotion anything seemed possible and I looked closely at every woman approaching or walking away, half-expecting to see her, but did not. And I didn't see her at the concert, either, because when the first concert was announced a few weeks earlier, it had sold out in twenty-five minutes. A second concert seemed called for, but Saturday afternoon and evening were already booked. So the second concert was scheduled for midnight on Saturday. That sold out, too. Neil (I imagine with at least an inner grin) assigned first-concert tickets to Astrid and me, second-concert tickets to Rassy, so that never the twain should meet.

Astrid and I dined after my walk and then walked up the street from our hotel through the crowds outside Carnegie Hall who were imploring passers-by for tickets. One young man offered me a hundred dollars each for our five-dollar seats.

Inside, it was the classic youth scene of the time: blue jeans patched, tight sweaters over young bosoms. We sat, I guess, like visitors from another world. But once the place was dark, we all could see this dark form approaching the front of the stage and then the spotlight came on him: tall and thin, blue jeans, checked shirt, work boots, dark straight hair to his shoulders or beyond, two acoustic guitars on a rack beside a plain wooden chair, a concert piano at his left. Moving gingerly as if his back was bothering him. No music to play except the songs in his head, all his own.

He sings in a way that twists my heart. It is a strange feeling to be on one's feet participating and then watching quietly a standing ovation for one's own son, as happened several times to me that night. It was all new to my experience, but when I thought of certain incidents later there was some connection with the old feeling Neil had about Buffalo Springfield: that the people who loved them really owned part of them and had a right to assert that ownership. Once he introduced a new song as being one that he would do in a week or so for a Johnny Cash show in Nashville, and there was a single loud argumentative voice from the audience, "Why? Why with Cash, man?" When he played a piano introduction, people applauded as if they knew from the opening notes which song was to follow. After about the third time this happened he stopped after a few bars and said, "Y'know, about these piano intros – I don't play so good. They're all the same intro. . . . I just wanted to let you know that I know." Laughter. Applause. Once he was applauded for rolling up his sleeve.

Maybe as part of his near-reverence for this hall where he was playing, he didn't hesitate to instruct the audience on manners. At the end of each song there would be shouted (or screamed) requests for this song or that. He told the audience to hold it, "You don't think I'd come to Carnegie Hall without planning? You're going to get all the songs you want to hear."

In the mob scene backstage, Neil waved at what looked for the moment like a jam-packed cocktail party (without the drinks), everybody talking at once, and suggested that we meet the next day for brunch. "Better make it in your hotel suite. It'll be quieter. Nobody will know where to find me."

Six of us met about noon in our suite: Astrid, Elliot Roberts, Bob, a friend of his, Neil, and me. We had a couple of easy hours although it was difficult for Neil to get comfortable because of the back brace he was wearing, which explained the careful way he'd moved onstage the night before. A few weeks earlier at the ranch he'd been lifting heavy slabs of polished walnut to fasten them to a wall. On one lift suddenly his back hurt. Before that he'd had some back trouble but had ignored it. "Once I simply couldn't move when I tried to move. I'd also had some trouble getting out of my car, but without any particular pain. But after the back started to hurt, when I was in the car I couldn't get out. When I was driving I couldn't get my left foot to go up to use the clutch or the brake. I had to lift the foot up with my hand. I could push down but I couldn't lift up. So I phoned my doctor in L.A. because I knew something must be wrong." He laughed. "I can take a hint, you know."

The doctor sent him immediately to hospital and into traction. An operation probably would be necessary, the doctor said, but meanwhile Neil could make his condition bearable, and fulfil his Carnegie Hall date, if he wore a back brace, got the hotel to supply a special bed, and was careful.

When they left, Astrid and I checked out and took a flight home. I can't even remember reading any reviews at the time, but that Carnegie Hall triumph is still mentioned in magazines and books and newspaper pieces about his career. What the concert did for me was bring me to realize fully for the first time that just as my boyhood dream had been to be Evelyn Waugh or John Dos Passos or John Steinbeck or Ernest Hemingway, many of today's kids want to be Neil Young. I look back on that night of December 4, 1970, as one of the great emotional experiences of my life.

12

Interlude

The relationship between Neil and Carrie Snodgress had a strange beginning and overall, as Neil once remarked wryly to me, lasted not much longer than Buffalo Springfield. At the time of the Carnegie Hall concert they had known one another a short time, after meeting in an unusual way. Neil had seen Carrie in the film *Diary of a Mad Housewife* (for which she received an Oscar nomination). He was captivated by the way she played the role of the housewife rebelling against the repressions of the stuffed-shirt lawyer she'd married. He got her phone number from a friend and called to tell her how much he liked her in the film. This happened to be a day or two before Neil's appointment with his doctor in L.A. They decided to meet and go out after he saw the doctor. When the doctor told him he had a crumbling spinal disc, shouldn't even be walking around, and put him immediately in traction, Neil called to cancel the date. Carrie came around to the hospital to see him. Sounds a little like a movie opening itself: rock star on the rebound, trying to recover after a shattered marriage that had shattered him; an actress he admired turns up in a hospital room to help him through a bad time. Both about the same age, Neil just turned twenty-five and Carrie twenty-four.

Not much happened right away. Uppermost in Neil's mind was his Carnegie Hall concert and a tour soon after. In between was Christmas. When I called him before Christmas, I couldn't reach him at home – he was in hospital, in traction again. An acquaintance of mine, rock journalist Ritchie Yorke, found him there a couple of days before Christmas. Ritchie reported that Neil had a lot of nurses for company the day he was there, as well as David Crosby, and Carrie from time to time. Even in traction again, Neil was minimizing his back problem. He had a tour to begin early in January. He told Ritchie, "I'm going to have to wear the brace for a couple of months, but we'll take a portable traction unit with us on tour and I'll get it together." In his hospital bed he was working on the song line-up for what he saw then as a double album. (This, as it turned out, was the first run at an album that was not to come out for years – his three-album retrospective, *Decade*.)

On the tour, he was going solo. No backup. Only Neil. Danny Whitten told someone not long before, "Neil likes to play in groups but basically he's a solo artist. I don't think he'll ever stay with any group for very long. Deep down, he knows he has to do the gig by himself." Which gave some perspective to Neil's remark from his bed to Ritchie Yorke, "I really wanna get this tour off, alone. I've done three tours with Crazy Horse, two with the bigger band (CSNY) and now I'm ready to just wrap it up. I wanna bring it back to the roots again, do my gig, and then I'm gonna take a year off from touring." By then he had already found that he could go into traction, wear the brace, take it off, as he had after Carnegie Hall, and have his back go out again. It probably would keep on happening that way until he had an operation. If that turned out to be true (as it did), the year off would be for the back operation and recovery, moseying around his ranch, working on *Journey Through The Past*, the movie he'd started in Topanga Canyon; writing and recording, but not touring. If Carrie was in his long-term plans at that time, he hadn't told anyone.

Ten days after that hospital scene, he was on the road. In another two weeks I was sitting with my family a few rows back from the stage in Toronto's Massey Hall. It was my first experience in my later official capacity as Neil Young's father. Strangers leaned over seats to talk to me about him. The next day I received a note from two young women along the row. The note said, "Thank you for your son." That was the first of dozens of letters I have received every year since from people who don't know where to write to Neil, so send me letters that pour out, usually not as tersely as that note above, the sometimes inchoate feelings they have that Neil may be speaking to millions but also speaks to them alone. When they enclose letters asking me to send them on to Neil, I do so.

I didn't see much of Neil during that stop in Toronto. At the airport on the way in he'd been put through the usual intensive search (the customs man also peered suspiciously into his harmonicas). Backstage was crowded, time for only a short chat. Some reports of the concert mentioned the similarity in our appearance, "despite the elder Young being well-groomed in a blazer and slacks, while his son was in patched jeans, a lumberjack shirt, and work boots." Another newspaper account described Neil's entourage as resembling a pack of "turn-of-the-century Mexican banditos who would have trouble getting rides if they were hitchhiking." But that was all beside the point. By that time, early in 1971, there seemed to be nothing that he couldn't do. We didn't talk money, or sales, or anything similar at Massey Hall, but certainly part of his persona at that time was the huge success of *After The Gold Rush* – with sales of more than a million albums by then – and his share of the huge success of CSNY's *Déjà vu*. The only fragment of conversation we had in that line at all was when I said to him, in the midst of the backstage crowd, "Different from the last time."

"Sure is!" he said. The last time in Toronto, two years earlier, he'd been playing in the half-empty Riverboat. For grand old Massey Hall, concert tickets had sold so fast that a second concert was scheduled for the same night. As young Astrid was only nine then, we were at the first one. After the late concert, Neil flew to Boston to play the Music Hall Theatre there the next night. The crowd backstage at Massey for both concerts had a lot of people who had known him when; when he was a stockroom boy at Coles and would play for twenty-five dollars a night if he got lucky; even when he'd been standing in front of the class at John Wanless School telling about his Pickering chicken-and-egg business.

When his tour ended early in February, he had things to do, songs to write, and a date to do a show with Johnny Cash at Nashville. (Echo from Carnegie Hall: "Why with Cash, man?")

But it was an ocean away that one could see what was happening to his career on a broader scale. After Nashville, where he also filled in a few hours by recording three songs for his next album, *Harvest*, he had a February 27 date in London at the Royal Festival Hall. Hundreds of fans lined up outside Festival Hall all through a raw winter night to get a shot at the 2,700 tickets on sale. *Melody Maker*, the London music weekly that has no real equivalent in North America, hailed him on his arrival as "the most sought-after solo star since Bob Dylan." When he flew in music writers were out in force at the airport. One was Allan McDougall, a reporter for *New Musical Express*, which battles hotly each week with *Melody Maker* for the United Kingdom's huge pop-music reading market. At the airport Neil said to him, "No interviews, man," but then invited him to ride in the promoter-supplied limousine from the airport.

McDougall: "When the limo drew up at the classy building on Grosvenor Square where Neil was to live in a vastly expensive flat, the doorman, considerably more resplendently dressed than Neil, stepped to the curb and said, 'Welcome, sir. Your neighbours here are King Hussein, Raquel Welch, and Mr. Michael Caine.' Whereupon Neil stepped back into the limousine and asked to be taken somewhere else."

That Festival Hall concert solidified, much more than his previous visit with CSNY a year earlier, his love affair with British fans. One of the most respected rock writers, Nick Logan, called him "likely to be the colossus of music in the '70s." A *New Musical Express* poll soon named him the "world's best vocalist," and later in an extensive reader poll *Melody Maker* named him top male singer (Rod Stewart was fourth, Mick Jagger seventh, Bob Dylan eighth), top composer, proprietor of the top album, and member of the top group, Crosby, Stills, Nash and Young. That springtime in London Neil's *After The Gold Rush* was number one on the album charts, and he also had a piece of second place, with CSNY's *4 Way Street*. The BBC filmed an *In Concert* show with him in a studio setting, and in an imaginative move that later was both criticized and lauded, Neil recorded with the London Symphony Orchestra the soaring backup music for two songs, one being "A Man Needs a Maid." Neil showed traces of the kid from Omemee, not realizing how big he had become, when he was telling me about that session with the London Symphony. "They were really into it, Dad. They treated me like *somebody*."

Several months later he and Carrie began living together. He went to some pains to explain to me (as if I might care, which I didn't) that they did not intend to marry. I knew her only from the movie then, but we spoke by phone a couple of times. She said she'd been reading a lot of new film scripts but hadn't seen anything she wanted to do. That summer – on August 11, 1971 – Neil had his spinal disc operation. The enforced immobility after the operation was one of the most difficult periods of his life. "But I had a lot of time to think about a lot of things – some that had worked out, and some I'd screwed up."

The doctor had told him that one reason he was having this trouble was that he didn't take the kind of exercise that would build up his back muscles. He decided not to let that happen again. He had a pool built on top of a hill behind his house. Even climbing up to it was pretty good exercise. It was one of the first times since Topanga that he'd had a non-musical project to take on. It wasn't your typical California pool. The underwater walls and bottom were dark instead of white to attract the sun's heat and supplement the heating system. For paths around the pool he selected a dark grey volcanic rock. The pool house, of weathered wood, had mattressed suncots for resting after a swim, and a big woodstove for taking the chill off cool days. It all blended into the surroundings.

While he was planning this and watching it progress we were in touch only occasionally, partly because in the meantime I was in somewhat of a scramble myself. The Toronto *Telegram*, where I was sports editor and wrote a daily column, folded. I had been warned but simply didn't believe it would fold. I have a stupendous lack of talent for expecting the worst. When I joined the *Telegram* in 1969 the editor-in-chief was J. Douglas McFarlane, an oldtime friend. We'd been together on the *Toronto Star* before either Bob or Neil were born. We'd also been together in Italy in 1944, he an army major and I a naval sub-lieutenant. He told me that I was crazy to leave the *Globe*; that no matter how innovative, bright, and interesting the *Telegram* was, the blander *Toronto Star* kept picking up much more lucrative advertising lineage. He said there was no guarantee that the *Telegram* could survive, losing money year after year; that maybe I was signing on a sinking ship.

I worked as hard as I could, in my way, to help make the *Telegram* the best newspaper in town. I was even the host at a huge and expensive dinner and reception for advertisers early in September 1971, telling them our big plans and assuring them that we would be around forever, if not longer. About two weeks later, John Bassett announced the paper's folding, to take effect at the end of October.

Practically my next phone call was from Dic Doyle, asking me to return to the *Globe* as a general columnist. I accepted. The *Globe* was solid. I had alimony to pay. And at the *Globe*, without the sports scene to cover, I could write from anywhere.

During this time I was not privy to what was happening in Neil's life, but a few months later I had a call from him. "Just thought I should tell you – you're going to be a grandfather!" Carrie came on the phone, also excited. They said the baby was expected in the autumn and why didn't I come out and see them sometime? We talked about it but made no specific plans.

Instead, in March of 1972 I took my family for a month in Florida, and was there just after Neil's new album, *Harvest*, was released and went straight to the top of the charts within two weeks. Every time I turned on my car radio in Florida I heard "Heart of Gold," the first single released from that album.

Then almost as often I would hear another from that album, "Old Man":

Old man, look at my life. I'm a lot like you were.
Old man look at my life –
Twenty-four and there's so much more
Life alone in a paradise that makes me think of two.
Love lost, such a cost,
Give me things that don't get lost.
Like a coin that won't get tossed rolling home to you . . .

Well, sure, "Old Man" pleased me a great deal. In Florida and back in Canada during the many months while "Old Man" was well up on the charts, people would mention it to me as if I were sort of co-proprietor, at which I would just nod and smile like Mona Lisa. Never question a compliment is my motto. "Old Man" was also such a nice change from some of the songs whose accusatory gist I had applied to myself years earlier.

A few months after my return to Canada, spending the summer at our country place and sending in my columns by telex, came the strangest near-meeting of our lives.

Early one Saturday afternoon Astrid and I were heading for a party an hour's drive away. The main east-west street of Omemee crosses the Pigeon River on what is called locally the Highway Bridge. Less than a hundred yards south is what is called the Mill Bridge. It was a wooden structure in Neil's childhood but had been rebuilt in steel. Neil had spent hundreds of hours fishing from the Mill Bridge, clambering around the timbers below it retrieving hung-up fishing lines. Once he and his best friend Henry Mason had pulled in a broken fishing line to find a sixty-pound snapping turtle hooked on the other end. It had been an afternoon's work to get it to shore and get it loaded on his wagon with all four legs hanging over the sides. As I recall, somebody – probably a tourist, prizing it for the meat – took it off their hands. Anyway, Neil had conceded, "It's too big for my sandbox." The area was very strong in memories for me.

As I drove across the Highway Bridge I glanced to my left and saw three people strolling onto the Mill Bridge. It was just a glimpse, but for an instant one of the figures seemed very familiar. But it couldn't be. He was thousands of miles away. "If I didn't know better, I'd think I just saw Neil back there," I said to Astrid, a mile or so later.

The party was at Pierre and Janet Berton's home north of Toronto. Many of the guests were the offspring of people who had visited us in Omemee and elsewhere when they and Neil and Bob were children. Almost as soon as I arrived, one of them, Jill Frayne, came up to me and said, "I hear Neil is in town."

"Jeez, I don't think so, not that I know of, anyway. Where did you hear that?"

"Well, there's a rumour that he's going to play at the Mariposa Folk Festival on Centre Island this weekend."

When we got home that evening we were met by Deirdre, who was twenty-one then. "Neil and Bob and Carrie Snodgress were here," she said. It had not been a propitious meeting. Young Astrid was riding, and Deirdre was washing her hair when they came to the door and was flustered when she came out wrapped in a towel. They didn't stay but left the name of the hotel in Toronto where they were staying. I hadn't met Carrie, at that point. I asked Deirdre, "What's she like?"

"Very pregnant," Deirdre replied.

I phoned Neil. They drove up in the early afternoon a day or two later, after Mariposa. Neil was driving a rented Chrysler. We rustled up some porterhouse steaks from Whitmore's in Omemee. Paul Whitmore had gone to school with Bob and Neil, when the business was run by his father, Carmen Whitmore. He cut some of the best steaks of his illustrious steak-cutting career to mark the occasion. My friend Jay

Hayes brought his mother, then in her eighties, out to see Neil again. Deirdre and young Astrid (then almost ten) hung around slightly awed. Neil wanted to look around my place, where he'd never been before. He and Carrie and I went for a walk back over the top of the hill behind the house and down through the hardwoods, catching up on a lot of things. His film *Journey Through The Past* was almost finished. The double-album soundtrack from it would be released in the fall, the film soon after. He was fairly reticent about what it was about, except that "It's pretty personal, an attempt to tell about my life in the last few years, and now." Carrie was in it, and the ranch.

Part of my place, the southeast ten or fifteen acres, is separated from the rest by an old road that had wandered across the property a century earlier so that farmers wouldn't have to negotiate a steep hill where the road should have run. The proper road allowance leads to a secluded trail up that hill and through the woods. We walked it, the tree branches meeting overhead to make it a long green tunnel.

"This is where the kids come to park at night, around here," I said, the three of us puffing along, swatting mosquitoes. "You know, they sit around and have a few beers, and . . ." Just at that moment when I was pointing out some bottle-caps and empties as evidence we came on a veritable plethora of used condoms. "I guess there's a little more than beer-drinking goes on," I admitted.

Neil (laughing): "I guess *so!*"

After the walk Neil and I stood beside my pool. Just the two of us. "Something I should clarify," he said. "You know that song, 'Old Man'?"

"Yeah. I love it."

"It isn't about you. I know a lot of people think it is. But it's about Louis, the man who lives on the ranch and looks after things for me, the cattle and the buffaloes and the feed and all that. A wonderful guy."

"Oh," I said. The Lord giveth and the Lord taketh away.

It was eleven o'clock or beyond, when they left. I have a photo on my wall of family pictures now that was taken of Neil at the Mariposa Festival, long hair, gaunt face, eyes half-closed. In the background across the stage, Bob can be seen.

A few weeks later, on September 8, 1972, Zeke was born. Carrie and Neil sent us pictures taken when he was a day or two old, looking a good deal as Neil had looked when he was a baby: big eyes, dark hair (which became fair on Zeke later), and balloon-like cheeks. From then on every few weeks we'd have letters from Carrie saying how happy she was, and how "little Zeker" had brightened their lives. They would see us soon when Neil took a major tour on the road. They didn't know at the time that Zeke had some physical problems, which eventually – but not for a year or so – were diagnosed as cerebral palsy.

13

A Sidetracked Journey
Through the Past

No doubt it is only a coincidence that this is chapter thirteen, which
some people consider an unlucky number. Neil had said before the
1971 solo tour, which ended in Royal Festival Hall, that when he
finished it he was going to take a year off from touring. The year had
stretched to eighteen months by the autumn of 1972, much of it spent
working on his film. But, riding the crest of *Harvest*, the music industry's best-selling album that year, he was planning his biggest tour ever,
gathering musicians at his ranch for rehearsals, scheduling concerts in
sixty-five cities (the last seven in England) in the first three months of
1973. He called it the *Time Fades Away* tour and chartered a Lockheed
Electra to alleviate the difficulties with schedules: into-the-aircraft,
out-of-the-aircraft, into-the-limos, into-the-hotel, out-of-the-hotel,
into-the-concert-hall, out-of-the-concert-hall (and on to the next
place), all the pressures of such a tour. But suddenly the universe was
not unfolding for him as it had during the past few years.

This period began with the partial foundering of the *Journey
Through The Past* project. Warners had put some money into the film
originally, and the double-album soundtrack was scheduled for release
in November. That did happen, but release of the film at the same time

did not. To telescope drastically the trials of the next few months, Warners decided to pull out of the film's distribution. Neil then negotiated full ownership for himself, but the soundtrack album – without the film's release to help explain it to listeners – was giving Neil his first real roasting from critics. Partly in response to these negative goings-on, Neil wanted to do the *Time Fades Away* tour so stupendously well that it would not only smother the doubters, but also bolster the faith that he still had, and never lost, in *Journey*. Zeke was only a few months old, and Carrie, living at the ranch, was being given many good scripts to read but turning them all down, when the musicians for the tour began to gather at the ranch – Ben Keith, Tim Drummond, Ken Buttrey, and Jack Nitzsche. Then Neil made one choice that was to haunt him.

Once *After The Gold Rush* was in the can in May 1970, Neil had severed connections, except those of friendship, with Crazy Horse, which then had added Nils Lofgren (guitar/vocals) and Jack Nitzsche (piano) to the core unit of Danny Whitten, Ralph Molina, and Billy Talbot to record an album. But after the album, called *Crazy Horse*, was released the planned tour to support it had to be cancelled. Whitten, who had written six of the album's songs, was too wasted from heroin to go on the road. Billy Talbot described Crazy Horse's next eighteen months as "just fumbling around." With Whitten no longer the driving force, or even a factor, Crazy Horse brought back George Whitsell from their old Rockets and eventually used another four musicians for two albums in 1972. But in putting together the *Time Fades Away* tour, Neil, out of his old friendship with Danny Whitten, his tremendous respect for what Danny had been before the junk got him, and the assurances from Whitten and his family that he had kicked his habit, asked him to be one of the group Neil was calling the Stray Gators. Whitten would sing, play lead guitar, and rejoin the world again. The reunion was a disaster. Danny had not kicked his habit. He was no longer even a shadow of the musician he had been. "He just couldn't keep up," Neil told me later, sadly. "Once in the middle of one song he slid into another and didn't even know it. I tried and he tried, but he couldn't do it any more."

When he had to tell Danny it was over, Neil gave him some money and a plane ticket back to Los Angeles. That night in L.A. Danny bought himself what turned out to be a fatal overdose. His longtime friend Ralph Molina, who had watched the long flameout from a closer range than most, said of his death, "It was the best thing that could have happened to him at the time."

Neil was deeply shaken, but if the music stopped every time a junkie overdosed, the world would be a different place and not necessarily better. Still, it caused the first incipient flaw in the band, leaving it under-manned by one, because Neil did not replace Whitten, whose lead guitar he had been counting on. Just as he and Stephen Stills earlier (and in times to come) electrified audiences with the competitiveness of their guitar-playing and singing, taking dead aim at one another and shooting it out with their guitars and voices, Neil had seen Whitten — if he'd been healthy again — supplying that energy.

Yet when the *Time Fades Away* tour landed in Toronto on a Monday, January 15, 1973, to an 18,300 sellout at Maple Leaf Gardens (which then held 16,400, including standees, for hockey), the tour seemed to be fulfilling Neil's original intent. It was being called the most successful tour in rock history. The previous night in Buffalo Memorial Auditorium had been another sellout. Even the vision-obscured seats behind the stages were all sold.

In Toronto I watched Neil as he sang the opening three songs, seated centrestage playing his old twelve-string from the Mynah Birds days, easing into the program that he always constructs so carefully. After the opening acoustic songs he brought in Ben Keith on steel guitar, Tim Drummond on bass, Jack Nitzsche on piano, and Ken Buttrey on drums, but stayed with the songs that his fans had come to expect from him. After that, the second half of the show was a shock. I thought at the time it might be only me being deafened, but the next day critic Peter Goddard called it "unbelievable, brutally loud, soaring rock 'n' roll." So whatever the fans had expected, crowding down by subway or from a hundred miles away by chartered buses, they got it: from the soft acoustic sound at the start to the deafening assault of the later music featuring Neil's blistering guitar solos.

The tour was moving to Ottawa to play Tuesday night and Montreal Thursday. The chartered Electra was waiting at Toronto International. Carrie's parents (her father a partner in a big Buick dealership) had flown in from Chicago. After the concert, Astrid and I joined Neil, Carrie, and her parents for a one A.M. dinner that Neil had arranged in the dining room of their suite at the Inn on the Park Hotel. Zeke, just over five months old, a smiling baby, was brought out to meet us all and then put back to sleep in the middle of a big bed, in a nest of bolsters and pillows. It was close to three when we got home, with plans that Neil, Carrie, and Zeke would come to our place before they left for Ottawa. For hours the next day we sat before the living-room fire as Zeke played or napped on a blanket at our feet. The conversation was easy and general, their lives and ours. Neil sat on the floor with his back against a chair and his long legs crossed in a way he has, heels tucked under his thighs, elbows on his knees. For him, it must be comfortable – he can sit like that for hours.

Those early concerts were the best of the tour for Neil. He'd started out knowing that nodes in his throat – small protuberances that aren't bothersome unless they are goaded into it (Bing Crosby had them, but didn't goad them) – might have to be removed eventually if he treated them badly. He did have an extra singing load because he had not replaced Whitten, who would have been singing as well as playing lead guitar. Then came trouble of a different kind. When gate receipts began breaking records for all tours, even those by the Beatles and Rolling Stones, members of his travelling outfit wanted more money. He felt let down. "They'd agreed," he said, "and they were highly paid, at that point probably the highest-paid musicians on the road. They still wanted more money. Everybody! The road manager quit halfway through the thing because of money. It was like the first time anybody had been close to the kind of money that we were making and it really affected a lot of people. It wouldn't have bothered me except that to me the band, without Danny Whitten, wasn't making it. All of this coming on top of Danny dying just before we went on the road, the *Time Fades Away* tour was a frustrating event for me."

He met the money demands but rapport was badly damaged – and was a factor in February when Ken Buttrey, one of Nashville's finest studio men on drums, said politely that he just hadn't realized the tour would be so stressful, and left. He was replaced by John Barbata, who had played drums with CSNY.

It was then, in the last third of the tour, that the final blow came. Neil's throat became big trouble: "If I wanted to sing at all I had to sing real loud. Otherwise I didn't have any control. It even hurt to talk." Sometimes for days he didn't talk. This increased his own and the others' sense of alienation.

Only a few of the critics sensed something was wrong. The public knew little of all this, or cared. *Gold Rush* in 1970, *Harvest* in early '72, had demonstrated where Neil stood with the fans. Few of them cared how Neil sang as long as they could understand the words, and they didn't care whether the other guys got paid in money or beaver pelts. Because of the long haul, the worn tempers, the damage to Neil's voice, the concert changed as it went along but it never stopped selling out. In March Linda Ronstadt joined to open with forty minutes or so of her lively songs. Later in the month, the tour was scheduled for San Francisco's Winterland. The fans there line up before every good concert to rush for the seats closest to the stage. Normally this line would begin to form in early or mid-afternoon. For Neil, the line was there at nine A.M. That audience got something extra as well. David Crosby and Graham Nash joined in mid-concert and remained for the rest of the tour, playing guitar and giving Neil vocal support. The next night, a Saturday, the tour went to Anaheim Convention Center (sold out), on Sunday to the Inglewood Forum (sold out), and on Monday to Long Beach Arena (sold out). Four concerts in four nights. Neil was now taking a few belts from critics for the trouble he was having with his voice. And soon he was in Oakland (sold out) where he made a controversially abrupt exit. He quit right in the middle of singing "Southern Man," put down his guitar, mumbled that he couldn't play any more "because of what's going on out there," stalked off the stage, and went home. This was not explained at the time in the U.S. music press, either because Neil refused to talk about it, or nobody could find him later to ask the question. But he did explain, eventually.

It might be just my imagination but I think that Neil is looser, more relaxed, when he is playing in England. He seems to talk more to English audiences, take them more into his confidence. That walkout in Oakland, catching everybody by surprise, was in the spring of 1973. Six or seven months later at the Rainbow in London, a house seating about 3,000, he did explain. In Britain and elsewhere in Europe, bootleg tapes of every concert are available, some of high quality. During a research trip ten years later, in 1983, I became friendly with Paul Makos, then head of an organization called the Neil Young Appreciation Society. The NYAS publishes what must be the most literate and well-produced magazine in the genre, called Broken Arrow, of such high quality that although Neil has no recognized fan clubs in North America, the NYAS in Britain (and with members in many countries including the U.S.) has been more or less anointed; it corresponds with his agents, gets details of tours in advance, gift albums to be used as prizes in competitions, excellent concert seats for members, and so on.

Paul Makos is in his late twenties. His late father, a Polish navy man, served with the British after Poland fell in 1940. With the help of his Scottish mother, Paul had two shoe-repair shops in Glasgow and lived with his wife and children in a pleasant row house in a nearby suburb. One night chatting in his living room, Paul told me he had a tape of a 1973 concert at the Rainbow in London that explained the Oakland incident six or seven months earlier and 7,000 miles away!

"Want to hear it?" Paul asked.

"Sure."

The part of the tape in question opens with a little harmonica music. There are insistent calls from the audience for "Southern Man." Then Neil speaks (this is unedited, leaving in all the *y'knows*):

"I could tell you a story about 'Southern Man.' It was at the Oakland Coliseum and I was playing away, you know, having a pretty mediocre time actually. (Audience laughs.) It wasn't that hot, you know, stop number 58 on the *Time Fades Away* tour, we were all tired, you know, and the band wasn't right in the first place, just one of those things, you know. . . . By the time we got there, 'Southern Man,' you know, everybody, every time, everywhere, would yell '*Southern Man*'! '*Southern Man*'! And I can dig it, you know, uh, nice, but you know, I sang it with Crosby, Stills and Nash, I sang it by myself, and I sang it with these other guys and by then I was starting to feel like a Wurlitzer, you know (audience and Neil laugh), uh, even though I believe the song, where I was at when I wrote it, you know. Anyway I was singing away, '*Southern Man, better keep your head, don't forget what your good book said,*' and this guy in the front row, he was about as far away as you are from me, he jumped up and yelled, 'Right on! Right on! I love it!' He felt really good, I could tell. And all of a sudden, you know, a black cop just walked up to him, you know, and he just crunched him! I just took my guitar out and put it on the ground and got in the car and went home, you know. A lot of those people in Oakland couldn't understand it because they couldn't see from the other end, you know, just thought I'd freaked out or something, you know, but ever since I've never sung that song, you know, I don't know why. I sang it a lot, you know, I sang it every night for a long time and I really . . . that's the story . . . I couldn't do it, I don't *feel* it right now."

Voice from audience: "Don't do it!"

Harmonica over laughter and a confusion of shouts.

At the end of *Time Fades Away*, there was some cleaning up to do. He cancelled the U.K. dates he had planned on the grounds that his throat was bothering him too much to face even another few concerts. But there was doubtless a supporting element. In a few days, *Journey Through The Past* would have its first public showing at the U.S. Film Festival in Dallas. Neil wanted to be there. As it turned out, *Journey's* reception in Dallas foretold its future fairly accurately.

Although Neil wasn't expected to attend, Dallas papers called it an indication of the power of his name that *Journey's* two showings on April 8 drew the biggest crowds of the week.

When the film began and Neil's name appeared on the screen, the audience burst into spontaneous, sustained applause.

At the end, the applause was much more restrained.

Neil had watched the film and listened to the response in the privacy of the projectionist's booth and apparently was not fazed by what he heard. When he walked quickly down the aisle to the front, the audience reacted with surprise and enthusiasm. He sat on the edge of the stage, dangling his legs, and for half an hour the audience fired questions. He said that the film had cost about $350,000 to make. He'd started it in Topanga, playing around with a new movie camera, and at first had thought he'd blow up some of his home movies into something to show the neighbours. "It grew over the years," he said.

Comments at the time from people in the film industry were guardedly in favour. "Neil's touch is great, as it is in his music," said Lou Adler, himself a star of several rock movies, but added that he would be more interested in Neil's next tries at the film medium. Bob Porter in the *Dallas Times Herald*, while calling *Journey* "simplistic . . . probably of value primarily to those searching souls looking for a view of the outside world from inside the hectic, confused and confusing world of rock music," went on to say: "Young expressed the determination to do other films. He is artist enough that he may grow with that." Producer Fred Underhill later told film writer Janelle Ellis, "It's a conscious attempt *not* to do a music film, a *performance* film. He ventured into fantasy and did fictional sequences. But it also has his music and some historical context for it, from TV films of Buffalo Springfield through today." Pause. "I keep asking Neil what it's about, too."

The bottom line really is something that Neil said to me once, "Once in a while I like to do something that has a chance of failing."

When he released the film later that year I took young Astrid to see it in Toronto. The theatre was almost empty. There was great cinematography, music, and images that made it as mysterious in its way as some of Neil's songs. His ideas were presented in the film through a character, the Graduate, played by Richard Lee Patterson. Once, in cap and gown, he is beaten senseless, dropped off in the middle of a desert and begins to wander through sequences in which the threats to his rights are represented as the church, the military, and big business. One scene shows Neil in a junkyard under a freeway, sitting in a 1957 Buick, opening his lunchbox, and talking about unnecessary waste in the way we live, and one simple way to allay part of that: "Like, man, you know, rebuilding old cars instead of manufacturing new ones." There was a long scene of a junkie fixing up (Neil had seen such scenes, backstage at concerts), shots of Jesus freaks in Hollywood putting the word on Neil, and a re-creation of a recurring dream he had: twelve men wearing black hoods riding black horses in a cavalry charge towards a man in a pick-up truck.

It was, in the end, more of a cult item than anything else. In some university communities it was popular, playing for weeks at the Orson Welles Theater in the Cambridge-Boston student area. The movie is still around, shown here and there at film clubs and elsewhere. In a way it heralded Neil's incipient urge to leave the safe middle-of-the-road, which he felt he had been tending towards in *Harvest*, and heading for the ditch. He didn't dive into the ditch at once, but rather sidled toward it, as could be seen by his fragmented spring and summer.

The appearance of Crosby and Nash in *Time Fades Away*'s last few concerts had heralded an attempted reunion of CSNY. But after a month or so of playing and recording at his ranch and Hawaii, Neil decided to pull out. He didn't want to start another cycle of recording up to a finished CSNY album and then touring to support it. He and Carrie were in trouble. When he said once that they hadn't lasted much longer than Buffalo Springfield overall, the "overall" was intended to mean from beginning to end, less absences by one or the other. Once Carrie spent several months in Hawaii. Neil was gone for months at a time, sometimes touring, sometimes hanging out with friends, without Carrie. When he wrote the song "Motion Pictures" in the summer of 1973 he was in an L.A. motel a one-hour flight from home, where he hadn't been for two months. ("*Motion pictures on my*

TV *screen, now home away from home and I'm livin' in between.*") He was groping for a new direction, pulled home occasionally mainly to see Zeke. For all these reasons he was having heavy trouble putting together a recording of the *Time Fades Away* tour. He decided to use all live cuts, and put it out knowing that in the long run it was going to be his most nervous record. "It makes you feel uneasy to listen to it. The only redeeming factor was that it truly reflected where I was at. It was a chapter that I wish hadn't been written, but I knew I had to get it out because I knew it represented something. So let it go! Get it out there. Some people like that about it, the ones who can tell the difference. Some people have come up to me and said, '*Time Fades Away* – I love that record.' All I can do is look at them. But (laugh) not many have said that to me."

At that time he had not seen David Briggs for the two years during which *Harvest* had been put together, *Journey Through The Past* released, and *Time Fades Away* faded into uneasy memory. David had spent those years in Canada. With backing from a member of Montreal's high-finance Webster family, David operated a recording studio in Toronto while living north of the city in the Mono Mills–Orangeville area. He counselled his backer not to get in deep, if at all, on a rock festival called Strawberry Fields, but it went ahead anyway, lost $750,000 and change, and the recording studio was one of the casualties.

David moved back to California and rented a house a few miles from Neil's ranch. "One day in the summer of 1973 there was a knock on my door. I opened it and there was Neil. He said, 'Hey, I was just on my way to a CSNY session and I just don't feel like going there. Let's go make some rock 'n' roll.' So we packed our bags and came down to L.A., and wound up with the *Tonight's The Night* album."

14

Tonight's The Night

I've heard all the theories of what happened next, some from more-or-less-innocent bystanders and others from the people most closely involved. But mainly I have my own ideas. When Neil went to Los Angeles with David Briggs in that summer of 1973 he found that Bruce Berry, his oldtime friend and roadie (with CSNY and elsewhere), had died from an overdose of heroin. Elliot Roberts has said, with chapter and verse, that Neil has a weakness for strange, impossible people. In half a year, two of these had gone that route to oblivion. But there was a lot more to Neil's reaction than the loss of Bruce Berry and Danny Whitten. There is a streak in him, which I know well, of wanting to be good, wanting to be the best. In the previous few years he had built a stupendous reputation for completeness in his field – great onstage, great in the studio, quick to react to events ("Ohio"), sure of his touch. But there is also a streak in him, a very wide streak, of hating the idea that people think they have him figured out. He despises what has been slow death for many artists – achieving success and then repeating the formula *ad infinitum*.

In 1973 *Gold Rush* and *Harvest* were the way people had him tabbed. His record company naturally wanted more of these tried and true bonanzas. He needed something soothing to that part of him that rebelled against middle-of-the-roadism, and even that was only part of the trouble. The difficulty he was having in his relationship with Carrie after only two years was partly a result of what to him was a way of life, and had been since boyhood: there were times when he wanted to hit the road like a carefree kid and hang out with his musician friends, jam with them, and partake of the other tribal customs. Why not? It was his life and his profession. Again, as with Susan, he had gone through the first warm flush of a relationship and had come out the other side somewhat wiser. (So was Carrie, no doubt about it.) It depressed him to try to balance his uneasiness about the home situation with his love and concern for their baby son. At home he would take Zeke out driving and show him chickens and horses and other things, and they'd enjoy each other's company. But deep love for a child can be separate from marriage. We all know that. It all added up to a need to rebel against what his life seemed to be right then.

This was a rebellion that went all the way. I'm sure he didn't have a plan at first so much as an instinct. In L.A. he looked up Billy Talbot and Ralph Molina, survivors of Crazy Horse, and Ben Keith and Nils Lofgren. They called themselves the Santa Monica Flyers and started playing some of Neil's new songs. Their first gig together was to join Joni Mitchell and the Eagles for a benefit concert at Topanga Canyon. "Tonight's the Night" hadn't been written then, but Neil liked more and more what they were doing. They were old friends, people who felt good playing together without pressure, playing solely for themselves but remembering Bruce Berry and Danny Whitten, guys who (in Neil's phrase) "had known that we're just here once." It was something he, in his own troubled situation, could relate to.

When he decided they were ready to record he did that in character, too, picking not one of the high-tech studios but a place where they'd feel loose and comfortable, the rehearsal hall at L.A.'s Studio Instrument Rentals, owned by Bruce Berry's brother. They got a mobile truck for recording, and started to play.

As Billy Talbot recalls it, one night Neil was just sitting around playing and started to sing the words, "Tonight's the night." Then he went back to where he was staying and wrote the rest of the words. The next day the group played it for the first time, along with a group of other songs that all somehow were in tune with his mood. In the rehearsal hall they met in the late afternoon or early evening, night after night. They would play the songs they were working on at the time and then they'd sit down and drink and smoke, and when they were good and high they'd play some more. It was a puzzling procedure to anyone not in the business. Friends wandered in sometimes to listen while partaking of the food and drink. One night at about eleven a friend of David Briggs brought Mel Brooks out to the rehearsal hall. Brooks had just finished making the film *Blazing Saddles*. When he walked in and found everybody sprawled around, drinking beer and tequila and enjoying themselves, relaxing, shooting pool, talking, and laughing, being a filmmaker he thought it was the end of the day, with everything done. About midnight Neil said, "Well, you guys ready to go?" Everybody said, "Okay." Two minutes later they were playing and recording. Brooks, spotting David Briggs the next day at lunch, dragged him over to his table and went on and on – he couldn't believe it: "You guys all looking like it was a wrap and all of a sudden everybody's up there making music."

What they tried to do with the drinking and smoking was to get into the frame of mind, or consciousness, that they thought Bruce and Danny might have been in just before they died. Neil: "To get out there we all got that high – not *that* high, but as close as we could. I mean, I'm not a junkie and I won't even try it to check out what it's like. When we got out there we just got into a place we'd never struck before, a spooky place; we really were spooked. We wanted it that way, as a tribute to people who'd been part of our force and our energy. We were right out on the edge, in such shape that we couldn't even be sure we could handle it as musicians, maybe fall right on our face."

Along the way he had shaken what he'd gone there to shake. He no longer felt like a lonely laid-back figure with a guitar, or whatever it was people sometimes saw him as; didn't feel that at all. "So I thought, wipe that out! Be aggressive and abrasive, leave a long-term message – that things change radically sometimes."

The only resemblance at all this had to the way songs generally are recorded is that they were playing and playing and playing, recording everything but waiting for the time when suddenly they'd get it as good as it was going to be, a keeper. Sometimes this only happens with one song one night, followed by a dry spell for a few nights, and then another keeper or two. But one night the five of them suddenly caught four or five tunes, soared with them, came closer than ever before to realizing fully what the album was about. Suddenly it was like a wake.

"When we really got it, we only mixed it once for the album," Neil said. "Most of the album was the rough two-track mix that we made that night."

The album begins with a few gentle piano notes and a brief murmur of voices and then Neil singing in a shaky voice the words, "Tonight's the night." Other voices join him as they sing those three words a total of eight times, then Neil swings into a strong and sure ballad style –

> Bruce Berry was a workin' man; he used to load that Econoline van.
> A sparkle was in his eye, but his life was in his hand.
> Well, late at night when the people were gone he used to pick up my
>   guitar
> And sing a song in a shaky voice
> That was real as the day was long.

The chorus, four times "Tonight's the night," follows, then:

> Early in the mornin' at the break of day he used to sleep until the
>   afternoon.
> If you never heard him sing,
> I guess you won't too soon.
> 'Cause people let me tell you,
> It sent a chill up and down my spine (this with a wail from Ben
>   Keith's guitar)
> When I picked up the telephone
> And heard that he died, out on the main line (this line a wail, a
>   scream).

Four times more they intone "Tonight's the night." Neil plays a driving riff on the piano. The band joins in. Neil sings part of the first and second verses again. Then sixteen times they sing (all or one or some, depending, and with different inflections each time) the words "Tonight's the night." The song ends with a loud groan from Neil.

In effect, "Tonight's the Night" is done twice on the album, like a pair of not-quite-matched bookends. The songs in between are mostly in the same vein of rough, abrasive, personal lament. "Albuquerque" has such lines as,

> I've been flyin' down the road
> And I've been starvin' to be alone

And independent from the scene that I've known . . .
So I'll stop when I can,
Find some fried eggs and country ham.
I'll find somewhere where they don't care who I am.

In the song "Roll Another Number (For the Road)" come these lines:

Though my feet aren't on the ground,
I've been standin' on the sound
Of some open-hearted people goin' down.

There was nothing light and easy in any of it. One song, "Tired Eyes," always hits me hard. It's a ballad, but a mysterious one:

Well, he shot four men in a cocaine deal.
He left them lyin' in an open field
Full of old cars with bullet holes in the mirrors.
He tried to do his best but he could not.
    Chorus: *Please take my advice,*
                  Please take my advice,
                  Please take my advice.
                  Open up the tired eyes,
                  Open up the tired eyes.
Well, it wasn't supposed to go down that way.
But they burned his brother, you know,
And they left him lying in the driveway.
They let him down with nothin'.
He tried to do his best but he could not.
   (Chorus)
Well, tell me more, tell me more,
Tell me more; I mean was he a heavy doper
Or was he just a loser? He was a friend of yours.
What do you mean he had bullet holes in his mirrors?
He tried to do his best but he could not.
    Please take my advice . . .

That song, always with its enduring echo in my head of "*Please take my advice, please take my advice, open up the tired eyes, open up the tired eyes,*" sets the listener up for the concluding second version of "Tonight's the Night." It has several differences from the first, including one place where Neil threw in an extra, too-early, "*And people let me tell you . . .*" and then caught himself and went on, "*Late at night when the people were gone . . .*" Also at the end he sang a two-line reprise of "*And early in the morning about the break of day, he used to sleep until the afternoon*" and from there went into the final long album-ending repetitions of "Tonight's the night." It was as if, that last time, they were leaving Bruce alive.

The original mix that Neil referred to as the most complete depiction of the way they felt never was released in that form. "It was just so far ahead of its time, so radical, that I hesitated," Neil told me. "There was all this talking between the songs. It was just a bunch of stoned-out musicians talking but it was all in continuity with what was going on. I should have let it go. We were just playing those guys on their way."

Maybe the original version would have come out, too, but the record company hated it, thought the sloppiness, the crudeness, the uncorrected errors of that mix were like a slap in the face to what the industry thought it was and had thought Neil was – smooth, professional, precise. They couldn't understand what had happened, how one of their very favourite sons suddenly was looking and acting like a rock star bound for disaster. Elliot Roberts was blown out by how destructive the music was to the image Neil had. (Everything had been going so *well!*) He wanted to hide the whole thing. The tour that became famous among Neil's fans and the cognoscenti of the rock world was booked, overriding all objections, only because Neil said to Elliot, "Listen! I want to go on the road, right now!" – causing Elliot to start a crafty hunt for the smallest and most obscure halls he could find.

A few weeks later Carrie wrote a letter one night saying that Neil was in his ranch studio listening "to music he rehearsed and recorded in L.A." and that he was taking it on the road, including some concerts in Canada and eight in the United Kingdom (to make up for the ones cancelled from the *Time Fades Away* tour that spring). She said Zeke was fine, and "Neil takes him on little trips . . . he is very trusting and content to be beside his pa in the Jeepster, driving off to 'who knows where.'" Neil scribbled a postscript at the bottom: "Don't know the exact dates but 1, McMaster U.; 2, Waterloo U.; 3, Guelph U. We'll be there a five-day total. Don't know the hotel yet. Looking forward to hanging out. Love, Neil."

When he arrived later in November he based himself in Toronto. The Ontario concert venues were not much more than an hour's drive away, at most. I drove to McMaster University in Hamilton one foggy and rainy night. I was politely treated but felt out of place among the half-stoned musicians and hangers-on in the smoky fog of the tiny dressing room. There were wooden benches around the wall. A shower area, I think, or some other kind of a little room, held the overflow from the dressing room. Hell, I thought, the old Olympic rink back in Winnipeg in 1936 (it was known as the Barn) was a very classy joint compared to this. Out in the audience it got worse. A dense heat and humidity and warm wet-wool smell was generated by the overflow crowd, most everyone having been caught in the downpour getting there. Finally, late, the lights went up on the sleazy set featuring a small mangy palm tree and a fake moon. Neil, in black shades, very long hair, whiskers uncut for weeks, moustache, and the general appearance of someone caught in a roundup of the usual suspects, strolled to cen-trestage and drawled, "Welcome to Miami Beach, ladies and gentle-men. It's cheaper than it looks."

I listened carefully but tentatively, not understanding what the hell it was all about. At that time all the songs were new to me, and to most of the crowd, but the crowd was comfortably dressed and had heady stuff to smoke and drink, and I was wishing I'd come in jeans or gym trunks. Actually I was saved by young Astrid, who was eleven then. She fell asleep. At that age when Astrid fell asleep that was it. I left the music of one offspring and took the other, the youngest and most vul-nerable, home. I went to have breakfast with Neil and the band the next day. He told me that he had been really shaken, thrilled when he mentioned from the stage that I was in the audience, and a tremendous roar went up. (This was, in effect, my home turf; besides my daily news-paper column I appeared a lot on Hamilton television.) "I just wasn't prepared for the way they thought about you. It must have made you feel good, too."

I had to laugh. Others had mentioned that crowd reaction to me, but I had left before it happened. It was a while before I heard the rest of the songs used in that tour. And yet something happened between then and the time two years later when the Tonight's The Night album was finally released and I heard it all. Either it had been ahead of its time, or I'd grown some. It instantly became my favourite album of all he had produced until then. Even in the summer of 1983 when a reporter from Kansas City phoned me for an interview before one of Neil's concerts and asked which was my favourite album, I immediately replied, "*Tonight's The Night*."

"Why?" The "For God's sake!" didn't have to be spoken.

When I was able to find *Tonight's The Night* tour tapes in England and read what had been written about those concerts at the time, it did nothing to disabuse me of the idea that whatever else Neil is, *Tonight's The Night* represents something essential. He was like a man on a binge at a wake, a long happy bout of not giving a shit. Those of his fans whose concept of Neil was set in concrete ("Sugar Mountain," "Cinnamon Girl," "Old Man," "Heart of Gold") might have developed a nervous tic for a while, but he had beaten the system. Not out of temperament and certainly not out of vanity, but as an artistic move, daring to be an *artist* and not just a hit-maker.

That's why he remembers that period so warmly even now. Ever since, he has felt that one of his best concerts ever was on that tour at the Hippodrome in Bristol. "We had gotten pretty good by the time we got to England. We knew what we were doing. That's where the Sex Pistols, Sid Vicious, Johnny Rotten, those guys and others saw us. Some of them mentioned it later. Not that I'm saying they eventually based their trip on us, by any stretch of the imagination. But they did remember. In Bristol none of the big music writers were there, you know, but it was one of those nights when we soared up to our best and beyond it." His mention of the early punk-rockers is part of his continuing respect for anyone, punkers, new-wavers, anyone who dares to buck the establishment whether it's with bloody-minded inventiveness or any other revolutionary move. In England he's one of the very few rock 'n' roll ancients who are widely respected among the yeasty young musicians there today because he has shown the courage to take chances, go out and walk the line.

As that tour went on, he kept building on the characterization of a rock star on the edge, throwing away everything his reputation was based on. From the stage between songs, the wry and often brief remarks of other tours gave way to so much talking that every once in a while he'd tell the audience, "If you worry about me talking so much, don't. I always play more than I talk. So the more I talk the more songs I'll play." At the Rainbow in London a few nights after Bristol, he explained the "Southern Man" incident from Oakland seven months before, and then after a few bars said the song he was going to sing he'd written in a Los Angeles hotel room earlier that year, a time when he'd been away from home for a couple of months trying to figure out his life.

Harmonica. Then Neil:

"Anyway, we're in this hotel room (harmonica), we're trying some honey-slides, you know. . . . You know what a honey-slide is? (Voice from audience: Yes!) Honey-slide, hmmmn! You know, real poor grade marijuana (he's playing soft guitar all through this), worse than you get on the street, and you take it and you get your old lady, you know, if you got one, to cook it up on the stove, you know, to put that grass in the grinder, you know, get it real fine, in a frying pan, put it on the stove, turn the heat up a little, wait till that grass just starts to smoke, just a little bit, take it off the heat, don't want to burn it too much (laughter and a few guitar bars), then you take the honey, you know, get a half a glass of honey about this big – I hope you ladies are listening to the recipes tonight – (audience laughter and a few words missing) just heat that honey right up until it's slippery, you know, and mix that grass with it, you know, the fine grass that you've cooked up just until it started to smoke and you took it off, mix those together and you get a spoon, you know (voices from the audience, laughter). I think you should eat it after that. Just eat a little of it, you know, maybe a spoonful or two, you'll be surprised, you know, it just makes you feel fine . . . (laughter) that cheap grass is great. You know, in these times, you have to think about prices and things like that (laughter).

"Anyway, back to the motel, we're just sitting around having a few honey-slides, and they slow you down quite a bit, you know, there's nothing to really get fast for, anyway, and this song is sort of . . . well, we're all sitting around playing this chorus, I'm playing with my friends Rusty Kershaw and Ben Keith, sitting around the motel room, the TV was on . . ." Neil then goes into guitar and harmonica and the song, "Motion Pictures."

I have examined that Rainbow concert in detail because it was fairly typical of how he went night after night on that tour. His recipe for honey-slides was part of it. His telling about the "Southern Man" incident in Oakland was part of it. The way he acted *off* the stage was part of it. One account by an innocent bystander from Holland helps give the atmosphere. A few days before the Rainbow concert this young rock music fan and occasional critic, Constant Meijers, was trying, from Amsterdam, to get a ticket. No luck. So he wrote directly to Neil, and a couple of days later got a phone call. His name had been passed from Neil to Warners in London to a Dutch record company, which called to say he could have a ticket to the Rainbow if he brought with him seventeen bottles of José Cuervo Gold brand tequila, which Neil had been unable to find in England. Meijers located only one bottle, sadly reported his failure to get seventeen, and instantly received a phone call from England saying, "Bring the one! Come at once! You'll be met at the airport and driven to the concert!" Thus buoyed up, he found three more bottles. In his later report, he said that when he reached the dressing room at the Rainbow and delivered his booty, he still couldn't get past the guard on the door. Then he saw Neil poke his head out.

"That tequila," Meijers asked quickly, "is it a good brand?"

"What tequila?"

"José Cuervo."

"Oh, you must be the guy who brought me the tequila," Neil said. They shook hands and chatted, arranging to meet in the dressing room later. Meijers' account of the concert, written in Dutch and not translated until ten years later, included comments that the sound was miserable, the coordination of the musicians miserable, Neil's piano and singing miserable, Neil's movements around the stage unsteady. "What on earth was happening to Neil?" Meijers wrote. "Where was the magic gone? He talked a lot, drank tequila by the wine-glass in one gulp and mumbled for minutes on end about anything." Later in the account, Meijers reports, "Picking up the guitar with some difficulty, Neil fought his way desperately through his set." The Meijers piece is about 2,000 words long, ending with Meijers in the dressing room where Neil, "looking like a beaten dog," is being reassured by David Briggs and the others that it had been a great concert.

Three years later, at a concert in Paris, Neil was asked about an insert being given away then with the *Tonight's The Night* album. It was the Meijers article, in the original Dutch. Neil explained how it had come about and, regarding the insert, "It seemed a good idea to print it in Dutch because in the U.S. nobody would be able to understand any of it. Because I didn't understand any of it myself and, when someone is so sickened and as fucked-up as I was then, everything's in Dutch anyway." (The article was translated into English by Mark Lyons and published in 1983 by the Neil Young Appreciation Society.)

Tonight's The Night was no big-deal limo tour. Neil and the others would walk to the gig from their hotel, drink in pubs, talking to anyone who came along. In Manchester after one show they set out to find a place that was open, which is not easy late at night in Manchester. "Eventually," wrote a reporter in *New Musical Express*, "they wound up in a really squalid place, the kind where night owls drop in for bad food. There were no drinks being sold but somebody scored some wine for them somewhere. Later, near dawn, Neil was wandering the rotting streets nearby muttering the appropriate west coast epithets."

In one concert he introduced a roadie only as BJ, so few knew that this was the old Baby John of the earliest days of Danny and the Memories, the Rockets, the early Crazy Horse. Neil (on a tape I heard): "BJ back there is one of my best friends! A wonderful guy! You can tell which one he is, he's the one applauding the loudest." And the crowd breaks up in general laughter. Yet the looseness at least once or twice turned to something intensely serious, close to his heart, untold until then. The "Tonight's the Night" song with its words, *"Bruce Berry was a working man,"* led him one night into a monologue that (on the tape I have) is not easy to make out, because he mumbles, plays guitar and harmonica, interrupts himself, but gives a series of images that I transcribed as best I could after playing the tape interminably to try for the exact words. It is confusing, but not *so* confusing when you know the plot – that once Bruce Berry turned up without a guitar he'd been responsible for, one belonging to David Crosby. The strong suspicion was that he had sold it to buy heroin.

Neil, to the Rainbow audience: "You've been hearing a lot of songs about a friend of ours named Bruce Berry and people that died." He then sings part of "Tonight's the Night," a long passage, and speaks again: "We could play like that all night . . . but now I'm going to get down and say something real, you know."

Some spoken passages about Bruce Berry are inaudible, but refer to his parting company with CSNY rather abruptly. Then Neil says, "We didn't see him for a while, then. Time passed by and Bruce came back one day."

Here he speaks as if he were an actor doing two roles, himself and Bruce Berry.

As Bruce: "Hey, man, need somebody to work for you now?"

As Neil: "Yeah! Yeah! Hey, wait a minute, though! Wait a minute!

Between 1976 and 1978 Neil
helped to tear down and rebuild
this boat, which he named the
W.N. Ragland, after his grandfather.

Neil had one son, Zeke (left), born in 1972 to actress Carrie Snodgress, before he met Pegi Morton (above) in the San Mateo County hills where his ranch is and near where she was born. They married in 1978. Their first baby, Ben, was with them wherever the *Ragland* sailed.

(Connie Moskos)

Left: Neil and Pegi on their wedding day, August 2, 1978. They were married at Neil's house on Malibu Beach, once owned by F. Scott Fitzgerald. The house was destroyed by a forest fire during the *Rust Never Sleeps* tour (above).

Opposite page: Ben suffers from cerebral palsy. Helping him achieve his potential was a seven-days-a-week, twelve-hours-a-day job for Pegi, Neil, and many volunteers. For the next four years, Neil did not tour; he and Pegi were bound to the ranch by their commitment to their bright but physically handicapped son.

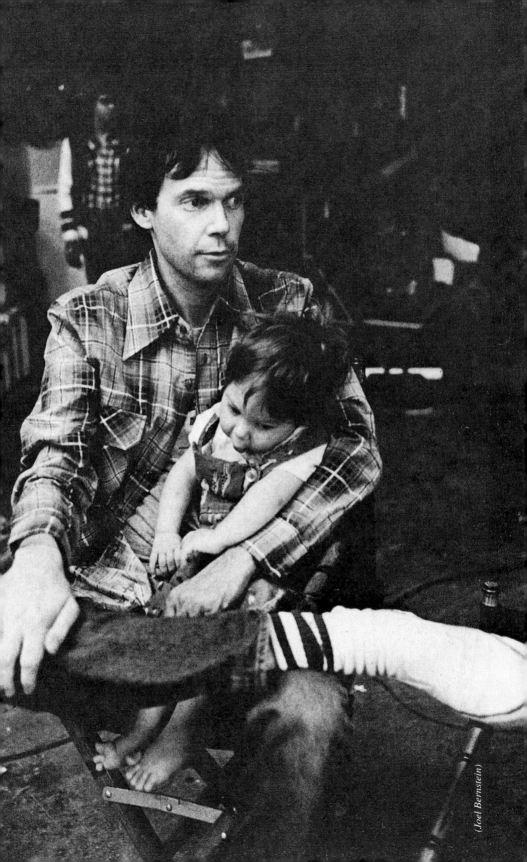

(Joel Bernstein)

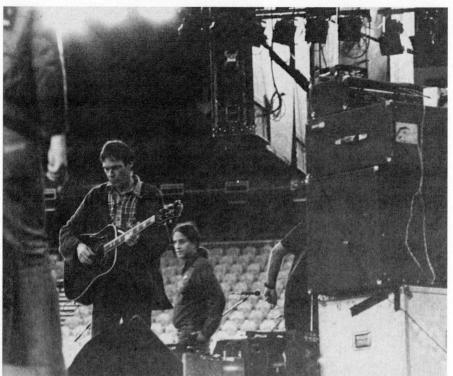

Opposite, top: Sound check in Birmingham, England, in 1982, the first time Neil had gone on the road since Ben was born. Joel Bernstein, who always tunes and travels with Neil's guitars, is in the background.

Opposite, lower: More than twelve years after Neil and Bruce Palmer last played together, Bruce came out of hibernation and Neil made him part of the Trans Band – that's Bruce with the beret, Nils Lofgren at left.

This page, top: After the *Trans* album, with its highly synthesized music – then called technopop – Neil made his next album about as far as possible from that style. He went back (bottom) to 1950s rock with a band called the Shocking Pinks.

(Geffen Records)

(Geffen Records)

(Joel Bernstein)

For about five years, when Ben's program was the main concern on the family agenda, Neil and Pegi were not sure they could do justice both to him and to a new baby – but then there was joyful news. On May 15, 1984, Amber Jean Young was born, bright-eyed and lively, and family photos had a new star turn. Left: clockwise from left, Zeke, Neil, Pegi, Ben, Amber. Below: Zeke, Pegi, Neil, Ben, Amber.

(Courtesy P. Young)

Didn't you lose, ah, didn't you lose David's guitar, man? You lost David's guitar!"

As Bruce: "I never lost anybody's guitar in my life. All I know, man, I left it in the back of the station wagon. It was in the back of the station wagon and I left it. I was in the bathroom and when I came back in five minutes the guitar was gone."

As Neil: "I'm sorry, man, you can't work for us now, you can't . . . because . . ."

As Bruce: "You mean after all the time I worked for you that you think one guitar, man . . ."

As Neil: "Sorry, man, that's the way it is."

The music and audience noise make the next few words impossible to hear, but the band breaks into "Tonight's the Night" again and Neil singing, almost screaming, full of anguish, *"People, let me tell you, I felt a chill go down my spine, when I picked up the telephone and heard that he'd died, out on the main line."*

In a variation of that monologue, at another concert, Neil's words to Bruce Berry included the line: "You took David's guitar, man, and stuck it in your arm."

There is one other reference in U.K. reports of the tour that struck a note with me: "After the death rumours circulated the previous month . . ." Reminding me that one October day in 1973, in my office at *The Globe and Mail*, an editor came in anxiously holding a piece of wire-service copy. "I hate to do this, but I thought I should ask you," he said, and handed me the story. It was datelined Paris and said that Neil had died there, overdosed. "Have you heard anything about this?"

I said no, but I had been talking to Neil a few days earlier in California and he hadn't said anything about going to Paris. I picked up the phone and dialled. He answered.

"Are you dead?" I asked.

"Not that I know of," he said.

The *Tonight's The Night* album was not released before the tour, during the tour, or for nearly two years after. This tells you, among other things, that no big wheels at Reprise Records were threatening to shoot up the joint if *Tonight's The Night* weren't put out pronto. Quite the opposite: they were dragging their feet like a fleet of sheet anchors.

They wanted something positive from Neil to counteract the nervous *Time Fades Away. Tonight's The Night* might have counteracted it for Neil, but not for them. Knowing that Neil was incessantly writing and recording songs, they felt if they could stonewall for a few months he'd have an album ready that they'd like better. This happened. *On The Beach* was it, released in July 1974. *On The Beach* was successful but its sales weren't nearly on a par with *After The Gold Rush* or *Harvest*. He was happy about it though, especially since although he had considered some songs from *Tonight's The Night* for *On The Beach*, each time he changed his mind and stuck to his resolve to bring out *Tonight's The Night* whole or not at all.

That's when Elliot Roberts stepped in with some ideas. He suggested changing the *Tonight's The Night* order, putting the songs in a different sequence, and adding three other songs – "Lookout Joe," "Come On Baby Let's Go Downtown," both with Jack Nitzsche on piano, and "Borrowed Tune." The version of "Come On Baby Let's Go Downtown" that was chosen fitted admirably, a Danny Whitten song he and Neil sang and recorded with Crazy Horse and Nitzsche at Fillmore East in 1970, a concert remembered by those who heard it as brilliant, crashing rock 'n' roll with Neil at the absolute peak of his powers. The record company was still uncomfortable. They suggested that he think about it again. They wanted to remix it. "I told them to shove it up their ass; they could take it the way it was or they would never hear from me again." They bowed, perhaps because Neil had another album ready, *Zuma*, that Reprise was high on and figured on releasing quickly after *Tonight's The Night*, as an antidote.

So *Tonight's The Night* was released twenty-three months after the first version was recorded. Neil then agreed to his first-ever album-launching party, and to sit for a couple of days in Elliot's office while interviewers from rock publications and radio stations filed in and out with their tape recorders and notebooks. Why had he never done that before? "I never had an album that you could party to, and interview to, before." One interviewer, Bud Scoppa, whose long piece in *New Musical Express* was a celebration of Neil and his strangest album, said to Neil what most of the people who had heard the album at that time were thinking: "It seems as if in this album you've gone against your superstardom musically. Where's the teen-idol?"

Neil: "We gotta tear down all that. It's gone now. Now we can do whatever. I don't want people to expect me to be a certain way. I have to be able to feel I can do whatever I want and it's not going to disappoint *me* to do it."

He tore it down, all right. But he had to keep working at it. The first printing of *Tonight's The Night* was much smaller than his usual.

Neil (to me): "They printed the bare minimum and tried to take it off the re-order lists. You couldn't even get it. We got on the case, and when it came time to renegotiate, one thing put into my contract was that everything I make stays in print. Whether it's selling or not, it stays in print. We keep making them. We never run out of them. Every time I sign, that's restated: 'Keep them presses up, boys!'" *Tonight's The Night* by the early 1980s was selling more than it did in its first few years.

There are a lot of reasons for going this deeply into the history of *Tonight's The Night*, one being that in 1981, eight years after the album was cut (and six years after it was released), Neil gave one of his rare interviews on a U.S. live radio phone-in program called *Rockline*. One caller asked, "Which album of yours is the most significant?"

Neil: "I'd have to say it's *Tonight's The Night*."

Disc jockey: "You still have those deep feelings about that album! It was your least successful record. It really means a lot to you, doesn't it?"

Neil: "Well, all of my records mean a lot to me, but that one means a lot just because it's the black sheep of the family. I just like it."

Ten years after the original recording, David Briggs and I talked about *Tonight's The Night*, on which he had shared the producer credit with Neil. At home a couple of weeks earlier he had come across the original tape, the one that wasn't put out. "I want to tell you, it is a handful. It is unrelenting. There is no relief in it at all. It does not release you for one second. It's like some guy having you by the throat from the first note, and all the way to the end." After all the real smooth stuff Neil had been doing, David felt most critics and others simply failed to read what they should have into *Tonight's The Night* – that it was an artist making a giant growth step. Neil came in during this conversation, which was in his living room. When David stopped Neil said, "You've got that original? I thought it was lost. I've never been able to find it. We'll bring it out, someday, that original."

15

Goodbye to Carrie

In 1973 Neil and Carrie were on one of those toboggan slides familiar to anyone who has ever experienced the break-up of a marriage or common-law relationship. This fact was not obvious to anyone at our distance, and no wonder. As John Mortimer once observed from his vantage point as a longtime English divorce lawyer and judge (before, during, and after his more illustrious career as a novelist, playwright, and screen writer), "There is no one cause you can write on the death certificate of a marriage; the patient is at the mercy of a multiplicity of sicknesses and . . . meanwhile there is a constant and increasingly hopeless search for a cure." That Neil and Carrie did not marry may indicate that the real commitment was never there, but otherwise has little relevance. Mortimer's law applies.

Through 1972 and 1973 Carrie's letters were full of warm news about Zeke and Neil but naturally she was not telling us the down side. Neither was Neil. As so often is the case, the fatal flaws lay not in either of them as individuals, but only in them as a couple. Music loomed so large in Neil's life that other attachments inevitably suffered. He was still picking up the guitar before the girl. In contrast,

Carrie decided to put her own career into total suspension. She read scripts and turned them down, sick of the Hollywood scene, she told me once. But neither (apparently) was she really ready to exchange the glare and flash of Hollywood, where many of her friends were, for one of the civilized world's most remote environments, Neil's ranch, with Neil not always there. Submersion of her own life and career into frequent periods of solitude – even with frequent visits to and from her Los Angeles friends – obviously took away an essential excitement. In turn, making Neil the designated core of her existence constituted a pressure on Neil that he obviously was not ready for. Her life fluctuated between the daily routine of the ranch and her absorption with Zeke to times when suddenly musicians and technicians would descend for recording sessions, to be fed and quartered in a totally work-oriented atmosphere not unlike that of an old-time threshing gang on the western plains.

Their friends could see the trouble brewing when Zeke was only a few months old. As Neil confided to the Rainbow audience during the *Tonight's The Night* tour late in 1973, the night of the honey-slides recipe, when he had written the song "Motion Pictures" a few months earlier he'd been sitting around a motel room with his friends Ben Keith and Rusty Kershaw, "and I hadn't been home for two months by then, trying to get my act together." Such absences were noticed by both his friends and Carrie's.

In the school break of March 1974, our daughter Astrid, then eleven, flew to California to stay a couple of weeks. Carrie and friends of hers who were at the ranch made her welcome, gave a very good time to a very aware little girl. When she returned she told us she hadn't seen Neil except for a night or two. "He was in L.A. all the time," she said, having picked up the terminology. But L.A. is only a quick plane ride away; it is possible to go down in the morning and be back at night – if a guy really wants to come back. "Some of the others said that Neil isn't at the ranch much any more," she said.

Neil himself once alluded obliquely to what he obviously saw as a lack of meaningful communication with Carrie. "Whoever I'm with, I like discussing things," he told me one day. "Even when I've almost made up my own mind, sometimes the ideas that come back in discussions are creative and help me. I don't like going deeply into something I'm thinking of, something that means a lot to me but maybe has some holes in it, and getting only the answer, 'Far out.'" So he had turned back to his tight network of musician friends for communication that he didn't feel he was getting at home.

One final factor: Neil was in pain with his crumbled disc when he and Carrie met. For nearly a year, always under heavy medication, he went through the pain of his back going out, the enforced immobility of traction, moving for a while into a back brace, taking the brace off, having his back go out again. This happened three times before he had his operation on August 11, 1971. At the same time he was involved in divorce proceedings with Susan. Carrie seemed the answer, and must have felt, in return, a need for Neil's love and companionship.

As time went on and the relationship was heading for the rocks, neither wanted to admit defeat – as in John Mortimer's "constant and increasingly hopeless search for a cure." The last two periods when they were together were in 1974. In March that year, while my daughter Astrid was in California, the rumours surfaced again that Crosby, Stills, Nash and Young were getting together for an album and a tour. Nobody took it all that seriously at first, because the four years since their original tour had been full of similar rumours. But this turned out to be different. Steve Stills said it was on, to start in July. David Crosby, interviewed in England, said it was on. Graham Nash said he was willing. Neil had been the most difficult to convince, probably because his work apart from CSNY had been successful and satisfying. But the persuasion was hard to withstand, even for Neil. Atlantic Records was eager for another CSNY album. Promoters putting the tour together offered the four a guaranteed one million dollars each against a percentage of gate receipts, for a two-month tour, thirty-one concerts. They decided (Nash told an interviewer) that, since their previous troubles had taken place not on the road but in studios, they would not go into a studio to record until *after* the tour, when the group presumably would be at its peak.

When the dates were set, Neil brought everybody to the ranch in June to rehearse. Carrie wrote in a letter to us, "The Country Kitchen is open again, cooking every day for 17. I have three girls in to help me." David Crosby: "Neil played host in the most incredible fashion. He had built this full-size forty-foot stage in the middle of a redwood grove right across from his studios where we could record. And the place, because it's so private and beautiful, was a natural to make us feel great and work hard." Neil, by that time, had added the adjoining

700-acre ranch to his original spread. The new part included the sprawling white five-bedroom ranch house I've mentioned earlier. Besides CSNY, the musicians for the touring unit included Tim Drummond on bass, Joe Lala on congas, Russell Kunkel on drums.

Neil had decided that when the tour hit the road, he would travel separately. He was having a General Motors motor home customized (later to be replaced by a more elaborate bus), but would need help with driving and other duties because he planned to take along Zeke, then about twenty-two months old, plus Art, their family dog of indeterminate ancestry. A friend from Santa Cruz, Jim Mazzeo, also known as Sandy or Maz, was working on alterations to the motor home. Needing help, he brought in David Cline from Half Moon Bay – a University of Texas business graduate who, still in his mid-twenties, had been a forest ranger and an oyster biologist, but right then didn't have a job. Neil was looking for someone to share driving and other duties with Mazzeo. He liked what he saw of the big, steady-going Cline. One night when the three of them were working around Neil's vehicle Neil asked David, "How about coming along and help look after things?" David knew nothing of music tours or the money involved. "Well, okay," he said, "but only if you'll let me pay my one-third of the expenses." He wondered why the other two laughed until they almost fell off their chairs. He found out: in the next couple of months he spent on Neil's behalf around $45,000 or $50,000 in cash, just on hotel rooms, travel, odd bits of expense. All through the tour David Cline never lost his uneasiness over not paying his share of personal expenses; he found it difficult being treated as a friend and yet not sharing the costs. However, they all survived.

The tour was a smash from its beginning in Seattle, where they sang forty-four songs and performed for a remarkable four hours. Crosby worked so hard that night that he was unable to sing at the gig the next day in Vancouver. Near its end when the tour reached Toronto two months later, September 2, accompanied by The Band, it had already become another rock legend; filling huge outdoor stadia wherever it went.

Carrie and Zeke came to meet Neil in Toronto, where 44,000 paid twelve dollars a ticket, with no seats reserved, to jam the 27,000-seat Varsity Stadium in midtown. A high stage had been erected during the day at the north end of the football field. Beginning in early afternoon of a day that turned cold and raw, people with blankets and bottles and tarpaulins and umbrellas camped in the football field's grass until no open space remained. Newspapers ran on their front pages the next morning air shots taken before darkness fell, showing the stands jammed and every patch of grass covered with young people.

Neil had given us tickets which would allow us on the back of the high stage when the concert began. When The Band opened the show, we were with Neil, Elliot, and others in a bus parked behind the stage for use as a dressing room. That's where I first met Stephen Stills (who wanted me to get him a real Hamilton Tiger-Cats game sweater if I could, which it turned out I couldn't), David Crosby, Graham Nash, Joe Lala, and Russell Kunkel. I'd met Tim Drummond the previous year during the *Time Fades Away* tour. By the time we all piled out of the bus and CSNY went to work, a cold rain began to fall, turning to sleet in a downpour slashing through the beams of the stadium floodlights. Up on the stage where my family and I huddled, Carrie and Zeke, then just two, joining us until she took him back to the warm bus, we looked out through the storm at the incredible scene. Crewmen brought us rain ponchos to wear. We stood behind scenery, amplifiers, anything that gave a little shelter. Out on the stage a few yards away the musicians played and sang with water running down their faces while the crowd shouted and cheered and the music crashed around us. Maybe some left but a friend of mine who was in the crowd said later, flatly, "No. Nobody left. It was just an amazing experience."

When it was over, we climbed stiffly down behind the musicians. We were shivering with the cold. If I hadn't been shepherding my family around, I would have bolted across the street to the rooftop bar of the Park Plaza Hotel for a triple hot buttered rum. As it was, I sent them to the hotel lobby to wait while I got our car. I stayed behind a minute or two, with Neil.

"Carrie and I will come over tomorrow," he said. "You better go and get warm." As I walked away a minute later I encountered Bill Ballard, who a few years before had put together Concert Productions International, which had promoted this concert. Bill and I had met originally through his father, Harold, principal owner of Maple Leaf Gardens where I'd spent so much time watching hockey.

"Want to see something?" he asked.

"Sure."

He passed me a damp slip of paper. "The box office statement," he said. It was a carbon of a handwritten note which read, "Gross receipts

$484,000." When you add to that some of the biggest stadia in North America, some gates a good deal bigger than Toronto, you begin to understand why, when it was all over and the fees computed, each senior partner in CSNY received about $1.4 million for his two months' work.

The tour then was not quite over. The next stop would be New York. Neil and Carrie did not show up at our place the next day, nor phone.

The tour's final huge move was from New York to London. It took a chartered Boeing 707 to ferry 72,000 pounds of equipment across the Atlantic. That concert in Wembley Stadium before more than 70,000 lasted ten hours and included The Band, Joni Mitchell, Tom Scott and the L.A. Express, and Jesse Colin Young as well as CSNY, Tim Drummond, Joe Lala, and Russell Kunkel. The music papers sent large teams to cover the action and filled page after page with stories and pictures. Ten years later it was still remembered as one of the major rock events of the decade.

To celebrate the end of the tour Neil bought a 1934 Rolls-Royce station wagon. "You could drive this to the other end of Africa," the dealer said proudly.

"So okay," Neil said to Mazzeo and Cline, "let's drive it to the other end of Africa!" He was obviously in no hurry to get back to Carrie and the troubled life they were having. After some shakedown cruises around England and Wales they looked at the maps and decided they'd go to Amsterdam. They had the Rolls flown there. They drove as far as Brussels before the car broke down – close enough to the Brussels Hilton that they coasted in. "Fate," said Neil, and they took a suite and stayed a couple of weeks, maybe three, while the disabled Rolls was flown back to England.

By then the African trip had been abandoned – it was going to take time to fix the Rolls. Neil's situation with Carrie was occupying more and more of his thoughts. Their meeting in Toronto had settled nothing. Warner Brothers invited him to use a place the company owned in Spain and he accepted, intending to go on to Italy from there. The night before they were to leave for Spain, the three of them sat around the Hilton suite all night drinking wine and coffee and talking about what is needed from both sides in a man-woman relationship. At one point late that night David Cline said, "You can travel around the world any time you want, Neil, but this may be the only time you can resolve what's going on with Carrie."

Maybe that stuck in Neil's mind. They packed for Spain, guitars, suitcases, a pile of luggage. They went to the airport. They checked all the luggage for Spain. Just as the flight was called, Neil disappeared for a couple of minutes. When he came back he said, "I'm going to California. There's a flight right now. I'll call. If it doesn't work, I'll be back."

With all the luggage, Maz and David went to Spain. Neil, with only what he wore, flew to California. A few days later I got a letter from Neil in his distinctive, big, felt-pen handwriting.

"Dear Dad and Astrid: Just got home to the ranch yesterday. I'm sure glad the tour is over. It's great to be back again. When you saw me in T.O. Carrie and I were going through pretty intense times. That is why we didn't make it over the next day. Sorry for not calling. Rock and roll and the life of a musician turn out to be pretty bad for a family. Carrie seeks the simple things that I sing about and have trouble reaching."

He had drawn a line under that part, then continued in a part of the letter that reflected much more deeply what he was going through, both sides of an agonized uncertainty.

"I just threw three months of stacked-up mail in the fireplace. I suppose it's an act of little care for the senders, but I can't face that mail right now. At this point in my life I seem to be just grabbing at straws hoping something lasting will turn up. I sure love Carrie and Zeke but the ranch is pretty lonely for a little boy alone. He should have friends. Funny feeling after all the love and work I've put into this place with Carrie. We're going to the doctor today to see if he's the one to take care of Zeke. I'm still writing and creating a lot which I'm grateful for. I seem to write more and more as time passes. First songs, now short little stories. The typewriter [one given him] helps a lot." The letter ended there abruptly and was not signed.

The postmark on that letter was October 12, 1974, almost seven weeks after the Toronto concert and five weeks after the tour's final gig in London. The letter did give some idea of what he and Carrie were going through but provided no final decision. As it turned out, within a few weeks Carrie rented a house in Santa Barbara and went there with Zeke, while Neil, needing something other than the ranch's solitude, moved into rented quarters at Malibu Beach.

Back in Spain, Maz was happy and David Cline was not. Neil had not called. David wanted to leave but had no money. After ten days he packed up everything of his own and Neil's that had to be taken back to North America and went to the airport, hoping there would be enough in unused portions of several months of airline tickets to get him out of there. There was, for as far as London. There, Warners came to the rescue. David flew home and delivered all the stuff to the ranch. Maz soon followed. At the ranch they found the financial arrangements chaotic, partly because Neil's accountants had never seen the place and didn't really know what was going on. David, not wishing to be tarred with that brush, couldn't get in touch with Neil but told Elliot he was quitting, and why. Then he and Maz phoned Rassy in Florida to tell her. She called to tell Neil he was being ripped off.

This obviously was the catalyst. Neil phoned his people at the ranch and was told everything was fine, not to worry. Then he phoned his accountants, who said the ranch was a disaster area financially. Finally he phoned David Cline, who said, "Did you know that I quit?"

Neil: "Well, you're the first person up there who has told me that anything is wrong. Would you like to come down here for a day or two?"

David met Neil in Malibu. They walked out on the beach and talked. Neil did most of the listening. David drew circles on the sand; the central circle being Neil and the income he generated, with connecting circles representing Elliot with his managerial responsibilities, the accountants with theirs, Carrie and Zeke, the antique car collection which then was small but valuable, and other projects. He suggested putting the whole operation into some kind of a rational accounting system.

Neil accepted that, took David to his lawyer, introduced him, and said, "When he comes into the office, treat him as if he is me." In effect, he was hiring David as ranch manager, although David says he was actually more of an overseer, as he didn't have the know-how to run the ranch. He listed all the people on the payroll and the jobs they were supposed to be doing. He fired some of them, and with Neil worked out a plan for picking everything up structurally. That way, the atmosphere would not change, but the old buildings would still be there in the future, instead of, in time, falling down. There were still problems, always will be, because Neil's volatile nature is naturally at odds with set budgets. If he has a new idea he wants worked on, like his tour bus, or his subsequent love affair with boats, and if that drains off funds that had been allocated elsewhere, it is Neil's newest idea that prevails.

Soon after his meeting with David, Neil phoned me to say that he and Carrie had broken up. Within days, Carrie's mother died suddenly in Chicago. Neil came back to go with Carrie to the funeral, and Rassy was along as well to help. But it was over. A sad letter arrived from Carrie. "Our lives are all messed up," she wrote. "Tried our luck, but weren't given enough time, I guess. This last year has been full of questions and confessions of inner self. It took us far apart, and now Neil wants to begin a new life. I understand."

When Neil looked back on it later he felt that when he and Carrie met, he acted without thinking. He needed somebody to be with and was going on instinct. "Maybe not even totally on instinct. I was just looking for some comfort. There was the situation at the time with my back, and the medication which I was on for almost a year. That's very important to remember! I keep telling myself, remember now, Neil, you did make a few mistakes but, ah, maybe with all those pills you just weren't yourself.

"Of course, having a son during that period made it . . . well, I love Zeke. He's the great thing that happened. It's too bad that he couldn't have a family living together but that's the way it was. It just didn't last very long. I don't even know if it was a mistake. It was just one of those cases." Always to be part of him, as such turns in a person's life are.

Through the 1970s I kept in touch with Carrie. We had a cordial relationship and she was the mother of my first grandson. We had Zeke in our home visiting both in Toronto and at the farm, sometimes with neither Neil nor Carrie present. Sometimes he was a handful but I don't think of him as more than slightly handicapped. Although he shows some physical effects of cerebral palsy, mainly a slight limp and one hand that doesn't work as well as the other, he can run fast, jump, swim, catch or throw a ball, doing all of these *better* than lots of kids without his quick reflexes. He is so bright and quick and full of energy that it takes a strong hand to keep him in check. I've seen him as a careful passenger on a motorcycle. He sat on my lap and steered my farm tractor. He rode with me on my snowmobile and didn't like it; I think mainly because he was only six at the time and had never seen one before. Later he went to a special school in Los Angeles, and wrote me his own thank-you letters after his birthdays and at Christmas, sometimes would call me on the phone, and in later years worked in many of Neil's travel crews.

16

Travelling Music

During the period when Carrie and Neil were in the process of breaking up, plans were being made for CSNY to get together and record the promised album from their tour. The idea was to do it in Sausalito, a few miles from San Francisco, early in the New Year.

Just before Christmas, Neil and Pegi Morton met for the first time through mutual friends. When she got home from spending Christmas Day with her mother in San Mateo her phone was ringing. "It was Neil to wish me a Merry Christmas." Neil, feeling more relief than anything at the end of his troubled relationship with Carrie, was in his house at the ranch making Christmas a happy time for Zeke. A couple of days later he and Pegi went out on their first date, with Neil bringing Zeke along as well.

Neil seemed to have come through the mood he'd been in a few months earlier when he wrote me questioning whether the ranch was really the place for him to live. His growing friendship with Pegi helped and had lasting warm overtones for both of them but soon was put on hold. "We both still had a lot of travelling to do," Neil said.

The recording sessions in Sausalito ended after several weeks when Stills and Nash had an immense argument over a single harmony note.

Neil left the studio and never returned. So in February 1975, once again the CSNY members went their various ways – and looking back at all the events of those two months, each ending with Neil on his own again, there is a pattern. Whether it was planned or not, he could not have lived the next two or three productive years as he did, if he had been tied down. By anything. "I'm enjoying the bachelor life," he said.

Part of this enjoyment was that he was back with a new version of Crazy Horse. By then Danny Whitten's 1972 heroin death was just a memory. Ralph Molina and Billy Talbot, the survivors, had tried to go on without him. But the band hadn't been the same with other musicians. Then early in 1975, the *Tonight's The Night* album still not released, Frank Sampedro arrived on the scene. He was unheralded, unsought, unsung. A woman friend introduced him to Billy Talbot, who tells what happened next: "I didn't even know at the time that Frank played guitar, but he was going to Mexico. I felt like going, too, and on that trip we started to play guitar together, acoustic, and I could see how he played. So we got back to my house and Ralph was there. We had the drums set up and George Whitsell had been staying there with his old lady, so George, Ralph, Frank, and I, and anybody who could come around – John Blanton, Van Dyke Parks, whoever – would get together and jam. Then eventually George split with most of his friends, and Ralph, Frank, and I were left and we kept playing together."

Neil was in Chicago that spring recording for a new country-ish album he was calling *Homegrown*. At the time he was still battling to have *Tonight's The Night* released, but wasn't getting anywhere so meanwhile was going on with other work, as usual. He called Billy, Ralph, and Ben Keith to Chicago to work on a couple of *Homegrown* cuts. Billy mentioned Frank Sampedro and asked if he could bring him along. The four of them arrived in Chicago. As soon as they began to play Billy knew a big corner had been turned. He was dazzled. "When Neil and Frank started playing all that heavy guitar stuff, with Ralph on the drums and Ben on the steel and me on bass, I couldn't even hear the steel any more! They were drowning out everything!" Neil had to go to Nashville with Ben for more recording, but as soon as he got home he brought along some still newer songs to Billy's house, suddenly more interested than anything else in playing with the new Crazy Horse.

At that point his unpublished work was piling up: *Homegrown* ready, *Tonight's The Night* still on hold, and these new songs destined for a newer album yet. But the record company was interested in something coming out, soon. *Homegrown* was the main candidate, and was ready on cassette to be played to a group of record people and friends. It happened that *Tonight's The Night* in its revised version was on the same tape. "After *Homegrown* he just let the tape run on and we listened to *Tonight's The Night*," Billy recalls. "I hadn't heard it since we played it first nearly two years before. Suddenly people started going up to Neil and telling him how great it was, he should put it out, why hadn't he released it? Frank Sampedro and I were just sitting in a corner listening to all these heavies telling Neil what he should do." They convinced him. That's when he shelved *Homegrown*, and insisted that *Tonight's The Night* should come out next.

Homegrown is still shelved, this many years later. Some of the songs have been used in other albums. *Homegrown* might have been next on the release list, except that the songs Neil had been playing with Crazy Horse sounded so good that he decided to record them as an album, too, called *Zuma* because at the time, David Briggs had a house in Zuma, California, and he and Neil chose to record there.

Two small footnotes belong in any account of the *Zuma* album. One is that one day David Briggs looked outside and saw Bob Dylan sitting in the driveway in his van, listening to the music from there. Briggs went out and said, "Come on in!"

Dylan: "Oh, I don't want to be in the way."

"You won't be, that's crazy. Come on in."

So Dylan came in to listen to one of his disciples.

Second footnote: The Briggs house was so big that it had two electrical circuits. The band was set up at one end of the house, playing into one electrical circuit. Tim Mulligan and David Briggs were at the recording console in the middle of the house, hooked up to the other circuit. Right in the middle of the band playing "Cortez the Killer" the electrical circuit being used for recording blew and the console went dead. The band was playing like hell and Mulligan and Briggs were dashing to find the circuit breaker and get it back on, which they did, after missing one whole verse. When the song was finished, Neil and Crazy Horse came down the hall exclaiming, "Boy, that was a great cut! That was really great!" Congratulating each other. Until Briggs said, "Don't shoot yourselves, but the power went off and we missed one whole verse."

Neil said, "Which verse?"

David told him.

Neil: "I never liked that verse anyway." So they went with the cut as it was, meaning that one verse of what was to be the big song on *Zuma* never has been recorded, to this day. Others on that album were "Don't Cry No Tears," "Danger Bird," "Pardon My Heart," "Lookin' For a Love," "Barstool Blues," "Stupid Girl," "Drive Back," and "Through My Sails."

A few months later when *Zuma* was released (*Homegrown* bumped again) Neil called Crazy Horse to the ranch, and they started on what Neil called the Northern California Bar Tour, which was when I arrived to stay a couple of weeks that winter. At first these gigs were impulsive, spur-of-the-moment. Neil would call a roadhouse and volunteer to pay off the house band for a night and come in to play. When word got out, the romance grabbed the rock world's imagination – Neil out playing little bars, staying after to have a few beers and talk with people. The music writers picked it up. Fans caught on and started crowding in. Some papers called it the Rolling Zuma Revue, a takeoff of the huge tour Bob Dylan was doing then, the Rolling Thunder Revue. The nonexistent budget and manner of the thing was such that one night when about twelve of us were having hamburgers and beer at the roadhouse where he was to play, I made the mistake of reaching for the tab – and they let me! That was a night when Zeke, then not yet four, warmed up the early crowd by playing the drums; a night when later three or four of Neil's neighbours and I stood and drank beer quietly in the parking lot while Zeke slept in the bed in Neil's camper and we hung around the back of it to make sure that if he wakened he wouldn't be alone. From outside we listened to the music bulging the walls. The tiny dance floor was so crowded that later when I danced we could hardly move which, given my dancing style, wasn't so bad.

It seems to me that in some ways the Northern California Bar Tour, as well as a similar attempt at near-anonymity more than a year later with the Ducks at Santa Cruz, should be seen not as anomalies, but as much a part of Neil as Carnegie Hall, as the 44,000 in the rain at Varsity Stadium in Toronto, as the 72,000 at Wembley. It's a little difficult for me to sort this out without sounding as if I'm reading too much into a few isolated events, but when Bobby Hull was widely accepted as the greatest hockey star on earth, I once saw him pick up a stick and play with some kids on an open-air rink, not to show off but to *be* there, to take it easy, be loose, and none of it for money. Neil is like that, or like Willie Mays slipping into the outfield of a pick-up game, just for the fun of it. Or if John Updike's character Rabbit in the novel *Rabbit Run* had been a great basketball star instead of a real good small-timer when (in the novel) he stopped to join a kid's game in an alley, trying to recapture something, I could relate him to the Neil Young who sometimes tries to recapture some needed feeling by acting as if he'd never had a spotlight on him in his life. So when he walked out, for instance, in a bar at Marshall, California, before fifty people, none of whom had paid to get in – there wasn't even what they used to call in country concerts a silver collection at the door – he was living out part of himself that perhaps he didn't want to lose in the rush of big events. That's why when anything gets to him, like the sheer fun of playing with Crazy Horse again after Frank Sampedro showed up, all his plans are changed so that he can do it.

Rolling Stone, which finally caught up with the Northern California Bar Tour, noted that after the Marshall gig Neil hung around the bar for a few beers, talking easily; the only thing he wouldn't talk about was where he'd play next; indeed, he might not have known. One thing he did not want was publicity that might turn the next concert into the kind of event that, for the time being, he was purposely turning his back on.

This element of privacy surfaced rather remarkably in another way about the time of the Northern California Bar Tour. Monte Stern, then twenty-three, heir to the Sears-Roebuck fortune, had leased a 600-acre ranch in the mountains of San Mateo County, a few miles from Neil's ranch. Stern spent a year trying to win over county officials and neighbours to the idea of outdoor rock concerts being held on his ranch. He ran into opposition but the idea was still alive until the day Neil, in old Levi's and two layers of lumberjack shirts, turned up uninvited at a meeting of the San Mateo County Planning Commission. He'd been stirred into action by an artist's depiction circulated by the Stern group of what the area would look like with a rock festival on it; it showed a couple of thousand people sitting around a beautiful stage on a hillside while kids ran around with balloons.

He asked to speak. "First of all," he said, "I'm just speaking for myself, but this is my home. I've been to more pop festivals than anybody in this room and this one is not safe. There's no proper access in and out on these narrow roads we have, nothing that could handle an emergency. If everybody leaves because of a fire, how are the fire trucks going to get in? What about medical facilities? What if somebody has some bad acid or everybody starts panicking, ODing and dying? How are you going to get help in there?" When he finished, the vote was thumbs down, all the way. The promoters gave indignant interviews, asking how Neil, who made a fair living as a rock star, could speak that way? One lawyer told *Rolling Stone* he didn't know how he could listen to "Sugar Mountain" properly any more, after hearing Neil speak as he had.

That incident made him an honoured citizen of San Mateo County a lot faster than if he'd just paid his taxes and gone his own way. A couple of years later one of the directors of the San Mateo Historical Society, Louise Buell, called him up to say she was retiring. She asked if Neil would come on the society's board of directors in her position, representing the county's coastal area. Because he liked and respected Louise Buell he told her he would think about it. But he tries to avoid publicity, which would be difficult to avoid in such a role. He attended one meeting but did not continue; not his line of work.

That spring of 1976 after the Northern California Bar Tour warm-ups he took Crazy Horse to Japan early in March and then on to Oslo March 15 to open a hugely successful tour that ended with four concerts at London's Hammersmith Odeon and one at the Apollo Theatre in Glasgow. At the time, a summer tour of the U.S. with Crazy Horse had been pencilled into his schedule, but anyone familiar with Neil could have seen a change coming.

He'd been playing with Crazy Horse almost a year then, steadily. But the previous summer, 1975, after he'd had an operation to remove the nodes in his throat, he had played with Stephen Stills a few times more or less extemporaneously – drop-ins. Stephen's career had been in the doldrums since the last CSNY tour. Early in 1976, Steve and Neil flew to Miami to begin work on an album. As studio sessions went on, Neil had an idea that it might be turned into a CSNY project. In California, Crosby and Nash dropped what they were doing and flew to Miami, but after a few weeks had to go back to the west coast to meet the deadline for an album they'd been working on. That, in effect, provided a gap in the CSNY reunion idea. The gap widened into a gulf.

Neil and Steve went back to their original idea of a Stills-Young album called *Long May You Run*, then toured along the route originally intended for Neil and Crazy Horse. After each concert they would get into separate buses – Neil his own tour bus and Stephen into another tour bus that he was renting from Neil. Travelling apart, which Neil had done originally in the 1974 CSNY tour, was now his standard practice. It allowed him to be alone for a while before going onstage again.

Some nights, like one in Cleveland, their music was great. The next night in Cincinnati was almost as good. Stephen has said since that he'd never played better than he did in that tour. But no one except the principals in the tour knew what was really going on. After three more concerts, in Pittsburgh, Greensboro, and Charlotte, it ended abruptly. Neil treads carefully, trying not to hurt feelings when he explains that, overall, the tour was hard to deal with. "I was having a pretty good time, but the reviews were playing us against each other. Stephen was reading the reviews. I was trying not to read the reviews. But even the headlines were . . . well, like, 'Young's hot, Stills not.' Then Stephen started thinking that other people on the tour were against him, trying to make him look bad to the audience. It just got real personal. Stephen did some things on stage, yelling at people and stuff, that I just didn't want to be part of. I made the decision to leave after the Charlotte concert: he'd been yelling onstage and there'd been a big fight afterwards. Not Stephen and me, Stephen and others. We were supposed to be in Atlanta the next night. Out on the highway I stopped, and David Cline and I sent telegrams to everyone involved. (The one to Stephen read, "Some things that start spontaneously end spontaneously.") Then I got back on my bus and dropped off onto a side road and made a big turn. One sign said Atlanta, where the concert was to be, and another said Memphis. I turned onto the one to Memphis. Then I got on an airplane and went to L.A. and stayed there for a couple of days to cool out. It was not a pleasant experience."

Elliot handled the upset promoters, telling them Neil was cancelling his part of the concert, but would give them right of first refusal the next time he travelled their way. If they wanted money, damages, they would be paid. If they wanted to give refunds to ticket-holders, Neil would pay the expenses involved in administering the refunds; he wanted everything taken care of with the least discomfort to the people who bought the tickets.

A couple of months later when the Stills-Young album *Long May You Run* was released, to largely indifferent reviews, Neil was touring again with Crazy Horse and Stephen was on the road as well. At that time Neil and I had another of our chance meetings.

I'd heard about his tour bus first in the winter of 1975-76 when I spent some time with him, the time he'd told me that it was my life, too, you know. One day he'd told me what he didn't like about the road – the hotels, the airline schedules that often made him go short on sleep. "I think I've got the answer: a tour bus that's as close to home as a bus can be."

In Boston a few months later, going by cab from the Boston airport on business of my own (a seminar on the effects of television on children, part of the research for a government-appointed Ontario Royal Commission of which I was a member), I said to the driver, "What's happening in music around here right now?" I knew Neil had been in New York a few nights before with Crazy Horse, but didn't know their tour schedule.

"Plenty doing!" the driver said. "Steve Stills was here last night, and Neil Young is coming in for two concerts tomorrow night."

The driver rattled on about Neil, with a few interjections from me that indicated I'd heard the name before.

"You a Neil Young fan?" he asked finally.

I hesitated a minute and then said, "I'm his father." I don't do that often, but the driver was excited enough about Neil that I owed it. That made for lively conversation on the way in, during which he mainly ignored the road and kept looking back at me to make sure I wasn't kidding. "Gee, wait'll I tell my wife!" he kept saying. At the Hyatt he only reluctantly took my money for the trip.

From my room I phoned Lookout Management in Los Angeles and left a message with the answering service. The next day Neil was on the phone, sounding upbeat, enthusiastic.

"How about coming over this afternoon?" he said.

"Where are you?"

"Well, the band is in the Copley Plaza and I'm in my bus parked outside the main entrance." He laughed. "Don't think you can miss it."

The cab driver was very impressed by the carved wooden sides and the two old auto chassis, a Hudson and a Studebaker, set into the roof as skylights.

I tapped on the curbside door. Neil opened it. He had coffee on. While traffic flowed around the bus like a river around a rock, he took me back to show me the bedroom area, spacious and comfortable; the electric piano amidships, baths, showers, power sunroofs on the auto chassis forward and aft, the compact yacht-like galley with refrigerator and freezer and microwave oven that ranged along one side of the forward area, across from the padded benches and table. A curtain could shut off the driver from the living quarters. When the coffee was ready we sat at the polished redwood table. We were fairly well caught up an hour or so later when Elliot Roberts came in.

"How about dinner?" Elliot asked. "The hotel dining room is big on neckties."

"Let's eat here," Neil said. "We got anything?"

"Sure. A manager can do anything," Elliot claimed. He broiled minced beef patties and made baked potatoes in the microwave. The five o'clock traffic was bumper to bumper around us by then. The security guard outside parried questions and would-be visitors. We ate. I had a beer. A little after six the band came out of the hotel. We all loaded into a chauffeured limousine – Elliot and Neil; quiet Ralph Molina, volatile Billy Talbot, husky dark Frank Sampedro, and me. In a big and bare dressing room below the Music Hall Theater backstage area was food and drink and the aroma of a joint or two, as well as a joking easiness that I came to know later as what goes with a good tour in progress, the bugs ironed out. They were doing two concerts that night. I stayed for the first one in the wildly enthusiastic crowd and then went to a much quieter group at Harvard where we ate cheese and drank wine and solemnly discussed such matters as how many murders the average child would see in an average week of watching television.

17

"There's more to my life than rock 'n' roll"

Between 1975 and 1977 Neil produced a tremendous amount of music. There was *Zuma* in 1975, as well as the revised *Tonight's The Night* and the unreleased *Homegrown*; *Long May You Run* with Stephen in 1976 plus hundreds of hours of work on the 1976 three-album *Decade* (sorting and sequencing, bringing in and pitching out until he had the thirty-five songs he saw as his representative work in the ten years since the old Pontiac hearse broke down in L.A. in the spring of 1966). Early in 1977 he released *American Stars 'N Bars*. All in all in about two years he had four albums of his own, one a triple, and also one with Stephen, along with taking part in the landmark film *The Last Waltz*, and starting work on his second film, *Human Highway*. At the same time his travels took him many thousands of miles, from Japan to Norway and points between. Yet, "there's more to my life than rock 'n' roll," he told someone once, and he wasn't just whistling Dixie.

When he was in Miami recording with Stephen he used to hang out nights at Coconut Grove. That's when he got interested in boats. He was helped, or at least not hindered by Mazzeo, his one-man entourage in Florida.

It is not easy to define the precise role of Neil's most trusted travelling companions. First they have to be friends and second they have to work their passage. In Florida, Mazzeo was a friend and companion; he also looked after money and phone calls, and headed off pests.

There was no professionalism involved when Neil bought his first boat. He and Mazzeo walked in and Neil pointed and said, "This boat. If it floats, I want it." It was a motor-driven yacht, which he fondly says was similar in appearance to the U.S. presidential *Sequoia* but smaller. All beautiful wood, it was a fifty-five-foot houseboat built about 1920 for cruising the inland waterways. It was also rotten to the core but he didn't know that. He and Mazzeo treated it like the *Queen Elizabeth* in her prime. They sailed all over the place, ran aground in some places and had engine trouble in others. "It was a wonder she ever took us anyplace, but she was a lot of fun."

Neil called that one the *Evening Coconut*. During one of its periods of sulkiness and intransigence, he met a couple of guys – Roger, a real sailor, and Chapman (which may not have been his name), something of an entrepreneur – who seemed to know a lot about boats. Chapman said he could find Neil a really dependable boat. As sometimes happens in Neil's life – "they see me coming" – Neil later felt strongly that the entrepreneur side of Chapman, tempted by possible access to a rock star's fat wallet, eventually got the upper hand. Neil thinks he must have been paid a separate commission from a man trying to unload an old Baltic trader in Grenada. Chapman painted a rosy picture of this craft, which stretched about seventy-five feet on the deck and more than a hundred feet overall. It had carried granite in the Baltic before being converted to a yacht in Denmark but had been tied up for some time at Grenada.

Neil asked Roger, the "real sailor," to go to Grenada and make sure it was in good shape, but apparently the real problems were well camouflaged. Chapman as captain and Roger as first mate brought the boat back to Florida for a refit. When they arrived, Roger immediately told Neil that on the trip he'd found a lot of defects that had been hidden from him on his inspection. On those grounds the deal might have been annulled. Instead, for days Neil and Roger roamed the boat inside and out. The list got longer and longer. Neil says now that maybe an expert would have run for cover, but he fell in love with the boat and decided to hell with the negative beginning. He had the bit in his teeth. "Roger and I talked it over and settled it then and there. We'd turn it around entirely, restore the boat, make it the beautiful thing we both could see was possible."

He fired Chapman and made Roger captain. They rented space in a Fort Lauderdale boatyard and eased the boat in. That's where Neil was to be found a good deal of his time in the next two years, a hammer in one hand and often a beer in the other. They tore the boat down to its hull. Some of the core planks had to come off. The supporting structure had been damaged. After the strip-down they began to rebuild. Because they hired their own crew to do the rebuilding job, and the boatyards could make more money by letting out not only their space but also their own boat-builders, they had to move from one boatyard to another a few times.

The phone number Neil gave me then was in Fort Lauderdale. Rassy came down from New Smyrna Beach from time to time. One October Neil threw a birthday party for her, her sixtieth. David Cline was there part of the time, Zeke was there sometimes, and for those two years Neil had this other obsession besides music. He felt good just working on that boat, suggesting refinements as he went along. Along the way, he learned a lot. That was part of the idea. He was to be the owner and felt to be a good one he had to know the essential parts of the structure, what makes a boat *work*. He says that rebuilding the boat with Roger and an expert carpenter was a wonderful experience. "We took it to the max. It reflects that."

Neil's part in restoring the boat was to come up with ideas, something he does well. Once filtered through the experts, these ideas showed in the beauty of the end result. He helped choose sails and other fittings as well as the distinctive interior design. Then, in what I feel was an inspired decision, one of love and family, he named it after his grandfather, Rassy's father, W.N. Ragland.

It's commonly referred to as the *Ragland* now, but when I think of it, it is always the *W.N. Ragland*, WNR as he'd been known by generations of people who worked for him, played bridge or poker with him, shot ducks with him. I knew him best as a friend, drinking and travelling companion, and father-in-law. I loved my own father, but almost equally I loved Bill Ragland. Years later when I found that there was no photo on the boat to show what W.N. Ragland had looked like, in the flesh, I wrote to *Sports Illustrated* for photos that Ronny Jaques had taken for an autumn 1954 article I wrote about the most exceptional duck-hunting expedition I'd ever had, travelling with Bill Ragland across the prairies in his company Ford with the ice chest (for drinks) in the trunk along with a case of shells and the dozens of mallard we'd shot. (He wouldn't shoot the smaller ducks.) I intended to give the photos to Neil one birthday, as one of my better solutions to the constant problem of what to give the man who has so much. But *Sports Illustrated* no longer had the transparencies. I'm still looking.

In my opinion, Neil's life in those middle years of the 1970s was closer to Jack Kerouac's *On the Road*, with its nearly anonymous cast, than to that of a rock star who rarely could move out of doors without being recognized. He acted often on impulse, as in, "If it floats, I want it." He was open to women again, but without any intention to cease being a bachelor. The realization that even with a son to show for it his time with Carrie had been yet another mistake in his love life was still a factor, but he soothed it somewhat by taking Zeke with him whenever he could. Working raptly on both his music and his boat, Neil thought nothing of setting out to drive half across the country on impulse. Once he drove a Ford station wagon from Fort Lauderdale to Nashville to do some recording.

Early in 1977 he made a phone call that was to make waves in his life for a while. He was at the ranch recording, and needed a woman backup singer for a couple of songs. He phoned Linda Ronstadt, I think in Chicago, asking if she could recommend someone. Linda said, "Sure. Nicolette Larson." When Nicolette left for the ranch, Linda decided to go with her. Which is how both came to sing on "Bite the Bullet," a long piece in the enthusiastically received album released in the summer of 1977, *American Stars 'N Bars*, with Crazy Horse. "We called the whole bunch of us Neil Young, Crazy Horse and the Saddle Bags. One day when we were in the studio working, they thought rehearsing, I had 'Bite the Bullet' recorded in the other room. They couldn't believe it when I said we were finished, that was it." It was not, however, the end for Neil and Nicolette.

That summer about the time *American Stars 'N Bars* was released, Neil dived again into anonymity. Mazzeo's home base was Santa Cruz, about seventy miles south of San Francisco. For a while as far as the music press (and I) were concerned, Neil vanished from the face of the earth, wasn't at his ranch, wasn't seen around L.A., hadn't been to his house in Malibu for a couple of months. What had happened was that he had gone to see Mazzeo in Santa Cruz and hang out around the music scene there. One group of people he knew from the old Buffalo Springfield days was the Jeff Blackburn Band, including Blackburn on guitar and vocals, Bob Mosley on bass and vocals, and John (Johnny C.) Craviotta on drums. Neil stepped in at lead guitar. They called themselves the Ducks and played various clubs and bars around town. Neil was not fronting, he was just playing, keeping a low profile, making music in a way that reminded him of the early days of Buffalo Springfield.

The only condition he imposed on the others was that he'd play as long as they stayed within the city limits of Santa Cruz. Mazzeo was managing them. They played not for a set fee, but a percentage. Neil lived that summer on what he made with the Ducks, using no other money. The most they ever made for one gig was $750, split four ways. That was at the Catalyst, the biggest place in town, where the admission charge was two dollars.

The two or three months they played together was made special not only by the music, but by the crazy persona they assumed. This maybe is not easy to accept as real if you weren't there, but a local legend (they claimed) was that once a surfer called Pussinger had driven wildly through a flock of ducks, killing seven of them. He was charged, tried, and given seven days in jail, one day per duck. However, an old duck named Master Mallard, representing the duck population at the trial, felt that the sentence was not heavy enough. He cursed the whole city of Santa Cruz and ruled that until all the people in Santa Cruz quacked together, under one roof, the curse would not be lifted. So when people came to hear the Ducks, they quacked! They quacked like hell. Neil: "Before the band came on, everybody would be quacking and yelling – quack, quack, quack, bring 'em out here! Then the voice would come up, 'All right, ladies and gentlemen, the Ducks!' And amid all the quacking they'd introduce the band – Buck Duck, Johnny C. Duck, Bobby Blue Duck – Mosley – and Young Duck. . . . It was ridiculous, totally ridiculous!"

The Ducks lived together in a couple of houses at the top of a cliff overhanging the ocean. Neil was driving an old Packard station wagon that looked like a duck and was called the Duckmobile. They'd drive it to each show and carry in their own equipment.

But anything so good can't be kept a local secret for long. People began to flock in. Phone calls were made by fans to friends in distant places when the Ducks showed on a program list. One night when they played the Santa Cruz Civic Auditorium music reporters from all over were backstage asking questions. Neil told them about a double album ready to go (it's still in his archives), but soon after that he decided that with anonymity gone, the fun was over. He took off in his tour bus with Zeke to Florida to work on his boat.

Zeke had just turned five. As a result of his cerebral palsy, he was unable to get the heel of his right foot to reach the ground (he could run, but only using the front part of that foot). He'd been examined at the Mayo Clinic in Minnesota, with the opinion that an operation would help, and before Neil took him to Florida this was done. When he was in hospital in a cast Neil brought him a pair of sneakers to show him what nice light stuff he'd be able to wear. Until the cast came off, Zeke insisted on keeping the sneakers in bed with him.

At the time, Carrie was just finishing a movie with Kirk Douglas, a Brian De Palma film called *The Fury*. When shooting was complete, she visited Florida for a few days in late September or early October and reported to us in a letter from a vacation spot in Mexico that, "Zeke is in Florida with Papa, living on the boat and going to school. It was joyful watching Zeke love his papa and learning new lessons that it seems only a dad can teach."

As far back as the summer, when he was with the Ducks, Neil had been working on some parts of his next album; in fact, one of the songs the Ducks did was "Comes a Time," which eventually was used – at the last minute – as the title for the album Neil was to release a year later. The theme of the song was upbeat and positive. While in Florida he recorded occasionally. Later in October when he went back to Nashville, Nicolette Larson re-entered his life for a while, and so did we.

At that time I had been separated from my second wife, Astrid, for a little more than a year. Our marriage had been good for ten years or so. We had a fine home at 17 Rosedale Heights Drive, having sold our first home on Inglewood Drive. Deirdre had a science degree from Guelph. She had married and (after four years) separated. Young Astrid attended Whitney School and then Deer Park. Her weekends at the farm were heady with having her first mount, a stubborn quarter-horse gelding of uncertain age named Diamond.

One of the troubles between her mother and me was the farm. It was my baby in more ways than one. When I bought the land in 1967, at the back of my mind was the idea that some time in the next few years I would get back to freelance writing. To do that in Canada, low over-head is an essential – at least as important as having talent. The farm would be the place for it. It had a house that I worked comfortably in (I'd written, all or in large part, several books there), a tiny mortgage, taxes of only $250 a year (they've gone up since). Also, the place was soothing to me. I liked fixing fences, cutting wood, drinking a lot of rum with my old friends from Omemee at weekend parties. In contrast, Astrid had spent her early years on farms in British Columbia and had been running from rural life ever since. In short, she had her prefer-ences as strongly as I had mine. She loved our city house, the neigh-bourhood, the parties we had when the joint would be brimming with fascinating people, from Robertson and Brenda Davies to Frank and Marie Mahovlich (I'd name them all but they know who they are). Meanwhile I wrote books and a daily column and was host of a televi-sion show and . . . and . . . and. . . . But instead I wanted to live on the farm and write every day at something that was not journalism.

Many people want things that they do not get. Certainly I can't have everything I want, either. But what I *can* have, I try not to miss. I was in my late fifties. I wanted to *need* less money, so that I wouldn't have to work for *as much* money, know what I mean? (Thanks.) I can't tell you the number of nights Astrid and I sat over a procession of large Scotches with neither of us giving an inch in our classy house on Rosedale Heights Drive with the new Cougar convertible and new Chrysler sitting in the drive outside. Once in the country when she and I happened to clash about country living while among friends, Astrid stated what undoubtedly was her right to state: "I married a Toronto newspaperman, not an Omemee farmer!" One year out of the three or four that this debate went on, she was not well, having some bone graft operations.

That winter I rented the farm to four students for eight months, but on Saturdays I would drive young Astrid up to the Saddlewood Equestrian Centre north of Bethany where her horse was boarded. She would ride all day and I would drive a few miles and walk around the perimeter of the farm, not unlike a Cavan township back-roads version of Charlie Chaplin's famished Tramp with his nose pressed against the restaurant window. I would eat my noon meal with my Omemee friends Jay Hayes, packing company salesman, or Edna

Deyell, bank accountant, and in late afternoon would pick up young Astrid and drive back to the city.

We lived the next two or three years with things really no better and often worse, although by 1976, when I began to think of divorce again, I seemed to have made my point about not wanting to have such heavy financial needs. That spring we sold the Rosedale Heights house and with the proceeds, plus a $10,000 legacy Astrid had received, paid cash for a new air-conditioned, sauna-ed, three-bathroomed, two fireplaced town house, and a few months later it was all over. I had started seeing some other women by then. When Astrid challenged me this time I said it was true. I'm skipping a few parts, man-woman battlegrounds about equally divided between what would make me look bad and what would make her look bad, so I think that's fair enough. One night a debate lasted until five A.M. I woke with a start two hours later, left Astrid sleeping, left a note in the kitchen, and walked out of the house.

My idea was that she could have that house if I could have the farm, and that came to pass. I lived in considerable emotional turmoil that winter (1976-77) at the farm with my two daughters, Astrid in a Peterborough high school (sprinting for the school bus each morning) and Deirdre – with a Doberman which insisted on eating all my favourite hats – pregnant and in the throes of divorce. Her son David was born in April 1977. That summer she moved out, back on her own. In the autumn, young Astrid and I moved (although I still had my frequent visits to the farm) to the city and in with Margaret Hogan, an editor and writer at the *Globe* (later we married), in a rented house on Harbord Street in downtown Toronto.

We were there in late October or early November of 1977 when Neil phoned me from Nashville, where he and Zeke had gone from Florida. Neil said he had a lot of recording to do for a week or two, which wasn't much fun for Zeke. Would it be okay if he sent Zeke up with Ellen Talbot (the one from Neil's ranch whose uncle was William Saroyan) to stay with us in Toronto for a while? Soon they arrived and Zeke had more women looking after him than he'd seen for a while. Astrid had known Zeke since he was a baby and with Margaret's three teenage daughters (later my step-daughters), Erin, Caitlin, and Maggie, we seemed to have exactly the right mix to give Zeke a good time walking, playing, riding the subway, going shopping. Neil phoned often. The reports were always good; Zeke was fine, so were we, and the little three-bedroom house with eight people in it was jumping. When Carrie got back and wanted Zeke home with her to get back in school, Ellen and Zeke flew back to her in Los Angeles.

A month or so later there was another call from Neil. He and Nicolette had been recording for weeks in Nashville and would it be all right if he brought Nicolette up for Christmas? Of course. Then came another call; he and Nicolette were going to Kansas City instead to visit her parents at Christmas, and would come to see us after that. Then silence.

I can't say that Margaret and I hopped from one foot to the other waiting for more definite word; our Christmas was too busy for that. When we heard no more from Neil we just figured he had changed his mind. Margaret and I flew west for New Year's to see her parents in Regina and my mother and sister, Dorothy, and her husband, Stan, in Flin Flon. On our return, there was still no word from Neil.

I'm not sure how other parents react when a family member goes silent for a while, but I really gave it very little thought and indeed the long silence was not mentioned until the last paragraph of his letter when I did hear from him again in May. This letter came in a registered parcel which included a cassette of what a few months later was released as *Comes A Time* (although the title he had written on the cassette's spine was *Give To The Wind*) with Neil's handwritten list of the songs in it. This letter read: "Dear Dad: Enclosed is my latest effort. Hope this letter finds you well and happy. As for myself, I've been here at the ranch since Christmas with a few quick trips to Fla. to check on my boat. I'm also collecting Lionel trains and I have a huge layout in my house. Zeke is fine. I see him almost every weekend when he comes up to the ranch from L.A. We play with the trains together.

"Life has held many changes for me this last year but I'm happy to be settling back into the ranch. I have a new girl friend, Pegi, and we enjoy doing a lot of things together.

"I'm sponsoring Bob in the PGA for a while and that seems to work out well. I just signed a 5 album deal with W.B. for $1 million guarantee per album over 5 yrs. Some deal. Hope I didn't hang you up over Christmas but things were a little confusing for me at that time. With love to you and yours, Neil."

Instead of going to Kansas City, Toronto, or both, he and Nicolette had gone back to the ranch. Their relationship was on the downslope.

They had made their music together and (Neil's words) "got a little carried away, and then, you know, we realized what had happened: a short romance." Just before Christmas, Nicolette was at the ranch. One night she and Neil and Tim Mulligan went over to spend an evening with Pegi Morton, who had a small house not far away. After that, Nicolette lived for a few weeks at the beach house Neil had bought a year or two earlier in Malibu, which once had been owned by F. Scott Fitzgerald and was the setting for the film of his unfinished novel, *The Last Tycoon*. It was then that he and Pegi, good friends for some years, began going out together again. While many of Neil's women friends had lives that tended to pull him away from his bent for country living, specifically the solitariness of his ranch, Pegi was the exact opposite: she had loved the San Mateo hills long before Neil fell in love with them, and eventually with her.

18

Pegi – and Rust Never Sleeps

It is generally rather fruitless, or even feckless, to try to understand what draws a man and a woman together. Even the flash fire of physical attraction is complicated enough when one considers the staggering assortment of shapes and sizes (usually somewhat at variance with those of Adonis or Miss America) of those who regularly take part in this tribal rite. When two people have known each other for years and suddenly all the bulbs light up, as was the case with Neil and Pegi, it can't always be the old girl-next-door or boy-next-door syndrome. When they clicked in the first place right after Neil and Carrie split, Neil didn't want to plunge right in again. "I had a lot of freedom I wanted to experience." Three years later when they put it back together, he'd made up his mind that he didn't feel like wandering around any more, just drifting. Pegi was the first woman he'd ever looked at, he says, in a particular way, "really thinking it through."

During the years they had not seen each other, Pegi spent a lot of time with David Briggs and Tim Mulligan at the studio on the ranch. Sometimes they worked late at night and Pegi kept them company, or helped when she could. This introduces a factor that might not be all-important, but certainly has *considerable* importance: the ranch area is really Pegi's home turf. Neil loves northern California, it's his home, but she's the one with northern California bred right into her. Her grandmother, as a child, had lived in San Francisco with her parents (Pegi's great-grandparents). Sometimes for a holiday they'd drive out to San Mateo in a horse and buggy. They liked the freedom from the crowded city so much that San Mateo became their second home, with a bit of land to go with it. Then when the San Francisco earthquake devastated the city, they fled to San Mateo along with many of their neighbours from the Irish neighbourhood of San Francisco. They camped out in tents all over Pegi's great-grandparents' place. Her grandmother married and lived there. Then her mother. Now Pegi.

When she was little the family used to come out of San Mateo and up into the hills around what now is Neil's ranch. Later she used to cut high school to go out there. It was her favourite place, just the peace and pace of it, so after leaving high school she started living in the hills. She wanted to travel a lot, so she'd work at various jobs, save her money, spend it for the next journey somewhere.

When Neil was with the Ducks at Santa Cruz in 1977, Pegi and some friends decided at the last minute one night to "shoot down there," but she didn't talk to Neil after. He didn't know she was there. "When they finish playing, many people want to press in. I didn't like to do that so we didn't meet, that time."

A few months later, just before Christmas of 1977, the time did come when Neil and Nicolette and Tim Mulligan dropped in at Pegi's place. A week or two later (she'd spent Christmas with relatives in Alexandria, Virginia) Neil called and they went out together several times, and on Valentine's Day, 1978, they went on their first trip together, to Florida to see the boat. "Whatever developed between us then, I don't think that you can put it into words," Pegi says. "I think words would spoil it. One unusual thing was that we had known each other for a long time. I think in our other relationships we didn't know the people that well. You think you're really in love and then when you get to know each other it gets worse and worse. Starting as friends, as Neil and I did, you already have a foundation. You know each other, you already really like each other, and then to have it grow into something else – that was unusual for me and I think for him, too. We didn't want to get into anything that wasn't going to work."

It was about three months after that first trip they took together that I received a cheerful, upbeat letter from Neil, mentioning Pegi for the first time. In the next few weeks we talked some on the phone. "What's doing with you?" he asked.

Well, I told him, Zeke and Carrie (who was playing *Two for the Seesaw* in Detroit) had been to my farm for a few days. Zeke and I played catch, and he rode with me on my old tractor, which he steered. One day I caught a ten-pound snapping turtle for him as it crossed a road near a little stream (at home later it escaped into the pool and when I netted it and turned it loose, it kept coming back). Astrid sold her second riding horse, Sam, for money to buy an electric guitar, a used Gibson, but was still working on oboe as well. Bob was preparing to fly to the Pacific for the Asian pro golf tour. After two years apart, Astrid's mother had filed for divorce . . .

"Just your standard Canadian summer, Neil. How about you?"

"Well, we're doing some shooting on my film, *Human Highway*. Doing a lot of shooting, in fact."

"Any chance you'll be coming up this way soon?"

"Yeah, but it isn't really definite yet. I've been thinking about a tour. If I do go out, we'll certainly be coming to Toronto."

The shooting he was doing for the film was at the Boarding House in San Francisco, during a five-night, ten-performance booking. The place held only 292 people. Neil performed alone, except for three wooden Indians parked around the stage. Seats for all ten performances were sold out within hours, and when rock writers flew in from New York, at least one, Paul Nelson of *Rolling Stone*, paid a scalper thirty dollars for a seat because it was the only way he could get in. Elliot told John Rockwell of *The New York Times* that this was Neil's 1978 World Tour: ten concerts in one place. It was still being called a one-stop world tour in *Rolling Stone* late in July, although Neil by that time had definitely decided on a major tour that autumn in support of his *Comes A Time* album. Apart from the one foray into San Francisco, most of the film's shooting was being done in southern California.

By then, Neil and Pegi had made their decision. They were married in the Malibu house with their closest friends around them on August 2, 1978. They didn't have a honeymoon. The *Comes A Time* album was being put together, a tour to support it was tentatively in the works, and Neil was still trying to work on his movie. With the album finished they went home to the ranch and then took off to go to the Bahamas for eight days, along with film editor Larry Johnson and

David Briggs and David Cline and wives. Pegi, laughing: "I guess that was our honeymoon – the maiden voyage of the *Ragland* from Fort Lauderdale. It was the worst seasick I have ever been, that first night. Five and a half months pregnant and going across one of the worst waterways in the world. Anyway, we came back, and within a week or so we went out on the *Rust Never Sleeps* tour."

The idea for staging *Rust Never Sleeps* came to Neil one day on the *W.N. Ragland*, almost impossibly close to the tour's take-off date. He scribbled it out on a single piece of paper in an hour or less. I remember him phoning me from the ranch early in September to tell me. When he has a new idea that excites him, there's no doubt about his excitement – it has to imbue everyone around him with the idea that no matter how unusual the concept it will work. He told me about giant amplifiers, how the roadies – "I'm calling them Road-Eyes" – would be dressed in hooded cowl-like garments, with flashing red eyes under the hoods. "I'll be, like, sleeping under one of the amplifier lids when the lights go up, like a child sleeping, and then . . . well, I hope you'll see it."

I said it sounded almost like mounting a Broadway musical.

"Yeah, just about."

"Can you do it all in such a short time?"

"It's going to be close. We've only got about two weeks to build the sets and get the costumes made and rehearse all the staging, but we'll make it."

When Neil was working up *Rust Never Sleeps*, only he and those closest to him, Elliot, David Briggs, David Cline, Larry Johnson, and a few others knew what Neil had in mind – until the whole tour crew gathered in the Cow Palace in San Francisco the day before takeoff and Neil announced, "Okay, guys, here it is – you'll be wearing blackface, headsets, and these costumes!"

You could hear it coming back from the veteran roadies, "What? What are you talking about?" Neil said that if anybody didn't want to go on those terms, it was okay, no sweat. But they all went, and when they got into it they became actors as well as roadies, contributing to the show by the purposeful way they moved openly at tasks that normally they'd do with as little notice as possible. The set was open from the back, so anyone with backstage privileges had to wear one of the outfits. Pegi was a pregnant Road-Eye. Reporters and other supernumeraries would be painted up and have uniforms slapped on as they entered – writer Cameron Crowe, the tour accountant, everybody.

After the initial hesitation the real roadies got into it so much that they wouldn't even change out of the uniforms when they had a chance. "I'd see them on a break," Neil said, "four or five guys in these costumes sitting around a packing crate with their coffees, talking, like a bunch of guys in a boardroom, as if this was just what they wore, you know, man."

In subsequent years Neil often mentioned the *Rust Never Sleeps* tour as being some kind of a bench mark, for him, putting his music into a setting that some found eccentric, some found enchanting, and he really liked – the opinion that counts, with him. The staging arrangements and sheer sweep and scope of these concerts looked as if they must have taken a long time to work up, instead of starting from scratch the day Neil walked off the *W.N. Ragland* with one sheet of paper laying out the whole thing. In city after city the concert opened with Jimi Hendrix's "The Star Spangled Banner," followed by the Beatles' "A Day in the Life." Then the set was lit up. Huge packing boxes were designed to look like giant amplifiers, and when the top of one of these was lifted it revealed Neil, prone, then rising with his cordless guitar, looking sleepy and spacey as he began to play and move down to centrestage among the busily moving, cowled and cloaked figures who looked like monks except for their blinking red electric eyes. One critic, Stanley Mieses, writing from North America for an English magazine, said the "enigmatic" stage set "provided a wonderfully incomprehensible edge to the evening's musical performance, which was clearly superlative."

Margaret and I first met Pegi in Toronto during that tour. She and Neil arrived in his bus late on September 30, a Saturday, and parked it beside the downtown Chelsea Inn. I saw them there briefly the next day and then went on to meet the family for the concert that night.

Margaret and I and our families had just moved into an old house on Albany Avenue, in a one-time working class district close to downtown, by then being infiltrated by a few artists, writers, teachers, and even men in three-piece suits. When Neil phoned on the morning after the concert I explained how to get there. Early on the sunny autumn afternoon Neil and Pegi parked a rented car nearby and we walked through the house out to the little back yard where grass grew long (we didn't own a lawn mower at the time) and sat under the big trees talking and having a beer or two. I had to go and write a column. Neil went to a recording studio on Hazelton near his old hang-outs on Yorkville. Margaret took Pegi shopping along Bloor Street, all to meet later for dinner.

Neil and I had discussed this by phone a week or so earlier. He'd bring some of the people from his crew, and we'd bring all available members of our extended family – Astrid, Deirdre with her eighteen-month-old son David, and Margaret's daughters (Zeke's pals), Erin, Caitlin, and Maggie, plus Don and Alyson Scott, our friends and neighbours from Neil's chicken-raising days in Pickering, and Sam Charters, a friend just out of a journalism course.

I'd told Neil by phone before his arrival that I wasn't sure where to book for this dinner for twenty or so.

"How about Ciccone's?" he asked.

That was the family restaurant on King Street near Spadina where Mary Ciccone still presided, as she had in the days when Rassy and Bob and Neil and I sometimes ate there; and where Bob and Neil and I had dinner the night I tried to explain to them why our family was breaking up.

The group at the long table loaded with food and wine was small enough that there was lots of intermingled conversation. At the time Astrid had switched finally from oboe to electric guitar.

Neil asked, "Do you have an amplifier?"

Astrid said no.

"Gotta have an amplifier," he said.

That Christmas he sent her a Fender amp. No doubt in retribution for my ancient sin of being a non-understanding father, that amp took me one day and ninety-six dollars in duty to get through customs. I loaded it into the trunk of my car, lid up, to drive back downtown, where soon Astrid's amplified guitar blasted through the thin-walled frame houses of Albany Avenue and for blocks around. When you got off the bus on Dupont a block away you could hear it. On the card Neil wrote, "Astrid – if your musical aspirations fade, you can use the case as a hope chest! Brother Neil."

Neil seemed to hit another level of public awareness with *Rust Never Sleeps*. In 1978 he had not yet started referring to himself as a dinosaur, as he came to do a few years into the 1980s. He was beginning to pick up young devotees. Many first had heard his music late at night when the lights were out and their parents put on *Everybody Knows This is Nowhere*, or *After The Gold Rush*, and murmured about the flower days of the late 1960s when they were in their teens or just out and heard him first. The rock music press is one thing; it covers everything. But in the 1978 tour a different sort of attention was paid; it was as if editors of some major magazines suddenly remembered him from the 1960s and, being reminded that he was one of very few from that era still not only on top but also still springing surprises, unchained their pop-music writers and sent them into the night. There was also in the concert a telling line. It could refer to you or me, but mostly it seemed aimed at those of his 1960s confrères who in the years after Woodstock had just been doing the same thing, over and over, becoming hollowed-out wraiths of their former selves. "It's better to burn out than it is to rust," Neil sang, obviously doing neither but showing himself, as one critic wrote, "alive and well and making great rock 'n' roll music."

It happened also that his tour criss-crossed many times Bob Dylan's major concert tour. They arrived in the New York area simultaneously. Inevitably, they were compared, and it angered Neil – Dylan being one of his own heroes – the way the comparisons sometimes were made. One critic who saw Neil at Madison Square Garden one night and Dylan there the next wrote, "One has to conclude that a living legend pales next to a thriving talent." Neil wanted to be good, but not to have this noted as part of a put-down of Dylan. Neil had been put down himself before and knew he would be again, so he felt badly when *Time* magazine's subhead on its November 6, 1978, coverage of the two tours bore the subhead: "The master gets drubbed with a disciple's reputation."

Later in the same piece *Time* summed up the Dylan-versus-Young matter more equitably than its headline did: "Dylan's reputation, in historical perspective if not in current application, is immense, possibly unrivalled. Young is a more insular artist whose stormy tenure with Crosby, Stills and Nash brought him his first fast shot of celebrity. Twelve subsequent solo albums, . . . all together, form a body of work hard to beat for reckless honesty and his own kind of compound romanticism, which can veer sharply from sentimental to sulfuric at the bend of a lyric. Dylan both mocked and gloried in his informal ordination as a generation's prophet. Young, fully as ambitious in his music, kept closer to the ground than Dylan and sneaked into rock's pantheon like a highwayman."

But the body of the story, to Neil, did nothing to allay the headline's heavy put-down of Dylan. Cameron Crowe, a boyhood fan of Neil's who by his late teens had become one of the best magazine writers about rock music and musicians, happened to be on hand just after Neil read the *Time* piece. As Cameron told it later, he and Neil's friend, photographer, archivist, and tour musician, Joel Bernstein, were at Elliot's house not far from Neil's ranch, waiting to meet Neil and Pegi, when the screen door opened and "a disturbed-looking, wild-eyed Neil Young bolts in: 'Show me this *pantheon*,' says Neil Young, pacing around his neighbour's kitchen, insulted that he could be pitted against his own mentor. 'I don't want to have to read that shit in *Time* magazine. That's irresponsible journalism. Disco attitude. Somebody somewhere is going to believe it. I did not see Dylan's show – but to think that all he's given, all he's meant to us . . . you can't cancel that in one night. . . . I don't know how to feel.' He sits down at a table, clasping his hands. 'I don't think I want to comment at all.'"

Neil felt better a week later when *Newsweek*'s two-page spread on his New York area concerts (Nassau Veterans Memorial Coliseum as well as Madison Square Garden) used his name and Dylan's in the same breath without treating them like the Rangers versus the Islanders. "Except perhaps for Bob Dylan, Neil Young, at thirty-two, is the most consistently compelling figure in American rock; certainly no one else has covered so much musical ground – folk, country and rock – with such originality. His songs are deceptively uncomplicated; stark, crisp guitar work (he is even more primitive at the piano); evocative, cryptic lyrics; a nasal, wistful, thoroughly distinctive voice that either grates or mesmerizes. His sound is easy to imitate; his spirit is not. Whether he is singing sweetly about love gone awry or angrily about a friend's death, brutally loud or quietly tender, Young aims straight for the heart."

I guess to round out the matter of Dylan versus Young is impossible, as well as being unnecessary. Dylan, being three years older, was a revered name around Greenwich Village when Neil was hauling his amplifier through the New York bus terminal late in 1965 on the hunt for Stephen Stills. When Jimi Hendrix surfaced first in the Village, playing for peanuts, playing his guitar left-handed (he had to hold it upside down to do this) and sometimes playing the strings with his teeth, Dylan already was a cult figure as a folk singer. Neil, Hendrix, Joni Mitchell – very few people who became big in music did not owe something to Dylan's trail-blazing, including his abrupt changes – such as when he went electric, to the dismay of the folkies to whom electric music was something from the wrong side of the tracks. Neil has always seen the daring in Dylan, and has known that was something he wanted to do as well, as he has done.

19

A Bright Little Boy
Named Ben

One night in the summer of 1983 I was sitting at a table in a one-room cabin on the shore of an Ontario lake with a group of friends, newspapermen or ex-newspapermen, who once a year gather, some from afar, to fish, drink, and talk. One, who is managing editor of a Seattle daily, mentioned Neil's concert in Seattle a couple of weeks earlier. A few others were chiming in when Gillis Purcell intervened. Purcell, as we all call him, or G.P., then seventy-eight, long my dear friend, was the man who had put up security for my borrowed down payment on my first house with Bob three years old and Rassy pregnant with Neil.

"Never mind the millions of albums he's sold and the millions of bucks he's made," Purcell ruled abruptly. "The most important thing I know about Neil and his wife is what they've done with their little boy. After he turned out to have a pretty severe handicap."

All present looked at him. Nobody interrupts Purcell, any more than they try to help him when he leans his crutches against a boulder and grabs the gunwale of a wave-rocked boat to ease himself, it always seems perilously, into his fishing seat. He was sitting at the head of the table with his fishing pants draped comfortably over the stump of a leg he left behind on a Second World War Canadian army exercise in

England in 1941, when he was thirty-seven. A parachute dropping supplies didn't open and his attempt to get out of the way of the supply
canister hurtling earthward didn't quite make it. He had love and care
as he learned to walk again on his peg, which he called Barney; and
then on his artificial limb. Part of his life ever since has been quietly
influenced in favour of people much more handicapped than he is. He
knows many through his membership in the War Amputations of
Canada: paraplegics, quadriplegics, people whose main chance for a
good life is through loving care.

"I've read just about everything that has been written about Neil since
I knew him as a kid starting out," he said. "I know all that stuff. But what
he and Pegi have done to care for their little boy *anybody* can identify
with, whether they go for what Neil does in music or anything else."

I don't know how Neil and Pegi would tell the story of Ben, but when
I'm with this bright-eyed and easy-smiling little boy, my grandson, it
seems to me that just the happy look of him tells a lot. It is not valid to
draw easy, poignant comparisons between the radiant Pegi of their first
married visit to Toronto in September of 1978 and her slow realization
a few months later (Ben was born in November) that he was not pro-
gressing as he should. Since then they have fitted their lives around
him, and what is good for him, both at home and when they travel.
Neil's 1980 songs "Stayin' Power" ("*Stayin' power, through thick and
thin*") and "Coastline" ("*We don't back down from no trouble, We do get up
in the mor-or-nin'*") are almost private assertions of their dedication as
parents of a beloved son who needs all their love.

Pegi
The birth was a month early. It wasn't a terribly difficult birth, but
Ben's face was really bruised. I thought it was probably just from
coming through the birth canal, and nobody told me any different, although later I found that it wasn't normal and I've tried to
get answers, but at the time all we knew was that it was ten days
before we could get a picture of him because he was so bruised and
swollen that his eyes never opened. He was really unhappy around
Christmas of that year when he was not even a month old, and he
kept being unhappy for a long time. When you're a mother for the
first time and a baby cries a lot it's worrying, but you hear about

cranky babies and we didn't know then that he was unhappy because he was in pain. I didn't think of cerebral palsy then but I knew something was not right, and this feeling started to grow when he was two months old. They kept telling me it was just developmental delay because of his prematurity, but I read baby books because I wanted to know what he should be doing. Even at two months he should have at least been doing what a one-month-old baby would be doing and he wasn't. So the developmental delay idea, I never really believed it too much. The one thing that really started me wondering what was wrong was that he didn't hold his head up the way a normal child will, he just never got that balance.

I discussed it with Neil, and everybody who saw him. "Do you think he looks normal?" I'd ask. "Do you think he's all right?" And everybody said, "Yeah, he's fine. Don't worry about it." But I did. He hardly smiled at all. He grimaced. One picture I took of him at the time, I sent out to the boat because he was smiling, what I *thought* of as a smile. In looking back at it later it was just a grimace, just pain, we came to see that the little guy was in such pain.

Those months dragged on in 1979 and finally cerebral palsy was diagnosed. We had a girl working for us, Jeanie, who had some training in therapy. She helped us give him the best care we could. Then I guess when he was about five or six months old Jeanie brought us some news clippings from the *National Enquirer* that I still have. The heading was something like, "A miracle boy who couldn't do this, but now could." First thing, seeing it was from the *National Enquirer*, we thought it was nothing, bunk. But we thought, well, we'll just call telephone information in Philadelphia and see if there is such a place as the Institutes for the Achievement of Human Potential that was mentioned in the clippings. There was. So we called there to ask questions and I was put through to Gretchen Kerr. Later I got to know her. I asked if the story was true and she said it was, that they had many cases like the boy mentioned in the story who'd been helped to overcome at least part of his handicap.

So we began to think about it. A while later, David Cline was building his house in Half Moon Bay. It turned out that one of the carpenters had some friends who were working with their child on a program from the Institutes. David told us and we invited the couple over to our house one day, to tell us about the program and how it worked. I guess by then Ben was about a year old, because we ended up going to their home just after Christmas of 1979 to watch them do the program with their child. All the time I was saying to her and her husband, quite honestly, "I don't think I can do this, it's just going to take too much time away from my life." But a few days later, even after what I had said, they sent in a card to the Institutes recommending us for inclusion in the program. Even knowing that I was not 100 per cent sure I could do it, they sent in the card.

A little after that we began getting communications from the Institutes. First thing you do is write a brief history of your child, everything that you think is important, to the best of your recollection. So I did that. I remember mailing it when we were away from the ranch while Neil was doing a little part in his movie *Human Highway* in a Dutch community where there are a lot of windmills. Actually, we were on our way to Los Angeles at the time to live for a couple of months while Neil was shooting for his film down there. While we were in L.A. I ended up volunteering to help another family with a child on the program. I'd go one day a week. One of the actresses in the film had been doing that, and I took her place. So now we had this other family writing in to say that we were capable of doing the program, even though in my heart I was still saying, "I really don't think I can do it, it's just more than I can do."

Then in the spring of 1980 just as we heard that we were being put on a short list I started getting terrible headaches. Nothing would help them. I had to go into hospital for tests, and soon I was told that I had what was called an arterial venus malformation, and that I would have to have brain surgery, or I could die anytime.

First thing I did when I heard that was to phone the Institutes and tell them about the brain surgery, and not to put us into a program at least until after August. My surgery was set for May 8 and my doctor had told me that if everything worked as it should, it would be three months after the operation before I'd be feeling myself again.

Late in April that year, Neil told me by telephone the darker side of Pegi's operation. The doctor told him there was a fifty-fifty chance of complete success. Anything less than success might leave Pegi partly or seriously impaired. Naturally he was deeply shaken. Pegi has said since how sorry for him she felt, two sons with cerebral palsy and his wife at risk, as well. The odds were staggering, not only in the case of Pegi's condition, completely unheralded, but against one man having two sons with cerebral palsy when there is little or no evidence that heredity is a factor. That was one of the few times I have heard him sound down, on the phone. "Seven out of every hundred thousand kids born in this country have this condition, Dad," he said. "And I've got two of them." Being from different mothers made the odds even more staggering. "But right now the only worry really on my mind is Pegi."

A few weeks later, that worry was removed. Pegi came through her operation perfectly. But soon I got a call from David Cline. "Neil's going to take Pegi and Ben on the *Ragland* on a cruise out into the Pacific to visit a lot of different countries, and we find that his passport has expired." A new one could be issued by the Canadian consulate in Los Angeles, but to get it they needed Neil's birth certificate and couldn't find it anywhere. Rather than risk delays that might foul up the trip, David asked, could I get a birth certificate for him? On sober reflection, I got him four copies at five dollars each (my treat) and suggested to David that they all be filed in different places. Head 'em off at the pass, so to speak.

Pegi

After my operation, I didn't just lay around in bed. I was ready to get back to living – I was really, really happy to be still here in one piece. I called the Institutes again just to check in and told them I was feeling pretty good but we were going on a little vacation early in August and would be back at the end of September. That was when we sailed to the Society Islands, Tahiti, and Mooréa and Huahine and some of the littler islands, snorkelling, sunning, exploring, having a lovely time, mostly. When we got back there was an appointment ready for us in Philadelphia. But we were all sick with colds after our trip. Ben was really bad. He ended up in hospital. I know there was some talk at the time that we'd been planning to keep on going on that trip, sail around the world, but I don't think we seriously considered anything that extensive on my first trip since my surgery. The boat did keep on going to New

Zealand but we flew back and when we were all feeling better again we went to Philadelphia, Neil and Ben and I, to see what we could learn about anything we could do for Ben.

I found that they have what they call initial visits by families once a month. That's what we were on. They bring in the children and their parents for ten hours a day for a week, to meet the staff, watch programs being carried out, look at kids who have progressed a lot – kids who have learned to crawl when they couldn't before, or even to walk when they couldn't before. I said earlier that I wasn't really sure I could do what the program says parents must do: the twelve-hour days, seven days a week, patterning the child to crawl, teaching him words and numbers and simple bits of information, doing all kinds of tasks to make him use and develop what his mind and body *can* do, rewarding him with stories several times a day while he rests for the next thing on the program.

But once we got to Philadelphia it looked different. Neil and Ben and I stayed in a hotel and were out to the Institutes early every morning and back dead tired at night. As soon as I could see the system working, my mind changed. It wasn't that the effort involved was less than I'd thought it would be, but somehow when we got to understand more about it and *why* we would be doing what we'd do, I lost all my doubts. Once you understand *why* you're doing it, to try to give your child a chance in life that he wouldn't otherwise have, it becomes crystal clear. There was no way you could go home and not do it. Or at least try it. Our group had about thirty kids. Some of the kids worse and some better than Ben. At some time during that week Neil and I looked at each other and knew we'd do it, knew that it would end touring for him maybe for years, and would radically change my life as well.

Neil told me on the phone from Philadelphia late that week about their decision. We had talked a couple of times earlier in the week and he had told me how impressed he was. "In all the people and organizations we've seen about Ben, we were never satisfied with what they told us. So much of it was just cosmetic. This is the first time I've heard something that makes sense to me – everybody pushing to the limit to make a child try both physically and mentally." When they went back home they went straight into the program which was to dominate their lives, they knew then, into the indefinite future. From then on, when anyone mentions it, it somehow comes out as if in capital letters: The Program.

A few months earlier I had returned rather precipitously to freelancing, intending to write nothing but fiction. I had no money and was in the hole at the bank. As you might deduce from that, I had not exactly planned my departure from *The Globe and Mail*, where I'd served two hitches totalling nineteen years. I had simply become furious one day, and quit.

What makes an S. Young, kindest and most equable of men, furious to that degree? I'll tell you. The *Globe* had a reporter about whom the less said, the fewer the lawsuits. One day in a general conversation I warned the editor, a longtime friend of mine, that we'd been danger-ously close to printing false and actionable material a few times, and if more careful editorial control were not exercised over this one man's work, "he could cost the paper a million dollars" in the event that someone successfully sued.

One morning a couple of weeks later I got back from a hockey game in Philadelphia, drove home to the country, and picked up the paper to find on the front page precisely the kind of thing I had warned against – the reporter in question quoting scurrilous remarks from unnamed sources. It seemed to me to tar by association those of us who took some pride in journalistic ethics. Just the fact that I worked for the same paper made me feel ill. I typed out my resignation and put it on a primitive fax machine, then called a remote copier, so it was in the office in minutes. Although the editor, with whom I have remained friends, and I had a long palaver by telephone the same day in which he asked me to recon-sider, I let it stand. Within weeks the other man was gone as well, and subsequently was fired from another newspaper, the *Toronto Sun*, over a front-page "exposé" in which, he later admitted, he had fabricated certain sources. This story resulted in a lawsuit by a Canadian cabinet minister, John Munro, for something close to $700,000. As I told the *Globe*'s editor later, in that case I'd been out by only one newspaper and a few hundred thousand dollars (which I admit turned out to be somewhat hyperbolic, as, although John Munro won the case, the money award was a little less than $100,000).

Soon after I quit the *Globe*, being broke, overdrawn, and having no income and substantial (to me) alimony, I had to retreat rather swiftly from my original intention to write nothing but fiction (the writer's lotus-land, which I once had inhabited). Luckily, within a short time one of Canada's most fascinating men, Conn Smythe, a flamboyant figure in hockey, thoroughbred racing and breeding, and veteran of two wars, asked me to help him with his memoirs. He was eighty-five and felt he wasn't going to live much longer, which turned out to be correct. The book turned into a year's loving work for me. We settled on a personal services fee, plus royalties, and then I surprised even myself by telling Smythe that I would put my 50 per cent share of royalties in with his for charity – his favourite for many years being the Ontario Society for Crippled Children.

He looked at me with tears starting to his eyes, and growled, "I didn't know writers had hearts."

I didn't tell him that I had given the matter no thought at all; in fact, the words of my offer had been as much a shock to me as to him. There I was, a penniless writer, giving away many thousands of dollars in royalties! Amazing. Yet I can't help thinking: Conn Smythe often said, "Cast thy bread upon the waters and it will return one hundredfold." From the minute I made my stupendously impulsive statement, I entered one of the happiest periods of my life. It makes me think maybe the old guy was right about bread cast upon the water resulting in more than just wet bread.

He died that November. For six months we'd been working intensely together. I had been writing chapters as we went along, so that he could okay them in our race against time. Just before his death, which then seemed imminent, I took him one of the final chapters. By then he wasn't able to read it, but asked me in a weak, slow voice to read it to him. He lay at my side, his eyes closed, the skin stretched tautly over the bones of his face; as I read I wondered if he was conscious. Then I came to a place that I knew amused him. As I read that story I glanced over and saw the big grin spreading from ear to ear.

Five days later I got the phone call that told me he was gone. I spent a few months tidying up the manuscript. After I turned it in at the end of March, I flew to California. I needed the trip. Working as closely as I had with Conn Smythe, coming to love him for his prickly strength and honesty, sometimes writing with tears in my eyes, and not coming to terms with his death nearly as easily as he had himself, I was somewhat of an emotional basket case.

Neil met me at the airport in a 1950 Plymouth in perfect condition,

On tour with the International Harvesters, Canadian National Exhibition, Toronto, 1985.

Poster advertising the Winnipeg show of the International Harvesters tour, October 10, 1984.

My mother, always "Granny" to Neil, had never seen him in a live concert. When he scheduled one for Winnipeg in 1984, she declared she would not miss it, and travelled from Flin Flon to get there. After the concert, Joel Bernstein lined up this shot, three generations, Neil, Mother, and me, in the depths of the Winnipeg Arena.

(Steve Babineau)

(Steve Babineau)

Three tours: Above left, 1986. Above right, 1988, with the Bluenotes. Below: 1987, with Crazy Horse, left to right, Poncho Sampedro, Billy Talbot, Neil, and Ralph Molina.

(Steve Babineau)

(Steve Babineau)

On tour, 1989

(P. Young)

A 1989 visit to Omemee. On the front steps of the house where we lived when Neil was a child. Left to right, Ben, Zeke, Amber, Neil, and me.

(P. Young)

Signing an autograph with our one-time house in the background.

Neil performing at two of the annual benefit concerts he and Pegi arrange to raise funds for the Bridge School for handicapped children, including Ben and friends, which they founded. Pegi is M.C. and the acts are usually people for whose own benefits Neil often appears.

Neil and Crazy Horse during their 1991 tour, "Smell the Horse."

(Jack Harper)

May 1992: Neil receives an honorary
Doctorate of Music from Lakehead
University, Thunder Bay, Ontario.

(P. Young)

January 1995: Neil and David Briggs on
the way to Neil's induction into the
Rock 'n' Roll Hall of Fame.

(Jack Harper)

Neil and me in Winnipeg, 1992, when I was inducted into the Manitoba Hockey Hall of
Fame. Bobby Hull, also inducted that night, cracked, "I used to be Bobby Hull, but now I'm
Brett Hull's father. And I look out there and see the one who used to be Scott Young. I mean
Neil Young's father."

Left: Zeke, Neil, and Ben at my daughter Astrid's wedding in California. Above: Others in the wedding party, clockwise from top left: Zeke, Pegi, Neil, Amber, and Ben.

When the new Scott Young Public School in Omemee was officially opened, our family from near and far turned out in force. A happy time of reminiscence with sons Bob and Neil.

August 18, 1993, Neil and Booker T. and the MGs played at the Canadian National Exhibition. That's my daughter Astrid in the background. Bob (inset) was also there.

In 1995, Neil toured Europe with Pearl Jam after the release of *Mirrorball*.

(P. Young)

Top left: Dublin 1996: On many tours, Neil gives the media a miss, preferring to head for where guests and relatives have gathered, what he calls "Meet and Greet." Our Howth friend May Crawford (peeking from the left side of the shot) joins Roseanna Leatham, Neil, Delores McCormick, and Jan Moore.

(P. Young)

(Steve Babineau)

Top right and above: "Broken Arrow" tour with Crazy Horse, Stockholm. Inset is Neil's new tour bus.

found he'd come without any money (he never needs it on the ranch), and bummed a dollar from me to get us out of the parking lot. We drove home talking. "You'll see Ben's program," he said. "It's amazing. You'll be able to help, if you want. We need three people on it all the time so we have a lot of volunteers who come in, but sometimes one of them can't make it and we need somebody."

"Count me in," I said.

We left my luggage in a small, well-provisioned (from Bombay gin to steaks) house near the sprawling ranch house where I'd stayed a few years earlier. "This house will be yours while you're here," he said. "And I'll leave you this Plymouth." Then we went up for lunch a mile or so to the place where they lived then, the main house in the third parcel of land he'd bought, bringing his total holdings there to about 2,000 acres.

The house was not large: their bedroom, Ben's, and one for an attractive and helpful Swedish maid, Britta, who had not been long in the United States. The living room was the main focus of their home and Ben's program – with a big bay window overlooking rolling ranch land, a big fireplace with its firewood piled outside a nearby side door, a piano, a guitar leaning against a wall, a television, stereo, a dining area, old comfortable furniture, clear floor areas for his crawling exercises, a slanted ladder where he worked at keeping his feet in place and holding on with his hands. At one end was the table where Pegi worked, it seemed endlessly, on the printed cards and pasted-on pictures of what was called the intelligence part of the program. And there I settled into the routine of being a pinch hitter for any volunteer who for one reason or other couldn't show up to help with Ben – this grandson of mine with the merry welcoming smile, the glint in his lively eyes at every joke. And I could see how the program dominated all their lives.

Pegi sometimes worked until midnight preparing the next day's mathematics cards and simple sentences with related pictures and going over the carefully timed and reported results of the previous day's program. She was simply a wonder, the gung-ho mother on which much of the program depended.

For the first time in at least fifteen years Neil had little or no freedom to pick up and go whenever he felt like it. He could not fly to L.A. Drive to Nashville. Go out for a few days on his boat. Hang out in L.A. or Miami or Santa Cruz with musicians and filmmakers or good friends who are neither. He was doing none of this.

At first, he and Pegi told me, they'd both worked whole days with

Ben, the volunteers being extra to the parental effort. When the strain of this began to show, they worked out a sensible system of shifts. If it was Neil's turn to be on with two volunteers (or Britta plus one), Pegi was free to shop, garden, visit friends, get away. Other days Neil would lead the program from when Ben woke for breakfast, around six A.M., until a few hours later when Pegi took over. Pegi told me that before the program began, Ben rarely went to sleep without crying and fretting. Now when he was put down, tired from his efforts, his eyes would be closed before Neil, Pegi, or Britta could get out of the room.

When Pegi was in charge, Neil would take off down to his recording studio, or check on the imaginative new house they were building around his small original one, or work with Larry Johnson and Amanda Hemming editing *Human Highway*. Both Pegi and Neil told me that these daily breaks after the endless pressure of the first months were like gifts from heaven. I could see that. Sometimes I worked on the program inside the house while Pegi tended her little vegetable garden or her house plants; she stayed in sight of what was going on but studiously removed her attention from it (at least, it would seem that way). If she left, she'd stick her head in the house and say when she'd be back. Her car, one of the two 1950s Mercedes convertibles Neil had given her, would be heard moving off. Sometimes she'd have a friend in and they'd swim and sunbathe at the pool on a hill above Neil's first little house, while Ben would be going through his schedule – the crawl-patterning for five minutes of every hour, the precisely timed two minutes every so often when he would breathe through a plastic mask with one tiny inlet about the size of a soft-drink straw; the idea being that this would cause his normally shallow breathing to become deeper and stronger. When the mask was removed he would keep breathing deeply for a while, giving him a rush of oxygen.

We'd show him cards with simple three- to five-word statements on them, cards with dots that represented numbers, picture assortments with spoken as well as printed identification of what was being shown. "These are cats, Ben," we'd say and then show him pictures of cats from lions to tabbies. Buildings, from the Empire State to the Taj Mahal, were in another series. Information grouped in such categories gave him the chance to see, over and over, the variety that could follow when one said, "cats" or "buildings" or "dogs" or "birds" or "horses" or "money" or "boats." He would fasten his fingers and feet on the rungs of the ladder and try to stay on for sixty seconds. As rewards many times a day he was read stories that even when I first met him, when he was not yet three, he knew by heart. His smiles would begin to fade when he saw that the reader was getting to the last pages. He would still listen intently but the smile gone, knowing that the story he knew so well was over once again, time for more work.

I guess part of what I am trying to say, overall, is that in Neil's life at the height of the Ben program, his music for once was not the end-all of his life, but was compressed into the space left to him by his over-riding concern, Ben's program. It had been decided, in an unspoken way, that Pegi ran the program and had first call on Neil to help her with it. Pegi feels it happened that way because she was the one (of the two of them) who had the most time for it. But she knew that Neil spent far more time on the program than most fathers can or do. Often she made her own decisions about the program. But every once in a while they had what were in effect business meetings, when they sat down and went over the whole program with a fine-tooth comb, weighing both procedures and results.

Because Neil worked so much more on the program than most husbands, Pegi saw it as essential that they have those kind of talks so that they could be sure they were doing everything the same way. Sometimes, Pegi confessed, it took a while for her ideas to get through; Neil was so used to being the one who had the ideas, which everybody else went along with. "He's not used to following someone else's idea."

Around then I first met Pegi's mother, Margaret Morton. She came up from San Mateo once a week to help with the program. I felt an immediate liking and friendship for her. Through Neil and Pegi we had concerns in common. When she left that night I walked with her to her car. We talked about Ben, and his progress, which was slow, and the tremendous effort everyone – Ben himself, his parents, and the nearly thirty volunteers who came, like Mrs. Morton, for a morning or afternoon once a week – made. I mentioned how cheerful Ben is.

"It has made a tremendous difference to Ben," Mrs. Morton said, as we walked towards her car. "Until the program started, he was such a sad little boy. I'd see his sadness and go home thinking about it. But when the program started and he had work to do every day, with the intense concentration of so many people around him trying to help, he just blossomed – that's what you see when you come into the room and he sees you and gives you that big happy smile."

20

A Day Off –
and Human Highway
and Other Matters

One Saturday we arranged that I'd drive up to the house in mid-morning and help Neil for the rest of the day. I got there to find that a friend of Pegi's had arrived unexpectedly. Pegi suggested Neil take the day off. He immediately had an idea – that if another volunteer could be found to take my place on the afternoon shift at 2:30 or so, he and I would drive to Santa Cruz. Some of his antique cars were being worked on there. One in particular, a sixteen-cylinder Cadillac, he wanted to have a look at.

The day I arrived Paul Williamson, who looked after Neil's fleet of antique cars as well as other vehicles, had brought Neil a 1949 powder-blue Cadillac convertible to replace the Plymouth he'd been driving, which he'd turned over to me. We left in the Cadillac to work around his electric trains for a few hours while Pegi tried to round up another helper for the afternoon. The old-style Lionel trains were a multiple by about 10,000 of the ones he'd assembled in Toronto twenty-six years earlier. The train barn had been called the car barn when I visited first in 1976 – holding about ten of his best vintage cars, including the two 1940 seven-passenger Cadillacs numbered one and two that year, when General Motors built so few of them (ten) that each one was numbered. One, equipped with bulletproof glass, had been used for years by a South American dictator. Now the cars had been moved to a San Francisco warehouse and the trains dominated the building. As some men can forget everything while hunting or fishing, or collecting stamps or antiques or paintings, Neil's relaxation therapy is the trains. That day he wanted to build the forms for a long concrete embankment, mix the cement, fill the forms, and leave the concrete to cure for future track-laying.

I swept the floor and then sawed braces for the wooden forms he had already cut. He stuck them in place with his hot glue gun. He *tore* into the business of mixing cement – using the kind of pail a cleaning woman uses for a wet mop. He had bags of sand, fine crushed stone, coarser crushed stone, and cement, which he dug into with a scoop like a sugar scoop from an old grocery store. He added water from a hose. It had to be mixed. He dashed outside and found a stick about five feet long, part of a tree branch. He used this to stir the cement. Due to the crooks in the tree limb it was extremely hard to handle. It was rather funny. He threw away the inefficient tree limb and plunged his hands into the mixture of cement and sand and stone and churned it around like a kid in a mud hole. He should have been wearing gloves; he should have been wearing safety glasses when he dashed over to use a power saw; he should not have been grabbing the pail and lifting it straight up in a weight-lifter's snatch to carry it across the room.

"Jesus, isn't that bad for your back?" I asked.

"Well, yeah, I guess I shouldn't do it." He kept doing it. "You gotta pour this stuff fast," he said. "It hardens up if you don't."

Totally involved, he made do with whatever came to hand. Filling the forms he would start ladling the cement out with the scoop, then with his hands, then he'd scrape the bottom of the pail with the scoop, then smooth it in the form with his hands. After two hours and six batches, mixed and poured, he had cement, mud, and God knows what all over him. At the end when he washed his hands, he started to laugh and came over and showed them to me. They were pale and wrinkled, as if he'd been in a hot bath for hours. He held them up for me to look at. "Think I'll get a movie job as a monster," he said.

Soon he called Pegi. Yes, she had another volunteer, so it was okay for us to take off to Santa Cruz.

"I think the back way might be open," he said, as we got into the thirty-two-year-old Cadillac.

The back way turned out to be all but impassable. Winter rains had washed out great gorges. Branches were down that had to be moved. My Omemee friend Jay Hayes once told me that I don't see it as fool-hardy, but as a challenge, to drive some road that others might think impassable. This was the first time that I'd seen Neil do the same sort of thing.

Once we reached the highway, we had a beautiful drive down the sunny coast. It is more than a coincidence that some of the better times I've spent with Neil in the last few years have been in automobiles. The open road seems to do something for him, as it does for me. There are sights to be seen and commented on, silences to be enjoyed, topics that seem easier to explore at leisure. About writing his music, he said, "The better the idea, the faster it gets done." I told him how I write – fast. He said when he has a good run of composing and starts thinking in terms of an album, he ponders which people could handle best the new songs he has, and gets them to come and record with him. "Every once in a while when there is a full moon, I get the band up here. I like playing with Crazy Horse." He likes recording during a full moon.

We passed more beaches, artichoke fields, wound through forested areas. Once after a long silence he mused, "You know, the songs I'm writing during the program we're doing with Ben indicate to me how much what I'm doing every day is the strongest single influence on my work." He was working then on the *Re-ac-tor* album. "The program with Ben is driving, implacable, repetitive. Very strong, very strongly motivated. The music I've been writing in the last few months since the program started is like that – driving, hopeful, repetitive." He thought about that and then said, "I think Ben is a very strong person already. He'll know that no matter how hard everything is, it can be done if you keep on working at it, that what seems unattainable might be attainable." I sat there hoping he was right.

We zoomed into Santa Cruz and through some back streets, pulling into Mazzeo's place, a large shed bearing the sign, LUCKY DUCK BOAT WORKS. Neil's Rolls-Royce station wagon, which Mazzeo had helped christen in 1974 in Europe, was having some of its wooden body replaced.

Maz, big and cheerful, had plans to build a series of twenty-six-foot boats he hoped would sell for about $20,000. The first one wasn't finished yet. Meanwhile, he was building a bed. The ornate wooden footboard was finished, featuring, in hand-turned wood, a number of easily identified phallic symbols. "When you're lying in bed, all you got to do is look down past your feet and you get the idea what you're here for," Mazzeo said.

I was introduced around. One of Maz's friends named Jerry had a boat that he'd bought as a wreck with a big hole in the bow. He'd patched it, painted it, named it the *Naughty Lady*. It was ready for its maiden voyage. The four of us headed through the streets to the public launching ramp at Santa Cruz's beautiful little harbour ringed with apartment buildings only three or four storeys high, restaurants with big windows facing the incredible array of about 2,000 boats tied up or moving in and out.

We got the *Naughty Lady* into the water, the outboard started first pull, and we rode out through the narrow neck of the harbour into the big Pacific swells. Neil was in the forward seat to Jerry's right. Mazzeo and I were in the back. For no special reason, or rather a lot of special reasons, everybody was laughing. Every time we came off a wave and hit a swell, it was like being hit on the boat's bottom with a mighty hammer. Water sprayed over the windscreen. Jerry was not exactly old Captain Ahab, handling those rollers. He was used to inland lakes. He took one turn too sharp and fast and I guess we came about as close to taking a boat full of water as is possible without actually doing it; a solid green wave came over the side and soaked me. When he corrected, spray soaked the others. But Jerry learned fast. Travelling parallel to the coast, Mazzeo lifted a dripping arm towards two houses perched on a cliff where the Ducks had lived in 1977. We landed alive and I took off my shirt and wrung it out, assuring Jerry it was nothing personal. Later at Mazzeo's house where his friend Mary Lou kept finches uncaged, as well as two pet crickets in a plastic box, some had beer and some smoked homegrown grass from somebody's back yard, pronounced by the smokers to be pretty good stuff. Neil's pot-smoking habits seem fairly standard to me, possibly on the light side as things are judged in the music world. In 1968, a jam session including Buffalo Springfield, Eric Clapton and others was busted in Topanga Canyon, and everyone was charged; but several charges were later dropped, including Neil's.

As for stronger drugs, his rule on tours is, "If you're wired, you're fired," but apart from tours he views drugs as neither a straight yes or no affair. "If you're trying to finish something that's going good and might be lost if you stop, maybe that time the answer would be yes." Yet once, talking drugs with me, he mentioned those native peoples who think they lose a little of themselves each time they are photographed. "I think drugs do that – each time you use them, you lose a little from the end of your life. Believe that, and you get careful."

So a joint or two passed around at Mazzeo's, and it was about eight o'clock when Neil said to me, "I think we'd better hit the road." As we headed north on the coastal highway Neil dwelt on what a wonderful day it had been. Said it several times. "It's a long time since I've been anywhere like that, just to hang out."

I thought later, getting ready for bed: we didn't see his sixteen-cylinder Cadillac. Or even mention it.

A couple of days later I became one of the first from outside the lodge to see Neil's film *Human Highway*, which he'd been working on for three years or so. I find it interesting that Neil can write ten songs, record them, and have the album out all within a couple of months (as he was to do in 1983 with *Everybody's Rockin'*) but does not lose patience with a film, even after years of working to get it exactly as he wants it.

One day in the studio he mentioned that while I was there I should see the film. He booked a screening room in Berkeley for nine P.M. Sunday, but we ran late, leaving closer to nine in the intense dark of the hills, with a lone coyote standing against the last light in the west. A friend of Pegi's, a woman I'd met before and liked (she laughed a lot, not necessarily at my jokes), was along.

On the drive, Neil said that, for better or worse, the film was in its final stages. The main thing missing, he said, was the opticals – the special film effects such as the rosy glow that would surround all the nuclear plant workers in the film in its final version. "It takes about two months to get the opticals, and they're expensive, so I won't order them until we know we have the final version."

The opening scene was a spectacular long shot of a truck convoy carrying radioactive waste from the nuclear plant which, in the film, was located only a mile or two from the corner gas station and restaurant in which the main action took place. Neil played a slow-witted mechanic named Lionel Switch. He was introduced wobbling along on a bicycle with a co-worker, heading for work. This followed an establishing sequence of nuclear plant workers emerging from an elevator, dressed in black with hoses running up their noses as part of their spacesuit-type uniforms. The film went on; it included a long sequence in which Lionel Switch was hit on the head by a falling auto part and fell into a dream in which he is a rock star. The film builds in a way that I won't try to describe, but is what Neil once called "a comedy about a tragedy" before the final, holocaust-like nuclear accident.

Maybe screening rooms are often full of sympathetic viewers, I don't know, but there was a lot of laughter from the group of us as the film drew to an end. Some had seen it, or parts of it, dozens or hundreds of times during the editing process. It was all new to me, and somewhat surprisingly I found myself shaking hands with Neil as we left the room. "It's good, Neil," I said, as I might have said to John Huston, or Francis Ford Coppola, under the same circumstances.

On the way home we talked animatedly. Pegi said she thought the opening was a little slow. Neil said there were a few minor things and one major thing he still wanted to fix. As we neared a roadhouse called the Belle Vista, one of their neighbourhood watering places, Neil said to Pegi, "Is it a hit or a miss?" Not referring to the film at all, but to whether we should stop for a drink or go straight home.

Pegi said, "I think it's a miss. I've got to get some sleep." The alarm went off every morning early, for Ben's program. As we neared home I caught a few words between them about what Ben would be doing on the program the next day. This had been their night out. But Ben's program was the reality.

One other fragment belongs in here somewhere, a distant echo from twelve years back when he'd had the remix done on his first album. One day Neil and I dropped into the big storage building where in 1981 he kept his two tour buses and some prime elements in his antique car collection – sixteen-cylinder Cadillacs, a 1934 Bentley, a LaSalle, a Buick Roadmaster station wagon, the Packard station wagon he'd driven in Santa Cruz in the summer of the Ducks (a big bumper sticker read: DUCK AUTHORITY). We wandered from there into a smaller storage area filled with scenery, his own travel trunks and some belonging to Joni Mitchell, boxes of the odds and ends that are found in vehicle cleanups after a tour – magazines, old notes, a battered cap that he picked out of one box and tried on and left on, making his ensemble read, from the ground up: green rubber boots laced to the knee over his jeans, three layers of checked shirts, and the cap. Also in the room were stacks of boxes full of records. "You know what they are?" he asked. I didn't. "*Comes A Time* copies that were no good," he said. The master tape of *Comes A Time* had been damaged. He checked it, think-ing it wasn't quite right, but not able to identify what. So he okayed it. A week or so later he found one of the tapes taken off the original master. Checking the tape against the album, then ready, he found that some frequencies in the high register were missing altogether from the album. He called the Reprise people to say that production had to be stopped. Aghast, they said they had already printed and shipped 200,000 copies. He said it was his fault, and they must be recalled; he would pay for this personally. They told him it would cost $200,000, at one dollar per album plus shipping albums back from Italy and Japan where they'd been shipped. He said he would pay that.

"I don't like throwing money around," he said. "But I wasn't going to have this album circulating around the world in bad quality."

"How do you make sure they won't get out sometime?"

He showed me. Each case of albums had been fired at with a rifle, piercing each record and making it unusable.

One time in Neil's train barn that week we were having the kind of conversation that goes on while other things are being done (Neil was carefully removing the plywood frames from the concrete embankment he'd poured a few days earlier). Larry Johnson, the film editor on *Human Highway* and also producer of the film *Rust Never Sleeps*, had dropped in from his house next door. We'd been talking more or less idly about songs when I said, "In one of your songs, you use the phrase, 'the darker side of me.'"

This is in the song "Lookin' For a Love."

But I hope I treat her kind
And don't mess with her mind
When she starts to see
The darker side of me.

"Yeah?" Neil said, without looking up, still tapping with the hammer.

"What do you figure is the darker side of you?" I asked.

There was a pause of several seconds and then he looked up and exclaimed loudly, "Well-l-l-l, Jesus Christ!" He laughed, a burst of laughter as loud as his original ejaculation, laughter that faded off into muttering and head shakes.

He could have sloughed it off, but instead he replied with almost a sigh, "Oh, geez. I don't know. The older I get, the more I feel like the darker side is realizing . . ." – he fumbled a little for words and switched from the first-person pronoun – ". . . realizing that you are as much of a clod as everybody else you've been criticizing all your life, or someone who always made you feel like, 'Wow! I won't be like that.' Then it turns out that you *are* like that, or are a clod in some other way. It's, like, nobody's perfect. Matter of fact, nobody is any more together than anybody else. They're all different. Everybody knows what their own little problem is. There's no way you can get around it. There's no way you can avoid thinking about it. The older you get, the more it comes up, starts looking at you and saying, 'I'm still here.' All the other problems are gone, but I'm still here – the darker side."

I said, "I took it to mean the way that we impose our lives on other people. We bend other people to our fancies sometimes. We don't even know that we're doing it, sometimes."

Neil, with a sharp look: "You mean, us Youngs!"

It was not a question and put the matter on a more personal plane than I had intended, but maybe he was the smarter one. "Well," I said, "I don't know whether we have any more of it than anyone else, but it's definitely there."

Neil: "It's just that you know there are some things that have to be done. That you have to do. Everybody has such things. Some have more of them than others. Sometimes doing these things requires selfishness on the surface. Whether it's premeditated or not is another thing. It's just that it's there. I've seen that as the darker side of me, to my mate. I guess in time, in fact all of a sudden, I've learned to temper that. I've learned that it's *not* most important. But it's taken me a long time. I always thought that my music was more important than anything, but now I know that music is important only in that it reflects where I'm at. If everything else is together, the music is good. By spending all your time on the music and not spending your time on anything else that's going on around you, you'll get the *façade* of the music being good, but the base it's built on is not solid. It took me a long time to figure that out."

Me: "When you say 'selfishness' it's another way of saying ego, because if you place your own number-one priorities ahead of those of everybody else, you could call it selfishness. I don't know. I think it's the only way that people – great writers, great artists, great singers – get where they're going."

Neil (interrupting): "They're driven there. They have to."

Me: "I remember you telling me about a girl you went around with and then you broke up. You said that sometimes when you got home, you picked up the guitar when you should have picked up the girl."

Neil (laughing): "Yeah."

Me: "But that's . . ."

Neil: ". . . true."

Me: "But doing it differently is a wrench. It helps to be married to somebody, or be with somebody, who allows you a certain amount of that selfishness as a matter of course, and yet who won't be ridden over roughshod."

Neil: "Right."

Me: "You couldn't be doing what you and Pegi are doing with Ben if you yourself still felt . . . if you were still putting that number-one priority as being yourself, your music."

Neil: "Yeah. That's not my fulfilment now. I can still pull my music through my life. That's the change. That's why I'm still here. I think that's maybe what has wiped out so many people, never being able to make the shift from thinking of themselves first. Although I still think of myself a lot, I think of my family first. The shift from thinking of my own projections and thinking of my family's projections for me was a very rough shift. It was a whole new area where everything, all the values, were being checked and rechecked. That's a very turbulent area for most people to get through and a lot of people don't. They end up doing themselves damage."

It seems to me that the importance of that thinking, when applied to Neil, is the "values being checked and rechecked" line. He is still obviously used to calling the shots. But when not everyone rolls over and gives with the "Yes, massa," he applies the brakes. I saw it work one night when we were sitting around the fire. Pegi was working over the records of what Ben had done that day in his program. She noticed that Neil, during his shift, had neglected to record one time check – the time it had taken for Ben to perform one of his tasks. She was quite firm, and annoyed. "We have to know that, Neil! You *have* to write these things down!"

I waited for Neil to bridle at this criticism, however justified it was. He was sitting in front of the fire, holding one leg bent up almost to his lap and resting on the other thigh, a habit he has. For a minute or two no one said anything. Then Neil said quietly, "I know you're right.

When that little guy tries so hard, it's wrong if he doesn't get the proper credit."

That reaction was very different from the impression given once when Larry Johnson answered my question, "What is a sound check?" by laughing, "It's a time when we do a lot of things and then Neil comes in and tells us what we've done wrong."

I remember once when he was a kid someone said how much they liked Neil, because he was "so biddable." He lost that somewhere along the way, gradually at first and then in a headlong rush. In that area, Neil has split the two sides of his life. In one, the music, the years he has spent ambling purposefully around concert halls and arenas and stadia listening to how this amp is working, or the sound from that piano, or where a microphone can be moved maybe only a few inches to get the effect he wants, he is still as adamant as he ever was because he is the only one who knows what he wants an audience to hear. In the other, his home, he still has strong opinions but the adamancy is gone. He'll argue, stand up for his opinion, maybe look for a compromise; but he thinks things through before he sticks to his position, and thinking it through sometimes causes him to change his mind. It is the difference between the simple (perhaps deceptively so) life he likes to lead with his wife and family – and which he values above everything else – and the life he leads when he goes alone into one phase or another of his professional life and refuses to back up an inch.

Even there, though, there are people he will listen to. If they make a point on the sequencing of a concert, or the inclusion or exclusion of a particular song, and he agrees, he does it. David Briggs was what he calls an "honest ear"; Neil liked to have him around. Elliot Roberts is another of the few in that category and even he makes a joke of it. One time when I was backstage hours before the concert and Neil was working on the song line-up, Elliot was watching over his shoulder. I heard Elliot make a suggestion for a change in sequence that Neil thought over and then said, "You're right. That's a good idea."

Elliot (laughing and winking at me): "Just an accident. Unlikely to happen again."

Once one accepts the fact that most of Neil's life, the music side, is not simple, one can see its true contrast with the outwardly simple lifestyle he seems to favour. As Pegi once said, "When we're here on the ranch we're one way. When we go out in the world, people deal with Neil a different way and I have to remember what it is. I don't undermine him. I don't think that's the wrong word. I don't, living with him, think of him as this gigantic person. But when we go out in the world, we see a lot of people who do feel that way about him."

In conversation with Pegi one day, I commented that when one of a couple is famous, people often rudely ignore the spouse.

Pegi (laughing): "Yes, and I've never been the kind of person that people ignored! Not because of any great achievements but just because of my basic personality. I had never been ignored in any group. That was something I had to get used to, not being the centre of attention. I don't know what can be done about it. (Shrugs.) Nothing, really. You just get used to it, and try to be graceful."

21

Thinking About the Road Again, and Getting There

We talked often on the phone that summer of 1981. Sometimes I called just to hear how Ben had done that day in his various tasks. The responses were usually positive, but there were interruptions – a painful shoulder cyst, other setbacks here and there, normal childhood illnesses. Too often his life seemed like a marathon swim in heavy seas, too often in control of elements other than the swimmer.

In autumn, Conn Smythe's memoirs, *If You Can't Beat 'Em in the Alley*, were published. I was asked to tour promoting the book. In October I was due in Vancouver for five or six interviews, newspaper phone-in shows, and an appearance on the afternoon talk show that was hosted for years by Alan Thicke before he went night-time with *Thicke of the Night* in 1983. The Thicke show taping was on a Saturday afternoon. The first flight I could get for San Francisco was the next morning. I had a couple of free days before the next dates made for me, back east.

Neil met me at the airport. Pegi's elderly Mercedes convertible was at the curb. Ben, in the back seat, was very much a presence in the car. We both talked to him and he smiled a lot and watched what was going on. Neil had just finished a new album, *Re-ac-tor*, due out in a few weeks. It had received a very positive response from the Reprise people but, he told me, he had not been satisfied with some vocals. He had felt a need to change his singing style here and there to fit some of the material. He had tried, but the change hadn't been great enough to suit him. Then as he'd been playing the *Re-ac-tor* master to the enthusiastic record company people (some of whom tend to think that anything of proved sales value should be revered, not changed), he'd had a new idea.

"I went out and bought a vocoder," he said.

"I don't know what that is."

"It's a machine that computerizes sounds so that I can hit any note I want. The machine takes my voice and locates it precisely where I've decided it should be. I've already used it to record a couple of new songs for the next album. . . . Listen."

We were on the narrow winding hillside road leading through the woods to his gate. He fumbled among cassettes on the seat, selected two, and pushed one into the tape deck. It bowled me over – strong, insistent, melodic, using both vocoder and synthesizers. He talked about a concept he had for a concert using mainly this kind of music, with the concert's story-line built around the idea that computers were running the world. Everyone on the stage would be moving with the stiff, mechanical action of robots. Ever since *Rust Never Sleeps* he'd wanted to do another stage show to go with the music.

"I might do something in a concert setting with those two songs I just played," he explained. "'Sample and Hold' is the first one I played. The second one is 'Computer Cowboy (aka Syscrusher).' Which is a guy's alias. Computer Cowboy is just a front; he has this herd of perfect cows, floodlit fields, even coyotes. But late at night he goes into the city and robs computer data banks of memory systems and leaves his alias, Syscrusher, printed over the information he's lifted. He is a twenty-first-century outlaw. That's where the big crime is going to be. It's going to move out of Las Vegas and into computer perforations. That's what all the talking in the background of the song at the end is. The computers are all talking to each other, reading what's happening; perforation, protection, security, all those words."

Listening to him, for the first time I began to get a glimmering of the mysterious thought-processes that had gone into songs and lyrics – for example, "*I was lying in a burned-out basement. . . . Flyin' Mother Nature's silver seed to a new home in the sun*" or "*Said the condor to the praying mantis, 'We're gonna lose this place just like we lost Atlantis.'"* It was just a fleeting thought as we drove on, playing "Computer Cowboy" again. Now I was seeing some images as Neil sees them, and as few others ever would. It's as if he has a seedbed of ideas in his head. The end results would be unforeseeable even if you took the seedbed a tablespoon at a time and looked at it through a microscope before finally pushing back your green eyeshade and saying, "Dammit, professor, I don't know what the hell is going to grow from this."

As he had been talking in terms of another tour, I asked if there'd been any change in what he'd told me in the spring – that to tour again was away off in the indefinite future. He said it was still in the indefinite future, but was now visible, a possibility. "Pegi and I have talked it over; we're starting to plan ahead a little bit, just to see how it looks. There's nothing specific. We're just trying to be realistic about making allowances for my life and Pegi's life in terms of how far we're getting with Ben's program. It's still full on, but we're watching it in a slightly different way."

Pegi and Neil had been working on the program for a year then. Their living room had been gradually transformed into an arena. The comfortable old furniture, the fireplace with the woodpile outside a side door, the desk where Pegi worked on the information side of the program, had been augmented by a runway that ran almost the full length of the room. Ben could work at crawling on it without running into chairs or lamps. "Ben's racetrack!" Pegi laughed. It was of smooth plastic with low foam rubber sides. A sort of trapeze had been erected near a big bay window overlooking the falling-away fields outside. The trapeze featured a secure harness mounted on springs. When Ben was in it he could bounce around, yet his body was fully supported, his limbs and head free. He seemed to love the freedom of movement it offered away from the frustrations everywhere else of trying to get his arms and legs to move in unison.

The sense of change, of looking ahead again, was fairly subtle. Neil had a different kind of drive. He went to the phone and tried to track down Crazy Horse. He wanted to get them up here to record at the full of the moon, Tuesday, two days away. He couldn't find them. He called to see if David Briggs could help. Finally he talked to Elliot. Neil had sent down a cassette of the two new pieces he'd played for me, wanting David Briggs to hear them. Somehow they'd wound up with Elliot instead. Elliot was very enthusiastic. Neil put down the phone, obviously buoyed up. A little later, after he had gone out for a while, Pegi expanded a little on the things Neil had been saying very tentatively about how the next few years might go for them.

Pegi

It's really a hard question. There're a lot of differences now in both our lives. I think all I can say is that we've come to realize that, and to balance it against the program in a slightly different way. Our first concern is Ben. If we were seeing a whole lot of improvement, that would be the answer in itself. But right now we just don't know. The time and effort we and Ben are putting into it, and the results that we're getting, are not even. Yet it's hard to judge. He had that cyst that we didn't know about for a while, we don't know how long, but the pain in his arm might have been hampering him a lot longer than we knew. We lost a full month because after the doctor did find the cyst, there was the operation and the healing process. If he started really picking up now, which he might, then we'll hang in there. I'm talking mostly about the crawling and patterning. They're the only things in question. The intelligence program is really wonderful and we'll keep doing that, whatever happens. It's really good. It keeps him from getting bored. I also think the idea of us spending time with him as intensely as we do on this program is good. So I think that if the day comes when we feel that we have done all we can as far as this full physical part of the program goes, it's certainly not going to be the end of the road as far as us doing what we can to help him develop in everything he *can* do.

I think I can put it another way. We have done every mortal thing that we can do to push him to the limit of what he shows he is able to do, or might learn to do. But there's a point at which we have to ask ourselves, is it really doing anything for him? Can we really say that what we're putting in is helping him, or would we be better rethinking, and taking another tack? We'll be up against that kind of a decision six or eight months from now.

The next day I walked through the morning sunshine and intense quiet to the studio to meet Neil. He and Tim Mulligan were at the vocoder. Neil sat down at the keyboard while Tim manipulated the controls. Neil explained that whatever note he pressed would become the control note for whatever he did with his voice, so that anything sung into the vocoder could be reproduced in perfect pitch as a deep bass, a falsetto, or anything between. Neil wandered off eventually into another part of the studio where Larry Johnson was screening some footage from *Human Highway*. Tim and I moved outside to the studio porch under the giant redwoods. Because he had been with Neil since the early 1970s, Tim had a perspective about Neil's working modes that few others have. Tim commented on what had been so obvious to me this visit: that Neil seemed to have a new enthusiasm. Tim said it was related to his new equipment. "Because he has to stay close to the ranch all the time, for Ben's program, we knew that we'd have to upgrade the studio facilities here to allow him to do more work here. This last album [*Re-ac-tor*] was the first one we'd brought right up to a master without going off the ranch. You can see how it jacks him up. Heck, years ago Neil would come in here many mornings with a bunch of new songs. That hadn't happened for a long time, until just recently, when he got into this computer stuff. He came in one morning and said, 'I wrote four songs last night.'" Tim was – there's no other word for it – elated, and felt that some kind of a corner had been turned.

Going away from the studio that day for a walk along the paved road that ran through ranchland and giant redwoods, over bridges, up and down hills in sunshine and in shade, I thought about all the ways works of art, and works of non-art, are created. It seems almost all my life, or at least since I got my first typewriter back when I was seventeen, I have been travelling through a cloud of impressions or ideas that I try to get on paper. There were ideas for all the short stories, some good; for the newspaper columns; for books, television scripts, whatever – and that's only counting what got written. Sometimes I'm sure the best have not been written yet, or may show up sometime as what Neil calls a fragment. He calls "Cripple Creek Ferry," the jaunty song that ends the *After The Gold Rush* album, a fragment.

Hey, hey, Cripple Creek ferry
Runnin' through the overhangin' trees
Make way for the Cripple Creek ferry
The water's flowin' down, it's a mighty tight squeeze.

Something about the island ferry in Toronto sparked it, and it hung around until he finished it much later in California and created a minor cottage industry for people who try to find the deep meaning below the cheerful lilt of the tune. To me, "Till the Morning Comes" on the same album speaks to every person who has ever had a deep and bitter argument in bed, but lacked the strength to get up and leave forever. At least, as I told Neil one day, that's how I saw it. Neil glanced at me and said it was one of those fragments that each listener could relate to something in his or her own life.

He laughed, "You just happen to hate arguing in bed, right?" Right.

This matter of publicly identifying real events with his songs is something Neil avoids so studiously that a fan, or critic, or even a father, can reach only two possible conclusions: (a) that as a matter of policy, he refuses to go into the genesis of each song because most them pass through so many layers of consciousness that explaining is impossible, life is too short; or (b) that he really means what he said during a phone-in *Rockline* radio show late in November 1981, when a caller asked, "Was the character in 'Powderfinger' inspired by someone in your life?" Neil answered: "There's no thinking behind any of these songs. I don't think about a song. So I can't say it reflects people in my life, or anything like that. I'm here, like, when it [the song] comes out, emerges. I just start writing and playing and when I'm finished, I'm finished. I don't really know why or when . . . don't associate it with what's going on in real life."

However, I don't think he would avoid the issue if questions of that sort were asked about songs that refer directly or obliquely to his sons; or, for that matter, to much of what is on *Tonight's The Night*. And he has said that one time when he was playing his "My My, Hey Hey (Out of the Blue)" with Devo, and the lyric sheet read, "*It's better to burn out than it is to rust*," Booji Boy of Devo added to that line the words, "rust never sleeps," and he thought, Well, all right, that makes a lot of sense to me.

As I walked along in California in 1981 I thought of things like that and of being told that Neil came in and said, "I wrote four songs last night." I was sitting in my place, the Little Red House, later that evening talking to David Cline and waiting for Neil; he and I were going to meet Pegi for dinner at the Belle Vista. I heard a car door slam outside and David said, "I guess this is him now." Neil came in through the screen door so deeply preoccupied that I don't think anything registered except the piano five steps away. He said nothing, but began to play, heavy and loud, pile-driver runs at certain chords, returning to run at them again differently. He played hard, driving piano for ten minutes before he came out of it and said, "Hi."

Often a song comes to him when he is walking and has no instrument with him. That evening, the music had come to him while he drove to pick me up. Hammering it out, experimenting, changing, seeing how it sounded, is his way sometimes. Other times it works up slowly. Pegi hears him trying something on the guitar or piano, then over a period of days or weeks she may hear it grow and develop. When he is working on lyrics, he sometimes sings around the house, but softly, little more than a murmur. "I hear it," Pegi said, "and it's interesting to watch it go from however he plays or sings it around here, on to the orchestra or to the band, whoever he's working with at the time."

When he is moving into something entirely different from what he's been doing, he might leave some trace of outside influences. His early work with the synthesizer and vocoder was a personal learning experience. He simply used them and laid himself open to ideas he could develop with them. But also he played some Kraftwerk records over and over again to determine how they were using synthesizers.

Also, his happy, jovial 1983 summer album, *Everybody's Rockin'*, might have been influenced by Pegi. Born in 1952, the third child in a family of three brothers and two sisters, Pegi was only seven or eight when she danced around the living room with her older brother and sister to Bill Haley and the Comets, Chuck Berry, the Platters, the Five Satins, Bobby Darin. Neil was amazed to find that she knew all that 1950s music so well. She thinks it is somewhat bizarre herself. I think some of it must have rubbed off on him, along with his own liking for the kind of music that came from those days when musicians went in to record (see the film on Alan Freed, *American Hot Wax*) and just played a song once or twice until they got what they liked. Then they put it in the can with no overdubbing or smoothing out.

And sometimes a song just happens, like "T-Bone" on the *Re-ac-tor* album in 1981. He was a little more forthcoming, but no more illuminating, in talking about how that one came into being. "We were just in the studio and had already recorded the songs that we thought we were going to be recording. We still really felt like playing so I picked up my guitar and started playing. If you notice, the song starts with a straight cut right through the middle. We'd already started playing before the recording machine started. I just made up the lyrics and we did the whole thing that night. It was a one-take thing. It seems like the lyrics were just on my mind. It's very repetitive but I'm not such an inventive guy."

That one was simple, as he tells it, yet one of his most intricate and image-rich songs, "After the Gold Rush," he wrote in half an hour. One time at Royal Festival Hall in London, February 1971, he told the audience, "I've got this new song I just wrote last night. I can't remember all the words and I forgot to bring my piece of paper with them on it. It's going to be the title song on my next album, *Harvest*." Which went to the top of the charts and stayed there.

Even in those days, many songs he wrote and some that he sang frequently in concerts were not released on albums. They went into his library, many to become a bridesmaid but never a bride. It's solely his decision. He explained it to me once, casually: "Usually the choice for an album is made from what's most recently recorded, plus anything else that I can draw on from my library to make a good juxtaposition, show off the new stuff better. I like to throw in opposites. They might be from a time I was feeling one way and then from a time I was feeling another way. You get an effect. The difficult thing is to decide which of the new songs to leave off. There's always a few that just don't get there. I've read some pretty amazing guesses at how much stuff I've got in my library, unreleased. But not counting new ones, it's got to be somewhere between ten and twenty finished songs. Plus many other different kinds of tapes and live albums that have older songs on them. I have a lot of finished projects that I didn't put out: the Ducks and about half the original *Homegrown* album, which 'The Old Homestead' came off of. But overall, it's hard even for me to make an estimate. I don't count 'em every New Year's Day, like stock-taking, you know."

A great deal happened, mostly without fanfare, after that brief visit in October of 1981. The six or eight months that Neil and Pegi had suggested in October would be the time it would take to make decisions about touring again, and what form the tour would take, turned out to be not long enough. On Valentine's Day, one of their anniversaries, they heard that a seminar was being held by the National Academy for Child Development (NACD), an organization headed by Robert Doman, a nephew of the founder of the Philadelphia Institutes where Ben's program had been set up. They went and listened and much of what they heard seemed to apply to Ben. It was a different approach, one that seemed to avoid many of the physical demands on Ben that they were increasingly finding to be unrewarding – in terms of Ben's development – in the original program. Late into the night, over a lot of wine, they talked about it and decided to switch. "It was a huge decision," Pegi said. Ben would be taken off the most strenuous physical parts of the program, which in nearly eighteen months had produced practically no measurable results. "The way we put it is that he has graduated," Neil smiled.

Soon Pegi was working as a volunteer instructor, helping others learn how to handle the handicapped, in the nearest one of the centres the NACD has across the country. She and Neil held a Patterners Ball for all the volunteers who had helped so faithfully in Ben's old program. (Eventually Neil and Pegi were named to the board of directors of NACD; Neil played a New York benefit for the organization, and in October 1983, they were named the Academy's Parents of the Year – this, ironically, happened within weeks after Carrie had taken some shots at Neil as a father in *People* magazine.)

When Neil and Pegi and Elliot flew to Toronto in April 1982, to accept the Juno Hall of Fame award, it was springtime again. Neil called me about a week before the awards dinner to say he'd be coming. He didn't know where he'd be staying, but said he would call when he got in. The Juno awards are a showcase of the Canadian recording industry, through its industry-sponsored Canadian Academy of Recording Arts and Sciences. As Canadians, and therefore qualifiers, year after year Neil and Joni Mitchell would be among the finalists in the Best Male Vocalist and Best Female Vocalist categories. This gave a façade of being fair to Canadians, wherever they were, but it was always a foregone conclusion that neither would win – it was a Canadian industry show and Canadians recording in Canada needed the hype much more than famous expatriates. So while Neil and Joni were honoured in the United States and United Kingdom as far back as the early 1970s, until the Canadian Music Hall of Fame award was established in 1978 the Junos made no bow at all to Canadians who had become international artists. There obviously was some catching up to do: Guy Lombardo and Oscar Peterson were inducted into the Hall of Fame in 1978, then Hank Snow and Paul Anka before Joni in 1981 and Neil in 1982.

I was reading late one night when my bedside phone rang. "Hi!" Neil said. "We're here. Just got in. Are you coming in for the Junos?"

I said I was.

"How many tickets do you need?"

This was a delicate question. The dinner tickets, at $140 each, were mostly bought by people or corporations in the music business – studios, record sellers, recording companies, concert promoters. I figured I could afford one, so I shilly-shallied a little. "Well, um . . ."

"You just tell me how many," he said. "I'll see that you get them."

So I told him six. I'd pick them up. He was at the Hyatt. The awards ceremony would be at the Harbour Castle Hilton. I'd be in touch when I arrived in Toronto.

"I've got a problem," Neil went on. "I'd hoped that we'd all be together at one table, the whole family. But I guess it can't work that way."

I understood. So at the Junos Neil and Pegi commuted between two tables – one at which Rassy sat with a couple of her friends, Elliot, and one or two others; the other with Margaret and me and our far-flung daughters. It worked out fine. When Neil was with us, some roaming TV cameras with commentators I knew came and interviewed him there. Once when I was out of the room, I came back to find that I was passing close to the other family table, so I stopped behind Rassy and said, "Hello, Rassy."

"Hello," she said. In my head there were so many images of times together. Maybe in her head too. But there you are. End of conversation.

When Neil was onstage in his rented tuxedo receiving his award from federal communications minister Francis Fox, he said he was proud to receive this award and "I'm sure that my relatives spread out across this country, and across this room, feel the same way." Not many would get the "across this room" line but those of us most concerned, at our table anyway, enjoyed it.

One member of the family who didn't get to the Juno awards that night was Neil's brother, Bob. I had tried unsuccessfully to get in touch with him. It turned out that he had been out of the city briefly, and as there was no pre-publicity on Neil's award (it was kept as a surprise to the public), he'd been unaware that Neil was in town. When the papers the next day were full of Juno award stories, Bob found Neil. Rassy had left the morning after the awards.

That evening a few of us, including Bob and his girlfriend, Susan, met Pegi and Neil at the Hyatt for a stand-up drink at the bar before a limousine turned up to drive us to a restaurant called Napoleon's for a long and laugh-filled dinner. When we finished, the limousine still waiting, Neil asked if there was any interesting music going on in town. Bob suggested the El Mocambo on Spadina Avenue near the garment district. The management there cleared a table for us in the jam-packed room and insisted on buying the drinks. We stayed for one set and part of another before we parted outside on Spadina.

Neil and Pegi flew out the next day for a brief stopover to pick up Ben and then went on to Hawaii. That started as a holiday. Before the Junos Neil had recorded at the ranch most of the songs for his *Trans* album to be released early in 1983, some with only synthesizers and vocoder, some with Crazy Horse. For that one he switched from Reprise Records to Geffen Records. In Hawaii he began to write again and phoned musicians – Joe Lala, Ralph Molina, Ben Keith, Nils Lofgren, Bruce Palmer – to ask them to join him for rehearsing and recording the new stuff. It was then he began planning seriously for the tour he would take to Europe later in the summer, his first in four years.

Why did Bruce Palmer surface again with Neil, after so many years? The story tells something of the nostalgic loyalty Neil always feels for people who were with him *when*. I knew little of Bruce's story since the times he was busted for drugs and deported. Bruce's last bust in the United States soon after the Springfield broke up had sent him to jail. In some desperation, he got in touch with Neil and Steve Stills asking them to buy out his share of the royalties for a lump sum. Although Elliot told me later that the royalties didn't have a great value at the time, Neil and Steve paid Bruce several thousand dollars outright for his share of future royalties. When Neil and Steve both went on to greater things, there was a related rise in Buffalo Springfield sales. In the early 1970s Stan Weisman, Bruce's lawyer, approached Neil and Steve about making a deal to reinstate Bruce's royalties. They did so, giving Bruce an income. In the nearly ten years after that, Bruce lived with a Sikh sect in Toronto and played nothing except the sitar. But suddenly in early 1982 he decided to return to rock music again. Later, when I got to know him (in 1983) I asked why.

"Boredom. Pure boredom." Bruce was then substantially heavier than the slim kid who shows on the old Springfield album covers. The day we first met he confessed he felt shaky from drinking. Sometimes he dropped French words into the conversation, as if they said things better. Our first meeting was in his lawyer's office. "Boredom," he repeated. "For ten years I hadn't played anything but the sitar. I just vegetated. Then I got thinking how Neil and Steve Stills, people I'd played with on a basis of equality, had taken their careers to considerable heights, while I hadn't done anything. I was *tired* of not doing anything. So I phoned Neil and suggested that we get Buffalo Springfield back together again, play a little, see if it worked, and maybe do some recording."

"It was like a voice from the past, to hear from Bruce," Neil told me later. "He had been good. We had a lot of old bonds. He called at a time when I was deciding what to do next, and I thought, why not? It might work." On the strength of Neil's okay, Bruce went to Los Angeles. He started playing wherever he could. He rented a small studio and pulled musicians off the street to play with him, help dispel the past. Weisman told me that Bruce's stay in L.A. cost him (the lawyer) $500 a week. Bruce got in touch with Richie Furay, Dewey Martin, and Stephen Stills, as well as Neil. A date was set – Stephen having the most difficulty in fitting it into his schedule.

Then, however, Neil's Juno date conflicted with the date set for the Buffalo Springfield reunion. When the reunion had to be rescheduled Stephen couldn't make the new date. So Bruce was in the back of Neil's mind when he went to Hawaii – and was the one major surprise among the musicians he called to come there. No promises, but a chance. The same chance Neil once had given Danny Whitten. Bruce himself felt nervous. He said later, "I walk into this room with all those world class musicians – Neil, Ralph Molina on drums, Ben Keith on pedal steel and keyboards, Nils Lofgren on guitar and keyboards, and Joe Lala percussion and vocals – and we start playing and I'm doing it as if I'd never been away!" They worked a few weeks rehearsing and recording.

When they returned to the mainland early in June, Neil felt the band wasn't right and for a couple of weeks dropped Bruce and tried to find a bass player to replace him. As with the Ducks in Santa Cruz and Crazy Horse in the Northern California Bar Tour, he began phoning around to various small houses in California, offering to come in and play. They started at the Catalyst in Santa Cruz. Then here and there small signs began appearing in club windows, NEIL YOUNG IN CONCERT, $5. Bob Mosley played bass for a couple of weeks before Neil phoned Bruce again and laid it on the line: "I need you, but only on condition that you control your drinking." Bruce promised. Reminding me of something Neil once said: "People that feel good to play with are hard to find. Usually I like people who are extremely erratic."

In another few weeks the narrow winding road into Neil's ranch was full of comings and goings as the technical equipment for the tour was put together. Late in August the equipment was flown over along with the forty-man crew to open on August 31 in the Parc de Sport at Annecy in southern France to begin a tour that lasted seven weeks and ranged all through Western Europe; after four years, he was on the road again.

22

A Trip to Dallas

One day deep in the winter of 1983, I drove through the snow down the rough and hilly lane of my home place in central Ontario, a hundred acres of woods and fields with a chalet-type frame house that faces east along a miles-long wooded valley. Four miles north is Omemee, where Rassy and I lived when Bob and Neil were kids. Driving slowly over the bumps I noticed that the red squirrel that lives in a pile of old cedar rails had eaten half the apple I had impaled for that purpose on a basswood twig among trees black with winter. I could see in the fresh snow where a jack rabbit had crossed at considerable speed (to judge from the six or seven feet between the clumps of footprints). A few yards on were the tracks of a walking fox. Sometimes at night I hear a family of wolves, and occasionally by day I see a wolf or two; one sunny winter day four of them lounged in a field and watched me watching them.

Then I was out on the road, figuring that if I did 600 miles a day or a little more, I'd be in Dallas in three days, about the time Neil would get there.

He'd sounded a little surprised the morning I phoned to say that would see him in Dallas. He'd been back from Europe only a week when he told me he was going out again. But when he reached Maple Leaf Gardens in February my wife, Margaret Hogan, and I would be in England. Besides, I'd never seen a tour just starting out, and I was curious about Neil's decision to take this one out solo, with no backup musicians, something he hadn't done since his old folkie days when he had been happy to have a roof over his head, any roof.

"I'm driving," I'd told him. "Probably leave Thursday."

"Great! Pegi and Ben and I are leaving the next day in the bus. We'll make it there Sunday. So, see you next weekend."

"Look after yourself."

"You too."

I crossed the U.S. border at Detroit, bought rum fifty miles down Interstate 75, had a couple of drinks and slept in a cheap motel at Troy, Ohio. After that, my long drive to Dallas in my sometimes recalcitrant stick-shift Olds Omega wasn't exactly like John Steinbeck's *Travels with Charlie*, but it had its moments.

For my second night I thought I'd try to make a long jump to Forrest City, Arkansas, because long ago when I wrote a daily sports column a friend among the many regulars at World Series and Kentucky Derbies and championship fights I'd covered was Raoul Carlisle, a lean and courtly columnist for a small paper in Forrest City. We could have a few drinks, if I could find him.

For hours that day I travelled more or less in company with a girl in a red Pinto. This happens sometimes on the road when two vehicles are going long distances at about the same speed. We saw one another hour after hour, in sight near or far, ahead or behind. But she dropped out of sight while we were skirting Memphis. I rather missed her. When she reappeared in my rear-view mirror west of Memphis half an hour later I impulsively waved hello. I saw in the mirror her instant response as she waved back. So she knew I was alive too. I guess I mention this as a communique from the state of being, at the time, nearly sixty-five but sometimes forgetting that not so long ago, it seems, I would have taken it as a good omen that she turned off at Forrest City, as I did, and indeed for a few seconds I did give some rein to the idea that it would be nice to have company for a drink or dinner, if it worked out that way. But then I thought of the reality so therefore lost her, or she me. Anyway, I had Raoul. I drove into midtown, hardly looking for the red Pinto at all, and said to the classically tall and willowy southern gentlewoman at the motel desk, signing in, "I have a friend here, Raoul

Carlisle. Do you happen to know where he lives?" Forrest City is small enough for that.

There was a long pause while she glanced at me, then said, "Three doors from my own home, but poor Raoul has met with a disaster."

"What kind?"

"You'll hear the trains on the railroad bridge going through at night. He used to short-cut across that bridge and one night coming home from a meeting . . ." She shook her head to beat back a bad memory. "If Raoul Carlisle had walked across that bridge once, he'd walked across that bridge a thousand times, and he *knew* when the trains came through. But that night he was on the bridge when the train came, and got himself killed. . . ."

Alone with good deep-fried catfish and rum in Forrest City that night. No red Pinto girl, no Raoul Carlisle. I wrote a letter home, instead.

The next afternoon, late, I arrived at a rather crummy north Dallas motel just off the LBJ Freeway. I woke long before dawn, read the Sunday papers, and checked with the airline on the arrival time of my daughter Astrid, who would be staying with the tour a while. In the Sunday morning emptiness I took a freeway downtown and circled State Fair Park with its silent Cotton Bowl, a railroad museum not yet open for the day, and the Music Hall. Neil's concert the next night was blazoned on posters. Two silver-coloured tractor-trailers bearing Neil's tour equipment were drawn up at the Music Hall's loading ramp, cabs empty and locked. Later in the morning after I'd found another motel nearby, I called the downtown Plaza of the Americas for Glen Palmer, Neil's tour manager, and found that the bus had spent the night at a truck stop north of the city, but would be in this afternoon for the sound check.

I met Astrid at the airport. She is small and pretty and exulted in the hot sunshine, excited about this trip. She plays guitar, writes songs, and sings, occasionally making a little money at it. The first time I saw her fronting for a heavy metal band in a Toronto tavern, I'm told I sat through a whole set with my mouth open; this little kid who used to ride her first horse five miles every Saturday morning from our farm to the equestrian centre where she'd have the company of others on horseback, the kid who had played good flute and excellent oboe in Toronto school bands, was now singing Black Sabbath covers with her fist in the air. When she was sixteen, having finished her grade thirteen, she'd gone out on her own. More than father and daughter, we were friends.

On the way through traffic to our motel I turned in at the Music Hall and said, "Hey, look." Neil's bus with the old Hudson and the old Studebaker set into the roof as skylights was parked with other vehicles around the loading doors. I chatted with Paul Williamson, the friend who drives for Neil and looks after his antique cars, and Donna Grant, a friend who travels with them and helps Pegi with Ben. Soon Neil and Pegi, Neil carrying Ben, ambled around the side of the Music Hall from an inspection of the railroad museum. I walked to meet them and there were embraces all around and a big smile from Ben. In the bus, Neil placed Ben in his body-moulded support chair on the counter. "There you are, Benny. Bet you're hungry." As we talked, Pegi opened the fridge and as Ben was fed we talked on. Astrid, across the table from Neil, was quiet. As good as Neil is to her, as much as she admires him from her own standpoint (she wants to do something not *like* him, but that he would like), I think she holds him in some awe.

In this connection, someone suggested to me once that Neil functioned in a way as our family's godfather – an individual to whom all others turned for decisions, favours, patronage. Nothing could be further from the truth. He prefers to stand back as much as he can, except in his love and care for his mother, which is natural and warm and perhaps can be demonstrated – at least in part – by a conversation we had not long before my second marriage broke up.

From the time back in 1965 when Neil told me that he had come to terms with the chasm that existed between Rassy and me, we didn't talk about it much. Then on the day in 1976 when my thinking about this book really began with our discussion about how I usually avoided even the appearance of exploiting him by writing about him, and he replied, "Well, it's your life too, you know," another topic cropped up. I told him that, after seventeen years of paying alimony to Rassy, I often considered going to court in an attempt to have it reduced or ended. At that time he already was providing a home for her in New Smyrna Beach and supplementing her alimony as well. "The only thing holding me back from trying to get the alimony stopped, or cut back," I said, "is that I know you'd probably wind up picking up the slack."

He thought that over very briefly then said, "Well, I guess by now

Mother is as much my responsibility as she is yours." A few months later, after the break-up of my second marriage, I wrote to Rassy and told her I could no longer pay her alimony. I knew I was going to have another, bigger alimony to pay to Astrid. I had no intention of doing what some parts of society consider to be the only decent course for a man in that position – to live on the crumbs left after the sacred obligations of alimony had been met. As a person of some experience in this matter, I am for a clean fifty-fifty split of all worldly possessions of whatever nature, followed by as cheerful a goodbye as can mustered. To me alimony is deadening for the receiver, while the giver develops new muscles as he or she keeps up with his or her added financial responsibilities. It is only with an extreme effort of will here that I resist saying piously, "'Tis better to give than to receive." Anyway, when Rassy called Neil over my no-more-alimony policy, he took over and thereby made unnecessary what could have been a difficult day in court, one that I might have lost. So I can't honestly say, without splitting hairs, that I have never accepted financial help from him.

He tried to help Bob by sponsoring him in golf, but when it did not achieve a long-term effect, it ended. He is liberal with concert tickets and backstage passes for all of us. Neil's stepsister, Deirdre, rarely misses one of his concerts and sometimes goes back after to chat briefly, but the relationship ends there. My wife Margaret and stepdaughters, the Hogans, Erin, Caitlin, and Maggie, are independent women who simply enjoy knowing him. The one Neil seems closest to is my daughter Astrid, his half-sister, the only one with a mutual bloodline. "She has an edge to her," he says in praise.

Astrid and Bob, however, probably have felt most strongly both the positive and negative sides of having a world-famous brother. Maybe Bob's adjustment was the toughest. The older-brother syndrome can be as difficult as the famous-brother one. Neil once had the former to deal with: Bob the rising young golfer, Neil his kid brother. Later Bob had the other. Bob eventually came to handle the famous-brother connection affably, but he had some hard times. One night when I was working at *The Globe and Mail* a friend of mine, columnist Dick Beddoes, came up with a grin. "I guess in some ways Bob has a tough life," he said, then laughed. A few minutes earlier he'd been standing outside the Globe building chatting with someone when Bob happened along. Beddoes introduced Bob to the other man, who could not have been too bright. They shook hands and the man said, "You're Scott Young's son?"

"Yes," Bob said.

"And Neil Young's brother?"

"Yes."

"My God!" the man exclaimed. "What a lot you have to live up to."

Whereupon Bob turned to Beddoes and said quietly, "I don't have to take this shit," and walked away.

But Bob in a more reflective mood could be wryly philosophical. Once he travelled to England with Neil and was interviewed by a *New Musical Express* reporter. Bob said that when he was a young golfer and I was writing a daily sports column, he had been known as Scott Young's son. "Then I became known as Neil Young's brother," he said. "I often wonder if Bob Dylan has a brother. If he does, I'd sure like to meet him."

Also, once in the late 1970s I found that Astrid, then fifteen, was skipping almost all her classes in high school. When I tried to find out why, it turned out that the Neil connection was the main part of the problem. "People come up to me and the first thing they say isn't, 'How are *you*?' but, 'How's Neil?'" She did not resent Neil – but the nitwits, however well-intentioned, who saw her only as Neil's sister rather than as her own strong-minded, bright, individual (my adjectives) self. I moved her to another school, and we had a talk about how to handle the Neil syndrome – gracefully, making it plain that she enjoys the connection, but has a life of her own.

For the next three days, there in Dallas and then at the University of Oklahoma in Norman, I watched and listened. The Music Hall stage was ready for Neil when he came out in mid-afternoon: a rack of guitars, a tray of harmonicas, drums, synthesizer, a banjo, two pianos (one upright and the other a grand with a huge chandelier over it). A sound check is, in effect, a run-through for all the systems and people involved. On the stage, Neil walked around in jeans and a checked shirt, asking questions, checking microphones, getting this or that moved. He wasn't a star strolling out to look around and nod after his seventeen-man crew had set everything up; he was more like a foreman. Pegi brought Ben out in his stroller and parked him in a corner of the stage where he could enjoy the sound and movement. Neil stopped and patted him and said, "How ya doin', Benny?" He wandered the stage apparently aimlessly but with a look of alertness about him, occasionally consulting a pad of paper in his left hand. He passed me down in the seats. "Everything okay, Daddy?"

The next night when the Dallas concert ended, a few of us went to Neil's dressing room — at first only Neil and Pegi, Astrid and me, and Elliot Roberts. A table of food and iced champagne and beer had been set out. Postmortems were held. Neil thought this song had worked well, that not so well. The line-up maybe could be improved here and there. Electronically everything had worked. The use of a giant mock TV screen before the concert and during the intermission had been a hit. This had been Neil's idea. On the screen was an actor name Newell Alexander. The set behind him looked like a Dan Rather news studio, with a big clock on the wall. His role was that of Dan Clear — clean-cut, smiling, telling people where the nearest fallout shelters were in case of nuclear attack, interviewing people live, or on tape, in the corridors. One of the live interviews was with me at intermission, cooked up beforehand. The opening question was "How long have you been a Neil Young fan, sir?"

"Since about a day after he was born."

Dan Clear's face registers amazement, shock, then realization. Even in the studio well behind the stage we could hear the surprised cheer from the packed, 3,300-seat hall. Let's hear it for procreation!

At the University of Oklahoma the next night (a field house seating 7,400, with 10,902 paid admissions) the space in front of the stage was jammed, the aisles were full, people were drinking from bottles, a low cloud of marijuana smoke hung over the proceedings. Early in the concert one girl was close enough to hand Neil some flowers. Another girl climbed to the stage and embraced Neil loosely while nuzzling the side of his face. He kept on playing, wearing her like a shawl until stage manager Tim Foster led her gently away. Later another young woman ran hard and fast from the rear of the stage and was tackled only a few feet behind Neil. It took Tim Foster and barrel-chested Lyle Centola, the production manager who is built like a half-ton version of the old fighter, Two-Ton Tony Galento, to get her under control. The struggle sounded like a tag-team wrestling match. Neil gave no sign until he was finished his song, then jerked his head back to where the ruckus had been and remarked mildly to the crowd, "I thought I heard some thumping back there." Girls, Tim Foster says, are not so bad. In Norway a few months earlier, big guys had jumped on the stage. After that, David Briggs gave Tim a key ring bearing a tiny pair of boxing gloves.

Once at Oklahoma, however, I thought something went wrong. Neil left the stage abruptly. It was noticeable perhaps only to those closest to him, including me, that it had not been planned. When the concert was over and we gathered in his dressing room for food and drink and postmortems, roughly the same group as in Dallas, Neil said he'd felt weak that night on the stage, once had had a dizzy spell. He hadn't slept well the night before and thought he might be catching the flu, as some others in the crew had.

We headed out to the bus. The next concert was two nights away in Houston, Texas. They would set out now and stop later for sleep. I was heading for home the next morning. We said our goodbyes and then I went outside to say goodbye to Astrid. Neil had said she could help around, earn her keep, while she travelled with his tour for a couple of weeks. Like other roadies, she'd have a motel room, meal money, air tickets. I left her some money, suggesting she keep some for bus fare home if required. At first she couldn't find enough to do. The crew was set, everyone with a job. For a couple of days she'd turn up with the others and go around the set looking for work, not finding much. Then a carpenter needed help. She helped. Some experience she'd had with video and recording equipment in Toronto then came in handy and she helped Larry Johnson and Dan Clear in the video studio (she had once quit a steady job with Bell Canada to work without pay in a Toronto recording studio, hoping to be put on the payroll when the owners could afford it, which did not happen.)

A couple of weeks later when the tour broke briefly and Neil went to Nashville, Glen Palmer handed Astrid an air ticket home and an envelope which, when she opened it in her room, contained five hundred-dollar bills. It was a form of accolade. Neil told me he had been really proud of her in those two weeks; I gathered later from others that the friends she made and the persona she had established didn't depend on being the star's sister, and that is a victory much greater than some might imagine. The truth is that a star's relatives (I speak academically here, massa) can be a pain in the ass if that's all they have going for them, which is sometimes the case. Astrid would like to work on more tours but being a female roadie is almost unheard of. When I asked her if she'd asked him she said, "No. I don't want to be like a member of his family mooching on him."

23

Five Concerts in September

From when I said goodbye to Neil and Pegi in Norman, Oklahoma, late on the night of January 11, we weren't in touch for a while. By the time Margaret and I flew to London late in the month the early part of the tour, mostly in small halls, was over. Neil was in Nashville to record, Pegi and Ben with him. During a few days off, the tour crew moved east from California. The slight cold or flu that had given Neil the dizzy spell in the Norman concert persisted. The crew had been swept by what seemed to be influenza. It didn't help to be moving from the heat of Texas to the frost of Colorado and back into the relative comfort of California. In early February when storms piled snow on the eastern seaboard, one storm causing cancellation of Neil's date in the Philadelphia Spectrum, he played the big arenas – still unable to shake the flu, seeing a doctor every place he stopped. As the concerts moved from Worcester, Massachusetts, to Buffalo, to a wildly enthusiastic concert in Toronto, the decision already had been made not to end the tour after Madison Square Garden late in February as planned, but to go on for another five weeks.

He didn't make it. A few weeks later, in Louisville, he collapsed.

For two months doctors had been giving him steroids and other medication. In Louisville he tried to sleep in the bus the afternoon of the show, but couldn't. His hands were sweaty. He had chills, then felt very hot. When he went out onstage and the lights went up, people started crowding around. "It wasn't any hotter than usual but I needed a wet towel to soak the back of my neck after the second song. So I'm out there with this wet towel around my neck. And I really was weak. At one point I couldn't both sing and play. I had to sing and stop playing just to finish one song."

He did get through the first set, but on the way offstage walked right into one of the monitors. "Then somebody grabbed me and supported me and I was mumbling, 'There's really something wrong with me.' I lay down on the floor of the dressing room. When the doctor came, it was the county coroner – it sure gave people quite a start, later, when the county coroner came out on the stage to make an announcement . . . but that was later. He told me that I was exhausted, and started giving me Gatorade and chemicals to try to get my blood sugar up. But during that time I was on the floor, I remember lying face down on the floor and seeing the carpet very clearly. My eyes were open and I was looking right into the carpet. I couldn't move. Then it was as if I was seeing the whole scene, myself lying on the carpet, the doctor leaning over me, Pegi with her hand on my back just telling me to stay aware, stay there, everything was going to be okay. Meanwhile, I was up there, up at the ceiling, watching. I could see the whole thing. I'd heard about that but I'd never experienced it. I was like another person in the room. I didn't feel like I was part of my body.

"But they got me back together and about half an hour, forty-five minutes later, I walked down the stairs out of the dressing room and into the bus. The doctor gave me a Halcyon pill and said he wanted me to take one every night. I took one, that first night, and slept fourteen hours. I didn't take any more – but for nights after that I had horrible nightmares. Horrible. I thought I'd be all right after a couple of days but it was longer than that. For days back at the ranch I was groggy, walking funny. I kept thinking of what the doctor had told me, 'You've lost everything; you need to get it back.' It took about three weeks for me to get straight, get back to the point where I could think straight. Then I immediately got back in the groove. Everything was okay."

He had hated to cancel the Louisville show. "I *really* don't like to cancel shows. It's harmful. It's never the same after you cancel. The crowd, they just don't understand, no matter what."

Neil was right about the harm of a cancellation. While he'd been feeling he was somewhere near the ceiling watching the scene around his prone form in the dressing room, paying customers had been booing, throwing stuff on the stage, some battling security people and the police. They calmed down only when the county coroner appeared, and they did not know until he spoke what his message would be.

I was in London when I heard of the Louisville collapse and cancellation of the last few dates in the tour – I got it in the form of scare rumours from Neil's fans. At the same time I also had a letter from Astrid saying that Neil was okay. We didn't have a phone in our Maida Vale flat so when I might have called on impulse, I didn't, although sometimes I wandered around our spartan quarters or sat in the nearby Truscott Arms, worrying a little and wishing he was sitting there with a pint of Yorkshire bitter, too.

I phoned Neil when we got back to Canada. No answer. I called David Cline. "He's fine," David said. "When he got here from Louisville he rested for a couple of weeks, doing nothing, and then he was back in shape, writing songs full speed, getting some musicians in to record. He had a good run. Just about got a new album in the can. He's calling it *Old Ways* – for now, anyway. Then he took off in the *Ragland* for a while."

A couple of weeks later I asked Neil, "When is *Old Ways* coming out?"

He dragged out, "Well-l-l, it isn't, right now. I got into writing some newer songs in the old 1950s rock style, a lotta fun. We recorded them and some others from that period and put that into an album. We had the record people up and played both *Old Ways* and the newer one, *Everybody's Rockin'*, which is about as far removed from the *Trans* kind of sound as it's possible to get. Anyway, we're putting out *Everybody's Rockin'* first. *Old Ways* will make it, later."

He told me he soon would take to the road again, starting on the first of July, breaking for a few weeks in August and then going on until New York around October 1.

They opened in Wichita July 1, travelled for a month, played Vancouver on July 31 and travelled homeward on August 1. The next day Pegi and Neil woke in their own bedroom on the ranch. It was their fifth wedding anniversary. The break in the tour had been

planned that way, so they could be in their own house, in control of
their own time, five years after the first day of their marriage.

Their July dates had been far from my home – Wichita; Kansas City;
Omaha; Minneapolis; East Troy, Wisconsin; Peoria; Memphis; Tulsa;
Dallas; Houston; San Antonio; Las Cruces, New Mexico; Tempe,
Arizona; Laguna Hills, California; Sacramento; Seattle; Vancouver.
When the tour resumed late in August the dates were better for me.
Besides, I like my own place in the summer, with kids visiting, seeing
my Omemee area friends, going to my desk in the cool basement where
I write a few hours a day. Instead of what I once had done, cut and
hauled my own wood for the furnace and fireplace, I hired some help. I
had my rituals, ten lengths per morning in the pool while the tea
steeped; tea on the deck with *The Globe and Mail* or, Margaret's addiction, the London *Sunday Times*. Congratulating God on the fine
summer. Still, I started getting a little itchy when I looked at some of
the tour dates – Saratoga Springs on September 4, Buffalo and
Pittsburgh later the same week, other places only a day's drive away.
But I felt like company this time. I asked Margaret but she had some
deadlines to meet. A friend of mine, Dave Toms, a television producer
in his thirties, lit up like a Christmas tree when I invited him along.
When Neil's *Trans* album came out the winter before, Dave had written
to me in London that when he listened to it the first time he hadn't felt
such awe since the first time, in the 1960s, he heard *Sgt. Pepper's Lonely
Hearts Club Band*. A few months later when Dave played *Everybody's
Rockin'* the first time, he laughed all the way through it. For a few years
he'd been a rock musician himself, until he got tired of being broke and
hungry all the time.

I decided that I'd be ready for a break about mid-September. We'd
drive to Dayton, Ohio, around the seventeenth. That was the plan, but
it didn't work that way. I got itchier. I looked at Neil's schedule again. I
know that when I have an instinct to do something I should do it. A
week before the Dayton date there'd be a concert at Pine Knob, north
of Detroit, and the next night at Lansing, an easy drive away. Two concerts would be fine. We'd come home in midweek. Again, it didn't work
that way.

My system for visiting Neil on the road has both good points and draw-
backs. We don't plan ahead much. I like it that way. I don't like my

every minute scheduled for me any more than he does. So any plans we make are on the spur of the moment. A good point is that I always know where his bus will be parked (unless, as sometimes happens, for mechanical or other reasons it goes somewhere else). A mild drawback is that when I find the bus with no sign of life I don't know whether he's been asleep for forty-five minutes or eight hours – as when Dave and I drove into the big shopping plaza parking lot near the Somerset Inn on Big Beaver Road at Troy, Michigan, about ten that morning. Neil's bus and the two others for crew and musicians were parked and quiet. I knew that Neil would be on his bus, all others in the hotel. I knew that they had had a long haul from their previous date in West Virginia, but I didn't know when they had arrived. Neither did the hotel desk. Tour manager Glen Palmer had a room, but I wouldn't rouse him at ten in the morning (a good decision, he told me later, as he'd got to bed at six A.M.).

I parked beside the bus, looking for signs of movement inside. Saw none. When privacy is intended, every heavy and impenetrable window blind is fully extended, as it was then. When the thick drapes behind the driver's seat are pulled together, even if someone is up moving around in the forward quarters, galley-cum-living-room, it is unseen. This closed-up stance told me Neil might or might not be on the bus, but that Pegi and Ben definitely weren't. Ben wakens as early as any other little boy. I didn't knock. Not a hard decision. I thought of taping a note to the door, but didn't. At the Somerset Inn's desk I left a message for Glen Palmer to pass to Neil that we were around and would see him later, we were heading for Pine Knob.

The concert stage at Pine Knob, thirty-odd miles north of Detroit, was spawned by rock music. There are dozens of concert bowls more or less like it across North America and Europe. Basically it's an amphitheatre with a partial roof. The few thousand covered seats slope down to a stage fully equipped for all the electronic and mechanical requirements of the modern rock concert. Beyond the covered seats the bowl itself extends in all directions up steep grassy slopes. In such bowls, if there are 5,000 covered seats (some have more) there will be room for 10,000 or 12,000 (or more) customers on the grass. They bring coolers and picnic baskets and – in cool or wet weather – groundsheets, parkas, umbrellas. These bowls are in the countryside, usually not even in the suburbs, but right out where if you were not growing crowds at thirteen dollars or so a ticket you'd be growing corn, grain, cotton, or whatever the local agriculture ran to. At Pine Knob there is not even a gas station within a mile of the main gate, let alone a village or store.

When we arrived about noon, eight hours before the concert, my 1973 Olds Cutlass was one of only four or five cars, all in a clump near the gate. Empty parking lots stretched for nearly half a mile around. Security would tighten as the day went on, but at that moment it consisted of two young men throwing a Frisbee back and forth at the main gate. Down the steep pavement that led to access doors behind the stage, I could see the parked semis. When we walked down there we found that much of the sets and equipment already had been unloaded.

In the next two or three hours we had coffee from a backstage table laid out with platters of Danishes and doughnuts, and talked awhile with Tim Foster, stage manager, and Tim Mulligan, vice-president sound. Then we took coffee into the rows of empty seats and watched the set go up, a sight that always fascinates me. Meri Took, an Australian who with his girl friend Deborah Vincent were sole survivors in this crew from the *Trans* tour crew of Europe a year earlier, was carrying joints and elbows and lengths of metal scaffolding aloft and fitting them into place at the rear of the stage. Meri climbed like a second-storey man. Deborah, strong and lean in shorts, was checking electrical connections to one of the recording consoles out front. Lyle Centola, the production manager, was supervising as giant speakers were lined up in groups of three, then raised five or six feet so another group of three could be attached. The process was repeated with three more until there was a bank of them on each side of the stage. Every man in the crew was strong, wiry or powerfully built. Mark Fetter, the lighting man, was dealing with power cables running everywhere, including back to Tim Mulligan's vast and intricate sound console set in the middle of the covered seats. A big crate was moved into place at stage right under the supervision of Tim Foster, the crew treating it as carefully as if it contained fine crystal. One side was unbolted to reveal Neil's grand piano standing on end. With extreme care eight men standing shoulder to shoulder began to bring it down, one of them Tim Foster, murmuring instructions as the piano was lowered gently to its legs. A quiet man at stage left began tuning an old upright piano there. A chandelier above the grand piano flickered briefly in a test to show that it was hooked up.

It was mid-afternoon before Neil's bus rolled in, Paul Williamson driving. He told me Neil was up there somewhere just back from golf with Anthony Crawford, whom I hadn't met then – one of the singing trio Neil called the Redwood Boys. Neil strolled down the hill with Anthony, a slim and intense man in his twenties who (he later told me) had switched while still in high school from being a miler (a 4:21 mile when he was fifteen years old) to being a singer. Neil and I hugged and Neil said, "Hey, Anthony, meet my dad." After a minute or two Anthony went to the musicians' bus. Neil said, "Come on in," and I followed him into his bus where Don Perri, Paul Williamson's backup, was standing in the galley filling a big saucepan with mince beef.

"Spaghetti sauce," Neil said, looking at it. "Great!"

Perri: "We're out of spaghetti, tomatoes, and stuff. I'll have to go and get what I need."

Neil said, "Send a runner." The promoter supplies cars and drivers for errands.

Perri also had a large serving spoon full of finely crushed garlic, which Neil made into a garlic sandwich. He bit into it, smiling. "Anybody comes over the edge of the stage, I'll just blow on him. Ever eat garlic sandwiches?"

I laughed. "No."

"I've got a little tickle in my throat. Garlic is amazing. Kills anything."

The night before, Dave Toms and I had stayed in Windsor, across the river from Detroit, with my brother, Bob, and his wife, Merle, Neil's closest aunt and uncle in his babyhood and early boyhood in Toronto. They'd helped him with food and shelter long ago when he'd been playing in Detroit around the time of the Motown recording, but hadn't seen him since. They'd asked me to line up something. "We don't want just a few minutes either – we want to really see him," Merle commanded. I was supposed to let them know whether to come to Pine Knob or Lansing. When I started to mention this Neil broke in, "Yeah! I phoned Uncle Bob and told them to come here. We'll get together after the concert. They're coming."

In a little while I went to find Dave Toms and bring him down to meet Neil. As we talked, Glen Palmer came in. Glen, strongly built, dark-haired, has an air about him that is vaguely military: neat shirt, knee socks, neat shorts, clean shoes. Neil said, "Oh, my uncle and aunt are coming tonight so I'm going to stick around after the concert to visit with them."

Glen: "So no quick takeoff? That changes?"

"Right."

Then Newell Alexander, the ultra-sincere Dan Clear of the pre-concert and intermission video shows, arrived through the open bus door in a sweat suit. "Ready for the walk, Neil?" he asked.

"Yeah. Right now." Neil asked if I'd like to come along. It's part of his attempt to stay healthy. Usually he walks four or five miles a day, but this day had played golf so would only do about two more. I said I'd hang around watching the setting up.

When Dave and I sat down again, still the only ones in the rows of seats, the preliminary sound check began.

"Gimme Neil's banjo!" Tim Mulligan called from his console.

On the stage, Larry Cragg, assistant stage manager, played a few licks on the banjo. The amplified sound rolled up the hill. Some early arrivals and people from the beer kiosks and food bars beyond the top rim of the bowl ran into sight at the top of the bowl to see who was playing.

"Now the guitar!" called Tim.

Joel Bernstein did a good imitation of Neil's guitar work, singing a little.

"Okay."

Neil came out about five. There were others with him: the Redwood Boys and the 1950s-style group Neil was calling the Shocking Pinks – Ben Keith, Tim Drummond, Karl Himmel. Most of the sound check was fairly perfunctory, but then there was a long jamming session on a new song Neil had been working on, one in the *Everybody's Rockin'* mode, with Neil playing some very hot guitar, Ben Keith on alto saxophone, Vito Toledo (the stage name for a Nashville lawyer named Craig Hayes) on baritone sax, Tim Drummond on an old upright string bass, the Redwood Boys singing into one microphone except when one of them, Larry Byrom, was playing trumpet or piano. In a new song, "Get Gone," Anthony Crawford and Neil sang chin to chin, Anthony giving Neil the same kind of work-out that he used to get playing guitar against Steve Stills. That part was as good as any concert.

I realize here that names don't mean much when you don't know the people. Some went way back in Neil's life, others he had met only a few months earlier. Tim Drummond and Ben Keith I'd met years earlier, I'm not entirely sure when, but it seems to me that when you know where they and Karl Himmel and the Redwood Boys come from, and why, it tells more about rock music than the wild crowds, the rushes for the stage, the adulation of the fans; maybe helps illuminate from a different vantage point the deep feeling this all-American music inspires.

Tim Drummond is a cheerful, medium-sized man in his early forties. When he was a kid in Canton, Illinois, he used to hang around after-hours clubs in nearby Peoria. One night, he says, laughing, he "saw a guy playing guitar, and the way the girls looked at him. So I went home and bought a guitar." Six months later he was playing guitar in a pick-up band. "One day a guy called me and said his bass player was gone, he needed a bass. 'Can you play bass?' I said, 'Can I call you back?' I ran down to the corner music store and took a bass from the rack and tried it. Then I ran back home and called the guy and said, 'Yeah, I can play bass.'" But like thousands of other hopefuls, he couldn't make a living at it then. He was working on a railroad gang laying ties when Conway Twitty, needing a fill-in bass player fast, called him. Tim spent three weeks that time in London, Ontario. "That was when I got a taste of what that echelon of music was like. I decided that unless I was good enough to play on that level, I'd do something else." He went back home and found a factory job and was working there when Conway called him again, this time with a permanent offer.

Later, touring with James Brown, Tim was the only white in the group. They travelled far and wide, including to Vietnam, where once they were under fire. When he got back he was sick of touring and decided to settle down in Nashville, where he had lots of sessions in recording studios.

One day early in 1971, a couple of months after Neil played Carnegie Hall, Tim was walking down a street when a friend of his, a photographer, called to him, "Hey, Timmy, Neil Young's over in the studio! Come and meet him." That afternoon after he and Neil played a little, Neil said, "Would you like to come back tonight and play?" Tim did, and was surprised to find James Taylor and Linda Ronstadt there with Neil, as well. They recorded "Heart of Gold" and "Old Man" that night, both to become big singles from the best-selling album *Harvest*. "I sort of liked the guy," Tim told me, meaning Neil, relating all this backstage one night. "I told Neil I'd go out with him if he wished, anytime." Now when Neil is putting bands together, Tim is often there.

When Neil got the idea for the Shocking Pinks, he told Tim he'd be playing string bass. Tim hadn't played that for twenty years, but was playing it now.

Ben Keith is tall, over six feet. His nickname is King. He has a kindly face with a lot of miles on it, and when I met him this time I remembered that long ago Nils Lofgren, describing Jack Nitzsche as difficult to work with, said that in contrast Ben Keith was beautiful, quiet, easy-going, "just one of those guys you like to be around." He was born in 1937 in Fort Riley, Kansas, and lived later in Alvaton, Kentucky. His father was an army officer with a talent for invention – he'd helped develop the famous Jeep, had helped design improvements for tank turrets, and in some things, such as when rock music came along, he was like a lot of parents of the time: he hated the noise and thought this music was corrupting the youth of America.

When Ben was fifteen, he bought a guitar for seven dollars. His father disapproved. Ben played so much that he injured a finger, damaging the bone. When it had to be operated on, he couldn't play normal guitar. But he'd seen people play what then were called Hawaiian guitars, sliding a smooth piece of steel up and down the strings. He found out how to tune his guitar for that method of playing. Then he bummed an empty lipstick tube from his sister to use as the steel. That's when he started becoming one of the best pedal steel men in the business.

One night backstage I was talking to Karl Himmel, to me the most intense of the Shocking Pinks. He'd been playing drums since he was seven, thirty years earlier. "And dancing," he said. "Not step-dancing or that country stuff, but like Fred Astaire, Gene Kelly. I dunno, I guess this business was in the cards for me from when I was a kid." He was born in Houma, Louisiana. "My grandmother, even, was in vaudeville. My mother was a good big-band singer, Dorothy Menville, back when the big bands were really big, on radio."

Another with the Shocking Pinks, playing horn, singing, and doing a cigar-chomping role as a gangster-type named Vito Toledo on a video part of the Shocking Pinks show, Nashville lawyer Craig Hayes is tall, burly, polite, affable, and not really a cigar-smoker. He grew up in Washington, D.C., across from Griffiths Stadium playing music and becoming a sports nut. As we got to know one another (he knew I'd been a sportswriter) he told me that as a kid he religiously read the sports column of a man I knew, one of the best in the business, Shirley Povich. Craig is lawyer to Ben and Tim. "When they were coming out on this tour and asked me to come along, I just said sure. I needed a break. I'd been working too hard. I love this."

Larry Byrom, thirty-four, and Rick Palombi, twenty-eight, were Anthony Crawford's cohorts with the Redwood Boys. Larry was born in Alabama and played lead guitar with Steppenwolf when he was only nineteen or twenty. In Nashville he is mainly a guitarist, but sings and also plays hot piano. "I never wanted to be anything but a musician," he said. Rick started playing and singing when he was in fourth grade in Detroit. Still, for a while, he wanted to be a scientist. He laughingly referred to his haircut as a "tour haircut" and said his family – now living in Toledo – kidded him about it: long sides, crewcut on top. Like Anthony Crawford, he is under contract to a music publisher in Nashville, which pays him a weekly retainer, enough to eat on. When the tour reached Dayton a week after I arrived, Rick would have his own cheering section – his mother and sisters down from Toledo to see their boy.

At Pine Knob when the sound check finished with that rousing new-song rehearsal, Anthony and Neil duelling with their voices at one mike, the stage suddenly was deserted for dinner break in a room behind stage right. Dave and I climbed up the hill and down the other side into the beer-and-food area, bought beer and burritos. We ate at a little table, watching early arrivals do the same while clustered around a small sunken area where two youths played and sang. Then we decided we should watch the gate for Neil's Uncle Bob and Aunt Merle. We didn't want them standing there baffled, not knowing where to turn. We never did see them, but our watch near the battery of turnstiles at the entrance area had its value.

As the crowds began to stream in we could see what a remarkable mixture of people made up Neil's audience: hippie-type women, some with babies strapped to their backs; young men in exaggerated combat outfits with tight pants and high well-polished boots; new wave purple-haired kids, probably *Trans* fans; Vietnam veterans with an air of indefinable something that set them apart; one family that obviously was three generations – a couple of teenage girls, their parents, and a grandmother. The majority were casually dressed young Americans, from jeans-and-jackets to trendies. But the question was, who else, except probably Bob Dylan, could bring all these contrasts together in one place?

Entering the gate, each person carrying a cooler would lift the lid unbidden for the contents check. No liquor could be brought in. Huge bins on wheels stood nearby and there was intermittent crashing as bottles full, half full, or almost empty were taken from their owners and tossed into the bins. Men and women alike stood, legs straddled, as the gatemen frisked their legs and bodies for hidden bottles. Nobody protested. They knew the rules. The ones who were caught trying to bring in liquor took its seizure with apparent equanimity. The only one who argued was a man with a camera. He pointed to the sign over the gate that listed forbidden objects and complained that only movie cameras were forbidden. But he had to leave his camera outside.

Near concert time Bob and Merle still had not shown. As the crowd gathered in the cool evening we went to our seats. Dan Clear was seen from time to time on the screen, with interviews and deadpan advice – such as telling people to "get down" if there was a nuclear attack during the concert. Near the end of his pre-concert video show, he always said that now they'll go to a camera in Neil's dressing room. "And here he is being fitted with his wireless microphone!" he announces as the screen shows a roadie wrapping a hundred feet of heavy-duty extension cord around Neil's neck. When Dan got to that point, and we knew that in two or three minutes the concert would begin, we were figuring Uncle Bob and Aunt Merle just hadn't made it. Then there on the screen was Neil, in a chair, Merle bending over him laughing and talking, while in the doorway Bob was reaching out and plucking at her sleeve, saying once in a while, "Come on, Merlie, we've gotta get out of here, he's busy." They didn't know they were on camera. Merle still didn't know it a few minutes later when Glen Palmer had them ushered down to sit beside us. Merle is a dear friend of mine from our teenage days in Winnipeg, before she met my brother, and she speaks her mind in a real auntie-like way. After all, she has known Neil since he was in diapers.

"What were you saying to him?" I asked her.

"I just told him I was glad he got his hair cut, but why did he have to play so loud?" she said, and then stuck her fingers in her ears as the first crashing bars came through the amplifiers and Neil began to sing "Comes a Time." She says she can hear the words better with her fingers in her ears. She spent the whole concert that way.

It was an interesting concert for many reasons. One was that Neil had rarely played better. His guitar work on "Down by the River" was stunning. Same on "Don't Be Denied" and "Ohio." But something was bothering him. It's something that bothers many artists. The people who would like to be in the front row, hanging on every word, hammering the stage, shouting in ecstasy, people who would rather starve to death or die of thirst than give up such a favoured place, aren't always there. Often the front seats are apportioned according to one form or another of favouritism to friends of the management. The ones who did have these prime seats were moving in and out a lot buying beer and food. Like a baseball crowd. Once Neil stopped and looked at two empty seats in the front row and read the numbers aloud: "One-oh-three and one-eleven, you're late!" (Joni Mitchell in Toronto a few days earlier looked at her concert's front rows and said, "I hope there aren't any freebies in these front rows – this is where the people who really want to hear, and pay for it, should be.")

When the concert came near its end, to the point where all through July and the last week of August and this far into September, Neil had sung "Sugar Mountain" and then introduced his 1950s rock segment with the Shocking Pinks, the Redwood Boys, and the dancing Pinkettes, he didn't. He simply left the stage, came back for an encore, and that was it. The crowd booed. He didn't come back. They booed more. But it was over.

When Bob and Merle and I made our way through the crowd back to the bus a few minutes later, a writer from *Variety* touched my arm and said, "Do you know why he cancelled the last part of the show?" I didn't. Inside the bus Neil was slumped back on one of the settees with a long-necked bottle of beer, talking to Astrid. She had come by train from Toronto to Windsor. Glen Palmer had sent a car to bring her and a friend the rest of the way. Neil hugged Bob and Merle and then sank back down again. The shortened concert obviously was on his mind. He burst out, "That crowd just didn't deserve the Shocking Pinks! I dunno, I guess I'll get criticized, but I just have to follow my instincts."

As we talked, Glen Palmer appeared behind my brother and said, "There's a music writer here from the *Detroit Free Press*, a friend of mine. He'd like to see you. I told him that wasn't possible, but that I'd ask if you had any comment on the concert tonight."

It was the gentlest possible way of giving Neil a chance to explain his cancellation of the Pinks – or to say anything else he wanted, even to give an excuse, if he wished, that he wasn't feeling well, or whatever. All of us waited for his answer.

"No, there's really nothing I want to say," he said. "Just tell him I hope he enjoyed the concert."

A little later in more private circumstances, he had a harsher word for the Pine Knob crowd, prefacing it by saying that he knew there were people out there he would have liked to play more for – but the total of the response . . . "Well," he said, "you don't put your best horse out on a gravel track, do you?"

Why did Pine Knob seem like such a gravel track to Neil that night? One opinion was that the enthusiasm from the thousands up on the grass simply wasn't getting back downhill. Otherwise, anyone's guess is as good as mine. There is never a provision on tickets or advertising that states: Neil Young will sing twenty-one songs tonight. They don't get listed, as on an album cover. On this tour each night he sang a mix with a lot of craft in it. The Buffalo Springfield fans got theirs; the *Harvest* fans got theirs; the *Trans* fans probably wish they got more of theirs, and every night except in Pine Knob the people who dance in the aisles at the *Everybody's Rockin'* stuff got theirs in the form of something many of them have never known: a dance party. He sang what he felt – there were no *Tonight's The Night* songs in the concert. But there was "Comes a Time," the gently melodic and upbeat song that he wrote not long before he and Pegi got serious, and there were the vivid images of "Powderfinger." And almost every night he gave them the Shocking Pinks, music in the genre of his nights as an eleven-year-old with his radio turned low under his pillow in Pickering, and tuned to CHUM. But not this night.

Half an hour or so later Bob said, "Well, I guess we'd better go," and, to Astrid, "are you kids going on to Lansing or what?"

"We're taking a train from Windsor to Toronto tomorrow," Astrid replied.

"Well, you might as well come with us then. We've got lots of room at our place and we'll drive you to the train tomorrow."

Astrid thanked him and said she'd just be a minute, she wanted to see a friend on one of the buses.

"We'll see you tomorrow in Lansing, Daddy," Neil said. "You driving over tonight?"

"No, but we'll probably be there by ten, ten-thirty in the morning."

"Good. We can have a game of golf."

"A long time since we played golf," I said.

"It sure is."

It was nearly an hour after the concert by then. As I started my car, Neil's bus went by. We fell in among other cars which were honking when they saw the bus and followed until we were out of the parking lot, and then went our own way for a couple of icy draft beers at the Holiday Inn in Pontiac. Then I read awhile – a reread, after thirty years or more, of Joyce Cary's *Aissa Saved*. Maybe a restoration of perspective.

When we'd been talking about playing golf the next day in Lansing, Neil said he'd be parked near the Harley Hotel, where the crew would stay. When Dave and I got there near noon the Shocking Pinks' bus was in the lot, but not Neil's. We figured Neil's bus had stopped along the way for sleep. We ate breakfast and called Glen Palmer at noon to say we were at a motel across the road, and did he know where Neil was? He didn't, but as we got back to our room the phone rang. Glen told us that the bus had just called and was at a 76 Truck Stop a few miles away. "Neil wants you to go right over and go golfing."

It took us half an hour of driving up and down highways to find the place. Away at the back of dozens of big rigs two buses were parked. Neil and Paul and Don Perri were up. Neil's bus had lost its air pressure just as they rolled into the place. Neil was shaving, cleaning his teeth, asking, "Where's the nearest golf course, I wonder?" I walked over to the busy truck stop restaurant for directions.

"Go out of here," the woman on the cash said, "turn right, go three lights, turn left, go four lights and you'll be there, it's right on the corner." Either she golfed there herself or a lot of her customers did. When I walked back the hundred yards or so to the bus, Neil was outside waiting for me. We left a minute later in my old Olds, Neil beside me, Dave in the back.

I don't know if Neil feels the same way, but it seems to me that each time we're together the give and take of our times past, times present, and time to come becomes easier. We were on this flat straight four-laner near Lansing with the trucks and vans and hot-rodders. Something, a boat on a trailer or on the roof of a car, reminded me of something you've gotta tell a man with a 105-foot yacht.

"Hey, you know," I said, "this year they've made a boat-launching place where the old swimming hole in Omemee used to be. The government did it, concrete launching ramp, parking lot, the works. They wiped out all those old boathouses that used to be under the trees at the side of the swimming hole."

As I drove I thought of the swimming hole. I used to swim across the deep part of the river on my back, with Neil riding my stomach. The nearest house was that of Austin and Bessie Hayes. One day, fishing from the Mill Bridge, Neil hooked himself in the abdomen, the hook going right through the fold of skin. He carried his fishing pole, held so the hook in him would stay steady, wouldn't pull, and walked across the road to where Austin Hayes, my friend Jay's dad, was sitting on his front steps, a round and cheerful man who had farmed much of his life before coming to live in town.

"Say, Mr. Hayes, do you think you could get this hook out for me?"

Mr. Hayes, with four sons of his own all raised and away, got pliers to cut the hook and carefully worked the two pieces out. He washed the patch of skin and put iodine and a Band-Aid on the cut. Then Neil went back to the Mill Bridge to resume fishing. There was no tetanus shot, no crying. Austin Hayes told me about it later. It became part of local folklore, not because Neil became famous, but because he was an Omemee kid who didn't cry, didn't run home, and didn't quit fishing because of an accident that could happen to anyone. He was five at the time.

We were still on the highway near Lansing, counting lights.

"I bought a boat trailer this year," I said. I'd got it as soon as I came back from England (if you don't get the things you want when you're sixty-five, you're not going to get them), and I was looking forward to getting my twelve-foot aluminum boat with the four-horse Johnson out on the river to fish and see the carp in their sex dance, and the big blue herons, and the rest of the familiar river scene. For a couple of years Margaret and I had been lifting the boat on and off the 1973 Ford pickup, and I thought I could indulge myself with a boat trailer.

Neil was still thinking about the swimming hole being gone.

"Did they fix up another place for the kids to swim?" he asked, looking sideways at me.

"Yeah. Over on the pond." That's the big mill pond upstream from the mill dam, where big muskies still live. "They trucked in sand to make a beach. It's near the school where you started. Past Cap's place."

"Cap's Cabins!" he laughed. "They still there?"

"Yep."

Cap's Cabins (where Rassy and Bob and Neil and I once stayed for a month after renting our house and preparing to leave Omemee) are on the edge of the pond and had been next to the old two-storey brick school. Some country kids used to ride horseback winter and summer to get to school. Its yard was a gentle grassy slope that ended marshily on the shore of the pond.

We turned left, as directed, at the third light.

"Is that old school still there?"

"No. It was empty, then burned, then was torn down. The high school kids are bussed to Lindsay, and the public-school kids come by bus from all around to Lady Eaton Memorial School back on the land we used to own, between our house and the railroad station."

We were counting lights again.

"Hey," I said, "I was past one of your other schools the other day, too. The two-roomer on the Brock Road at Pickering. Somebody sells air-conditioners there now." The place where Neil had played the rich shepherd in the Nativity that Christmas.

"Yeah?" His icons were disappearing one by one. He laughed. "That was the neatest school I ever went to. At recess we'd go down to the edge of the water, a little creek, and catch frogs." He laughed again. "We had a baseball team and we'd go and play other schools in little towns like Brougham."

We were at the fourth light, and could see golfers to our right. We turned in and parked.

The greens fee for nine holes (all we had time for) was five dollars, including club rental. Good repaint balls were three for a dollar, tees fifteen cents. It cost eighteen dollars and change for the three of us. There weren't many people around. We took off, Neil hitting the ball pretty well. It was a long course, with difficult par threes and fours and two long par fives on the first nine.

When we holed out, Neil had shot a forty-nine, not bad on that course. I was sixty-one in my first game in fifteen years. (I used to have a sixteen handicap.) Dave was sixty-nine, in his first game since he was a kid. Neil asked the time. He was thinking about time, now. In the car, he was drumming his fingers on the roof, not so much in impatience as in something, a tempo, he was working out. I could hear him singing something softly in the passenger seat.

When we wheeled into the truck stop the buses were gone, so we drove downtown to the Lansing Civic Center. Getting there, Neil left the car all but on the run. "Thanks, Daddy," he said, and shook hands with Dave. "Enjoyed the game!" he said. "See you!" He disappeared into the bus, parked with the semis and other buses; back in his routine.

That night the crowd obviously had more of what Neil wanted. A white-haired man in his forties or fifties sat next to me with an impassive expression and his arms folded, but everywhere else the place was jumping. Dan Clear had told me after the Pine Knob concert that he'd expected me in to do an interview that intermission. But he hadn't asked me and I'd not even thought of it. This time he did ask. Soon after Neil ended the first set with "Don't Be Denied," Dan Clear introduced me with, "I know, but the audience doesn't, that you're Neil's dad."

I said yes, I was, and found myself saying, "Yeah, I'm the bad guy in those first four lines of 'Don't Be Denied': '*When I was a young boy, my mama said to me, your daddy's leaving home today, I think he's gone to stay, we packed up all our bags and drove out to Winnipeg.*'" From sleepless nights and worried days to a vaudeville turn in only twenty-four short years.

I knew as we went on that I really didn't want to go back to the seat I'd had for the first set. It would mean people coming up to me and wanting to talk about Neil. That's all right, but some other time. When they were talking to me I couldn't concentrate on the stage. So I went to the far back of the hall. It wasn't far enough. Two beautiful young women came to me and talked. When they left one of them put her arms around me and kissed me and said, "Pass that kiss on to Neil. Tell him it's from Norah Lopez." Ushers came up and sat with me to talk. Others came by. I was someone they could touch as a surrogate for Neil. When people asked me for autographs I signed them, but that rush was pretty well over by the time I first saw the Shocking Pinks segment of the show. Neil was brought back late, near the end, by cheers and flickering lighters to say, "Thanks for bringing me back," and then saying that he'd like to roll back the years and they could help by singing with him. He sang "Sugar Mountain," and on the video screen behind him the numbers 1983 appeared. He went back to the screen and made a pushing motion with his guitar that started the numbers rolling back, 1982, 1981, 1980 and on. When he left the stage not everyone in the audience knew what was happening. Pink-garbed roadies began swiftly changing the set, bringing in an old-fashioned microphone, old-fashioned instruments. When the screen had rolled back to 1957 Neil charged back to the stage dressed in a white suit with his hair greased and shoved up at the front like Elvis used to, and stood at the piano and hammered out 1950s rock accompanied by Tim, Ben, Karl, Vito; the string bass, the saxophones, the drums, the Redwood Boys singing, the dancing-girl Pinkettes doing kicks (Pegi was head Pinkette when there). The crowd danced wildly through five, six, seven songs in the *Everybody's Rockin'* style. All I could see from the back was dancing humans and the silhouettes of arms held high shaking in unison against the stage lights.

24

I Just Couldn't Leave

I'm not sure of the exact instant when I decided that instead of two concerts, I'd stay for five. Eight months earlier in Dallas and Norman, Oklahoma, I'd found myself wishing that I didn't have to go to England right then, or otherwise think about making my living, and could stay for the whole tour. The feeling now was the same. Which meant looking at the map and finding that from Lansing's Tuesday night concert we would drive past Chicago and northwest to the Poplar Creek Music Theater near Arlington, Illinois, for a show Thursday, South to Bloomington for the University of Indiana concert Friday, east for the Sunday concert to be filmed in Dayton. Once decided, I felt light and free, like a travelling fly on the wall. This feeling was not based on the prospect of continued daily contact with Neil and the others, or even entirely on the fact that no concert is the same as the last. I had felt the same way at Olympic Games, World Series, Stanley Cups, many other major (at the time) sports events long forgotten now, and even the summer I travelled by ancient bus with the old Winnipeg Maroons through Fargo and Duluth and Wausau and Eau Claire and Crookston for class D baseball games when I was nineteen or twenty. I always just wanted to *be* there. Eyes and ears open.

It was early afternoon Wednesday when Dave and I arrived at the Arlington Hyatt. We weren't intending to stay there, and had watched for cheaper places as we got near, but parked and went in to check at the desk whether the crew had arrived. As I was talking to a clerk, another woman behind the counter was on a phone nearby. She put the phone down and asked, "Are you Mr. Young?"

"Yes."

"Glen Palmer wants to speak to you." She handed me the phone.

I'm told I have a distinctive voice, some say as recognizable in its way as Neil's singing voice, but this was ridiculous. While I was talking to the woman, Glen had recognized my voice in the background. He told me that it wasn't definite yet, but he'd been thinking that a night off would be good for a crew party. If it happened he'd like me to be M.C. So that I would be easily available if this worked out, he asked me to check in at the Hyatt. My room would be paid for. I said okay. The crew was ambling more or less aimlessly in and out of shops around the lobby, much like a hockey or baseball or football team on a day off, relaxing, having a few beers, cruising, maybe looking for a Miss Right. Some found her, or reasonable facsimiles. The crew party didn't come off. I never heard it mentioned again. Maybe it was just a ploy to keep me out of cheap motels. But I've been on the road on days off before and know how to handle it in accord with my own, if you can call it this, lifestyle. I decided I was tired. I spent the afternoon in my room with a huge bag of potato chips, a bottle of good rum, and a sheaf of computer print-outs covering every mention of Neil in *The Globe and Mail* in the last six years. You can call that research, mostly of things I already knew. One thing bugged me. I had heard of it a few weeks earlier. Here it was again, an Associated Press item dated August 24 from Los Angeles and headed: "Neil Young sued for child support."

The item said Carrie was asking $10,000 a month because of Zeke's "special needs." Her lawyer said it was about double what Neil had been paying under a longtime informal arrangement. The report said Zeke was six (he was really two weeks short of eleven and had been in school for years) and that Carrie and Neil had lived together from 1974 to 1979 (it was really 1971 to 1974; Neil and Pegi had married in 1978). Neil's lawyer noted that Carrie and Zeke were living in a house provided by Neil. The story didn't mention that this house, paid for and maintained by Neil, had also been home to the man Carrie married in 1982.

I was annoyed by the omissions and inaccuracies (AP is not supposed to be inaccurate) but more annoyed later by a sob-sister interview with Carrie in *People* magazine where the writer appeared to have been taken to the cleaners. He had Carrie living on $500 a month and considering bumping off, for food, a couple of chickens said to be in the back yard. The story didn't mention that taking all her support into account, Neil was providing about $6,200 a month. It was a totally one-sided story. It's hard to know in this case whether to blame Carrie for talking, the reporter for ignoring Neil's side, or the magazine editors for goofing off. I don't think the other major Time-Life publications, *Time* magazine and *Sports Illustrated*, would knowingly put up with that kind of editorial cop-out. At any rate, the eventual judgement by the Superior Court, which learned only at its courtroom hearing about Carrie's 1982 marriage, set the support sum – agreed to by both sides – at around $5,000 a month plus the house, less than Neil had been paying directly or indirectly.

When the *People* reporter had tried to get Neil's version, he had been referred to the court record where it was all set out. What Neil and his lawyers had not found out until weeks after publication was that the court record was sealed, unavailable. However, I have worked for many a city editor who would have laughed in my face if I had turned in a one-sided story with that kind of excuse.

The morning after the day off at Arlington, I found the bus parked outside the Hyatt. Neil and I talked and drank coffee there for a couple of hours. I mentioned *Old Ways*. "Want to hear it?" he said, and played it on a cassette tape. He talked of changes he might make, but I liked it as it was. Later back in the hotel I had a late breakfast with Anthony Crawford and Ben Keith. Anthony commented that Neil pushes him to the limit in his singing; once, not satisfied with one of their duets, Neil had told it to him plainly, "I want blood."

That was a terrible night at Poplar Creek for weather, a great night for the concert. It was almost as if the weather psyched everybody up. Backstage Neil was going around responding with something upbeat to every remark about the weather: "I go my best in the rain! I'm really one of those singin'-in-the-rain guys. A real mudder." As the concert began, latecomers could be seen running towards the theatre with their open umbrellas held directly in front of them against the flat-out rain. The windswept edges of the covered-seats area were wet. Out in the open on the crowded grassy slopes it was that much worse. Onstage, Neil's hair blew straight sideways as he played and sang. His breath streamed out frostily the same way. Balloons from the audience kept blowing onstage; he'd kick them off without interrupting the music.

He opened that night with "The Old Laughing Lady," an old song, and the whole concert was like something done on the deck of a schooner in a storm. The crowd rushed the stage late in the concert and danced. In one hectic Shocking Pinks segment, Vito Toledo ran to the front of the stage and started passing out *Everybody's Rockin'* albums. One was tossed back on the stage and hit Larry Byrom above the eye. It drew blood but he winced only for a second and never stopped his stand-up hammering on the piano. (Vito, later: "I learned something tonight – only give the albums to the front rows. I tried to hand that one back and so many people grabbed that it got broken and then somebody threw it back when they were fighting over it.") Two girls from the audience climbed onstage and began dancing side by side with the Pinkettes. The rain and wind also added to the finale – the video screen showing Neil and the Pinks running offstage into the storm and climbing into a vintage Cadillac, Dan Clear racing alongside for a last few words from Neil. Neil stuck his head out the window and said, "Y'know, this leavin' ya just don't *move* me. I wanta play one more song." Wild applause from the video viewers out front. The band ran back to the stage, and did chorus after chorus.

When they finally left, the car taking off, Neil's last shouted words were "Buy our album! Help us out!"

In Bloomington the next night the video failed in mid-concert and everybody had to improvise from then on, getting through the show without the sound and visuals of the video. "Well, if things were going to go wrong," Neil said, "better here than in Dayton when we're trying to film."

That night before the video failed, Neil drastically flubbed some lines referring to his mother and me at the start of "Don't Be Denied," tried to carry on, then stopped and said to the audience – "That's about my dad and mother, you know. My dad's in the audience tonight and maybe it's the pressure." He started the song again but the effect was not the same: the *feeling* that makes the song so strong had been marred by the correction and repeat. I saw him couple of minutes later, backstage at intermission.

"Shame on you," I called.

He stopped, laughing, and we bantered back and forth. Then, leaving, he called, "Wouldn't it be wonderful if life was as easy to fix as the wrong start to a song?"

I'm winding down, now. I've never known how to finish this, and I still don't. In effect I have been rummaging through my past and sometimes relating it to Neil's present, but when it comes to the time of this particular parting I still have no final judgements springing to mind. I don't even know what I am supposed to be seeking. Once in a while I still think of what I muttered to myself outside Carnegie Hall in 1970, as valid now as it was then, "What the hell happened?" In reality, human beings get to know as much about one another as either wishes to reveal. Irwin Shaw once had a character in a novel think to himself how, late in life, you suffer or profit from the consequences of the acts, or non-acts, of your early manhood. "Nothing is lost, nothing forgotten. The man who had devised the first computer had merely organized the principle of inexorable memory into a circuit of wires and electrical impulses." I am part of Neil's life and he is part of mine. It may be that I have gotten farther below the tip of his iceberg than he has of mine, but even of that I'm not sure. I know of his life only what I can see and feel. The famous are fair game for gossip and rumours and half-truths, or outright lies based on hidden truth, and I hear much about Neil that I simply balance against what I know of his life. I do not care whether it is truth or fiction, what's the difference? What I know is that what he has now is good, his life with his family, and how he relates that to what he is in public. Otherwise, he remains as mysterious to me as he is to others, and as I must be to him if he thinks about it in those terms. Yet I have a slight edge from a non-personal standpoint in that from time to time I can consult the judgement of others, as when I read the book *All American Music: Composition in the Late Twentieth Century*, by *New York Times* music critic John Rockwell, published in 1983 by Alfred A. Knopf. In that book Neil is the only rock 'n' roller given the full treatment, a chapter to himself, as accorded other major composers in genres other than rock 'n' roll. Rockwell remarks that some readers might find Neil's inclusion in this company surprising, but "Young is noteworthy for several reasons: the quality of his songs, the idiosyncratic charisma of his performing style, his elevation of rough simplicity into an art. But another distinction is his sheer, determined longevity in a field that prizes the transient fashions of youth. Neil Young got started a little later than the oldest still-functioning rock stars, men like Bob Dylan, Paul McCartney, and Mick Jagger. But he has sustained a first-class body of work longer than any of them."

In Dayton, once again I stayed – at Elliot's request, this time – at the same hotel as the crew. I drove back and forth to the Harrah Arena. I laughed at Elliot in the hotel lobby. He had ordered a taxi. The pressures on him in this concert, during which they were filming for theatres, video cassettes, and pay TV, were greater than on anyone except Neil. So he was edgy. The girl at the desk, summoning his taxi, held the phone and called to Elliot, "What's your name?" Elliot reacted somewhat as Gene Wilder might do, called upon to play the role in a movie: "Elliot! Elliot! But I'm just looking for a taxi, not a roommate!"

Pegi and Ben flew in Saturday night and were met by Neil at the airport. He took them to spend the night in the bus parked behind the arena instead of using the suite reserved for them at the hotel. He wanted to be near the setting up. Later Saturday night he strolled in to look around and immediately said, "How high's that stage?"

"Five feet."

"That's too high for the film crew to get the shots we want around the front of the stage during the concert. It should be three and a half feet, not five."

The crew worked all night striking sets, pulling cables, waiting for the dismantling of the stage, its rebuilding, putting up sets again, stringing cables again, checking lighting and effects again. He told me about it Sunday morning. "I was popular. I'm going to have T-shirts made with 'Mr. Popularity' on the chest, and below that, 'Pull It Down And Put It Up Again Lower.'"

There were thirty-five people in the film crew under the director Hal Ashby, a calm man of long experience. The film crew and tour crew had to cope with each other. There were no more hitches. On Sunday Neil sometimes stood like a quarterback at an open huddle on the stage: talking, pointing, making hand motions while camera and sound people stood in front of him with Ashby in a hollow inverted U, listening. Neil got into the saddle of the crane camera directly in front of the stage and took it up to full height to look through the view-finder. He squatted on the stage, wearing his guitar, and talked to Tim Mulligan, Larry Johnson, Tim Foster, Joel Bernstein, Lyle Centola, and others of his crew. Once he sat on the stage for a while with his legs crossed like a man at a campfire. He was oddly difficult to pick out among the throngs on the stage; his white shirt hanging over black torn-off shorts seeming to blend with the background. Once he tapped a microphone, found it live and said, "Okay, what's stopping us from continuing?" And later, "Joel, I need a couple of harmonicas – a B flat and a C." And later, amplified, for everyone: "I don't want to do this run-through at show levels. I don't want to sing at all until tonight."

I checked out of the hotel and phoned to book a motel room thirty or forty miles north, so that I could drive that far towards home before I slept. I was around the bus a lot, chatting with Pegi, Ben, Neil, and whoever came by. Pegi had been away from the tour for a week and was tidying and checking the bus supplies, grumbling kiddingly at the mess, making a list of what was needed. "It's awfully hot in here," she said once. "Isn't the air conditioning working?"

Neil, on a settee: "I opened the sunroofs to let some moisture in. It seems awfully dry on my throat."

"Well, it's sure hot."

Neil got up and pushed the buttons that closed the sunroofs. No sign of the temperamental artist.

Pegi, a little later: "I wonder how far it is to a market where I can buy some stuff?"

Me: "About a mile away. I'll drive you."

As we went shopping, Neil put Ben in his stroller and took him for a walk. The large paved parking area around the bus was fringed, in the distance, with trees. They headed that way. Elliot joined them. When we got back Elliot met us, holding out some apples. "You should taste these – picked them right off a tree over there! Never tasted anything like them, so crisp and sweet!" Elliot, a New York and Los Angeles guy, might never have picked an apple off a tree before. Neil looked at me and grinned. He had.

Just as an athlete, an actor, or a musician will key up for a big occasion, Neil had been leading up to this filming all week. It was a hidden or perhaps even recognized part of his cancellation of the Pinks segment in Pine Knob, of his fingers drumming on the car roof after golf in Lansing, his "I want blood" to Anthony over their singing, his fluff in "Don't Be Denied" in Bloomington, even his relaxing while pushing

Ben's stroller that afternoon. In recent concerts I had taken to standing along the wall near the stage. As this one got underway with the six fixed-position cameras and the hand-held one on the stage all rolling film, turning, moving to follow the action, the smallish arena jammed and deafening, Tim Mulligan's hands were flying over the switches, Tim Foster at stage right was wearing a headset, Larry Johnson and Dan Clear at work out of sight in the video room. All the other people I had come to know were crouched, running, standing, making it all work.

Near me a woman stood on her wooden folding chair. Her face wore an expression of such overwhelming happiness that I could not take my eyes off her, except to note that the man she was with did not stand up. It was later I saw that he was in a wheelchair. When the crowd rushed the stage, the woman got down from her chair and pushed her man up to a safe position near the edge, and Dave sprang to link hands with her and keep the crowd back from overrunning the several people in wheelchairs. When the dancing began she came to me. Maybe she had noticed me watching her. She put out both her hands for mine and I went with her and for a long, long time, as long as the Shocking Pinks were up there, we danced. I had been pretty good at jitterbugging around 1939: it wasn't so different now. I sweated and sang and realized that I never had seen a woman that happy, that transported – and that it came from Neil and his music, and in that way she represented all the millions, and I had been holding her hands.

When the concert was over I went backstage. Elliot thanked me for doing my intermission turn once again on the video with Dan Clear. I walked out to the stage where the dismantling was going on (tomorrow night, Kalamazoo), said many goodbyes, and then went backstage again. Pegi came up to me and said, "You're leaving?" I said yes, and we embraced. Holding her I said thanks to her, for a lot. Nobody was being allowed in Neil's dressing room. The woman guarding it knew I was Neil's father. She opened the door for me. He was sitting alone on the floor over by a television monitor, his back to it, leaning against the stand, slumped, a bottle of beer on the floor beside him, looking happy and wrung out.

"Hi, Daddy!" he said.

I sat on a settee facing him and told him it had been wonderful.

"You're sweating," he said.

"I was dancing."

He laughed. We talked on for five or ten minutes. I got up finally and thanked him for the hospitality and said I'd be going now, hitting the road.

"You're going, tonight?" he said, looking up at me. "Right now?"

I nodded. He put down his beer and got up, all in one motion. "Well, you can't go without a hug," he said, and we stood holding each other tightly for a few long seconds, clasped together, father and son no matter what else.

Postscript: Before Christmas, Neil told me happily that Pegi was going to have a baby. Amber Jean was born, alert and pretty, on May 15, 1984. I visited during Pegi's pregnancy and sometimes fussed about telling her she should not sweep this, or lift that, even though she was being very careful. I slept in a room across the hall from Ben and, being a light sleeper, would hear him stir and make his first morning noises, sometimes crying a little. I would look at my watch: six, six-thirty. Then he would become quiet, right away. I never heard anyone come, but each time would stay awake listening to the birds outside and thinking of my morning tea. I would wait a few minutes so as not to disturb Ben, then silently open my door and see the reason he'd settled down – Neil was lying there with him, both asleep again. This would happen each morning. At the first sound of Ben on the room intercom, Neil would make a silent dash from his and Pegi's room. And I would see them, Neil in his long robe stretched out above the covers, one arm holding Ben, the two heads close in sleep, early morning in a good family in California.

Afterword to
the 1997 Edition

In 1984 the original manuscript of this book ended with the birth of Neil and Pegi's daughter, Amber Jean, and it moved into the publishing process, at which time Neil had not read any of it. That possibility had not even been discussed between us. From my standpoint, if anything in the book caused heartburn in the family or elsewhere, I thought it better that I take full responsibility. But there was one nagging doubt. I was uneasy about a single telling passage for which I was the only source. It was also, in a sense, hearsay, even though the hearsay in question was something his mother had said to me, with no other witnesses. So I knew I would feel better if I had some kind of backup (such as, I thought fleetingly, the Royal Navy).

Here I have to go back a bit. Years earlier I had been asked by the editor of *Rolling Stone* to write an article about Neil – his boyhood, early musical experiences, influences, and so on. I declined for a lot of reasons, one being that I didn't really know enough of the answers firsthand. During the course that he had travelled from his first plastic ukulele to where *Rolling Stone* would ask me for an article about him, his mother had been the main parental influence. I didn't want to suggest anything to the contrary. Instead, I kept turning down magazine and newspaper offers until – after Neil's comment that "its your life too, you know, Daddy" – I did write a long piece for *Toronto Life* magazine.

By that time, Neil and Pegi had been married for years, but in the *Toronto Life* photo layouts – not my domain – actress Carrie Snogress, Neil's companion for a few years and mother of my first grandson, Zeke, got more play than Pegi. This angered Neil, as he hotly pointed out to me by telephone. Pegi and their son Ben were at the heart of his life then. But I soon had a chance to right that wrong. The article led to my being approached by McClelland & Stewart in Toronto to do a more complete account, with up-to-date photo layouts, for book publication. I agreed. When the manuscript was ready, some publishers showed interest in buying U.S. rights. As a result, on a visit to New York, I took the manuscript with me.

Neil happened to be in New York at the same time and we saw one another frequently. My wish to check the one sensitive passage eventually got an airing.

I took the manuscript to Neil's hotel room and found the passage. He was having some painful back trouble at the time so, to make himself comfortable, he put a handful of pages on the floor and stretched out belly-down on what I recall was a long footstool, turning pages as he read.

Suddenly he stopped and went back a page or two.

"What have you got?" I asked.

"This didn't happen."

He was pointing to the passage that had bothered me, in which I mentioned some letters that Astrid, whom I would eventually marry, had written to me. Shortly after Rassy and I separated, Astrid had flown east and we had spent some time visiting my brother, Bob, his wife, Merle, and their family in Windsor while I was covering a hockey series in Detroit.

When Astrid went back home to Victoria, she may have thought I was staying on in Windsor with Bob and Merle until the hockey playoffs were over. Or, as I had not yet found an apartment in Toronto, Windsor may have been the only address Astrid had and believed that any letter addressed to me would be forwarded. She could not have known that before we even met, there was some history that involved Merle and Rassy. Merle did not like Rassy, and Rassy did not like Merle.

Over the years they had found more ways to show this antagonism than any of the rest of us could have imagined. They were always taking verbal shots at one another. War was always breaking out. Merle did not like Astrid, either, and once told her flatly, "If it was my husband you were stealing, I would have torn your eyes out."

Against that background, when those letters from Astrid to me arrived at Merle's home, I can only assume, knowing Merle's dislike for both Astrid and Rassy, that Merle saw it as an excellent opportunity to get even all around. Merle was absolutely sure that if she forwarded Astrid's letters (distinctive handwriting, Victoria, B.C., postmark) to me at my old pre-split address, Rassy would open them and read them.

That is exactly what happened.

I had a call from Rassy at my new apartment.

"Some *love* letters have arrived here from your *little lady* in Victoria," she told me. "I'll leave them in the milk chute and you can come and pick them up. And you should know that I read them and gave them to Bob and Neil to read, so they could see what kind of a cheating so-and-so they have for a father."

Then she hung up the phone.

This was the part that Neil was reading on the hotel-room floor in New York. "But she never showed us those letters!" he exclaimed.

I exclaimed right back, "But she told me she did give them to you and Bob to read! Otherwise I never would have put that in the book! Why would she tell me that she'd shown those letters to you and Bob if she hadn't?"

There was a brief silence while Neil's expression slowly changed to a little grin.

"She just wanted to make you feel good about yourself," he said.

In one of the many books written about Neil after he became famous, the author spent some time on the battles that were part of our family life (actually most authors don't know the half of it). One wrapped up those troubled times and our eventual divorce with the line, "They were never reconciled." That is correct, although there were a few grace notes along the way. In the summer of 1984, a couple of months before *Neil and Me* was published, I was at my desk at the farm working on something else when the phone rang.

"Scott?" The voice was a lot deeper than I had remembered, but I knew who was calling. "Rassy. I hear that your book is supposed to be published this fall. I just want you to know that I've talked to a lawyer about getting an injunction to stop publication."

I was shocked, momentarily. "On what grounds?"

"I was promised that I would be able to *edit* the book before publication. As you know, that hasn't happened. I don't know what kind of lies you've got in there."

The use of the word "edit" was rather outlandish, but I had made no such commitment to let her okay the book, and why did she think I would? She said Neil had assured her that she would see the manuscript before publication and, if she wished, object to anything that didn't accord with her version of the facts. As it happened, both of us knew that Neil and Pegi were on the ocean somewhere on his boat, the *W.N. Ragland*, and could not be reached to comment on what she was treating as a guarantee. She kept mentioning her conviction that publication could be stopped legally until she had made sure I was not misrepresenting the facts.

I didn't think there was much chance that she could stop publication, but I did have a little ammunition. I had written to her during my research, suggesting that I visit her in Florida to discuss my approach and to make sure that she had her say. She didn't answer my letter, but she had had a long interview with another writer working on a book about Neil (which was never published, although the writer, Cameron Crowe, had written about Neil in *Rolling Stone* from time to time). However, she was going to see my book eventually and I did not want publication to be halted, or hampered, by any protest she might make, in the courts or otherwise. So I made a decision.

I reminded her that I had given her a chance to say her piece, and that she had ignored the opportunity. "I don't think there is anything in the book that you can argue with but . . ."

"But what?"

"I have the manuscript right here. If you can believe the Purolator commercials, I can get a copy to you by tomorrow," I said. "If you find anything that you feel isn't true, you get back to me about it. I'll consider any objection you have and, if justified, I'll make changes. The only thing is, there isn't much time, so I have to insist that you get back to me by phone two days after you get the manuscript."

She agreed to that condition.

Two or three days later the phone rang.

"Scott? Rassy. Page twenty-two."

I had the manuscript at the ready.

"On page twenty-two you write that when my grandfather died, leaving mostly bills, my father, who was attending Virginia Military Institute at the time, quit school and went to New York and got a job on the Bowery and sent his wages home to pay tuition for his two sisters at Sweet Brier Academy, and did that until they graduated."

"Yes?" I said.

"He had *three* sisters at Sweet Brier."

I waited. "And that's it?"

Well, there was one other place. It involved Carrie Snodgress. Carrie's mother had died, and although Neil and Carrie were no longer living together at the time, he had decided to go with her to the funeral so she wouldn't be alone at such a difficult time. Rassy wanted me to add that she had also gone to the funeral with Neil and Carrie.

I made that correction and, after a few minutes, our conversation having become quite civil, she said that *Neil and Me* was a good book. "You never had to prove to me that you can write," she said. "I hope you sell a million copies."

When I recall that conversation now I remember how emotional I felt about Rassy saying that. In all of our life together, which was rarely really easy for her, she had never been other than behind me in what I was doing, trying to make a living as a writer to support our family. So many years after our separation and divorce, her few words about the book made me feel elated, on top of the world, that many wounds had healed. A few weeks later I mentioned to Neil what Rassy had said about the book and how much her approval had meant to me.

When he listened, that little grin signifying an imminent shoot-down showed again, and turned into a chuckle just as I was saying, "I was really surprised. I think I'd been expecting anything from her except that she liked the book."

"Well, Daddy," he said, "you're the only person she ever said that to."

I saw Rassy and Neil together for the last time in 1984. He was touring Canada with the International Harvesters in support of his country album, *Old Ways*, and Winnipeg was on his schedule. I drove to Ottawa for his concert there and phoned my mother, well into her eighties, in her longtime home of Flin Flon to pass on my reaction.

She was excited. "I'm going to the Winnipeg concert!" she said. "I can't miss this chance!" Flin Flon is about five hundred miles from Winnipeg and she had already arranged a ride. She had all Neil's albums, and a network of friends tipped her every time a radio station played one of his songs, but apart from on television she'd never seen him in action.

Rassy would be in Winnipeg as well. Mother had not seen Rassy for many years and was a little nervous about meeting her again after so much had happened – the breakup of our family, and the years of distant turmoil. But Neil had arranged everything and the only anxious moment, for me anyway, was when I and one of the backstage crew were guiding this frail old lady as she climbed a steep ramp to reach the backstage area just behind the band. From where we sat, out of sight behind the band, I could look out into the crowd and see Rassy in a front-row seat, actually in what during hockey games was the penalty box.

Neil had started his musical career in Winnipeg, of course, and in some ways this was a classic case of a crowd showing pride in a home-town boy making good in a big way. One of the best parts in that memorable evening was when Neil told the crowd that his next song would be dedicated to his mother, as he pointed to where Rassy was sitting, before the group played and sang one of his most familiar songs, "Heart of Gold." Then Neil said that his dad was "right back there" (indicating the backstage area) and the band members all turned and lifted their hats towards me and motioned to me to stand up, which I did, as they played another of his enduring hits, "Old Man."

I stood smiling, remembering a time years earlier when "Old Man" was a new hit. Neil and I were alone in front of the house at the farm. To set the record straight, at least as far as we were concerned, he told me that while a lot of people, including me, thought that song had been written for me, causing me occasionally to bask in that kind of warmth, in truth it had been written for a well-loved old hand at his ranch, Louis Avila. Many times later, when anyone mentioned the song as having been written for me, I made the correction, apparently without changing anyone's mind – people still refer to it as the song Neil wrote about me. So be it. It is still one of my favourites among his songs, "Heart of Gold" being another, because he had dedicated it to Rassy.

But there was more to that memorable night in Winnipeg. After the concert, when I helped Mother safely back down the ramp, all of us with close connections to our original family through blood and arguments and dislocations and broken marriages gathered in a sort of hospitality room, a big lower-level area away from the crowds. Mother and Rassy walked straight towards one another and clasped hands and chatted warmly. In a moment or two, when I approached them, Neil came behind us and put one arm around Rassy and one around me and hugged us both as he called out to cheers and applause, "This is something I've been wanting to do for years!"

I remember that scene as a turmoil of emotion. Shortly thereafter, Neil spoke to Joel Bernstein, his official archivist and photographer, and got Mother and Neil and me into a nearby corridor for a photo that we would later have framed and has ever since been hung prominently in every home we've had.

The next day, Mother, Pegi, Rassy, Neil, and a few others met for coffee and goodbyes at Mother's hotel. I wasn't there but Mother often talked later about what she called one of the big moments of her life.

I don't think Rassy and I spoke again. After Neil and family had taken off in his tour bus for the next concert farther west, at one point I saw Rassy at the airport, both of us carrying bags, holding tickets. I tried to catch her eye, for what I'm not sure. She passed a few feet from me but we didn't speak. I don't know if she saw me. I realize that if I'd been a writer of country songs and breaking, or broken, hearts, I could have made something of that. Or has it already been done?

The publishing history of *Neil and Me* had a few twists and turns even before the first hardcover edition went to press in 1984. At that time, I'd had to cut one longish passage because it concerned a complicated drug case before the courts involving eleven defendants including, in a minor and disputed role, Neil's older brother, Bob. At the time the charges had been laid, early in 1982, Bob, a golf pro, was in the United States. After discussions with Neil and me by telephone to the effect that Bob's best move would be to return voluntarily to Canada and defend himself, he did so, believing that the charges against him could not be substantiated. After he turned himself in he was freed on bail that Neil and I provided. That stage of the case did not end until June 1985, when convictions were handed down to all eleven defendants which, after numerous appeals, including Neil testifying on Bob's behalf, wound up with Bob serving about two years in Joyceville penitentiary, among the least of the eleven sentences.

With that court case out of the way, and the earlier cuts we had made to the full story no longer embargoed, McClelland and Stewart decided to publish a mass-market paperback edition in 1986 in which I could use much of the previously prohibited material. This new edition included an account of a visit Neil and I made to Bob at Joyceville. Neil was on a concert tour of the U.S. and Canada, heading for western Ontario, when he phoned me from somewhere in New York state to suggest that if he changed his schedule and crossed the Ontario border at Kingston instead of farther west, we could meet and could go together to visit Bob. We set it up.

The next day I drove south from the farm, parked my car at the Cobourg railway station, took a train to Kingston, and waited near the rendezvous Neil and I had agreed upon. Neil's tour bus turned off the highway right on schedule. I climbed in, with welcoming hugs all round, and I told his driver the moves to make from there to get us to the penitentiary gates, a first for both of us. Soon we were going through the heavy security routine, and then spent the sunny afternoon sitting outside in an enclosed area chatting some hours away until it was time for all visitors to leave. As we did so, at Neil's request, his driver let out a parting blast on the bus's horn – just to let them know we were gone.

Once during an earlier visit I made to Neil's ranch, he and I were out for a long walk around his property. At the time, he had made a switch to writing country music, which would lead to the album named for his song "Old Ways." He had played that song for me first on cassette in his tour bus during one of his travels to the American Midwest, but it was a while before I came to realize how serious he was about going into country.

He told me that he had done or was doing some recording with such great country musicians as Willie Nelson, Waylon Jennings, and Hank Williams, Jr. He spoke enthusiastically about the impact the country stars had on crowds. "They've been around for a long time, a lot longer than me, but to the country audiences they just get bigger and bigger. There's nobody in rock 'n' roll has that grand-old-man kind of impact on the public."

I said that by the time he and some other rock 'n' rollers had been around a few years longer, some would have the same kind of grand-old-man following, which has turned out to be the case.

But at the time he stuck to his guns and put together the International Harvesters for a big and successful tour of the U.S. and Canada.

In that and other ways, Neil did well by country. He didn't just skim off what advantage there was as a country music drop-in; he made himself a permanent part of the country music world, always one of those present at such huge fund-raising events as Farm Aid, and in other ways identifying, sometimes politically, with country concerns and country music people.

One of the perils of being the star's old man, as one veteran roadie confided to me somewhere in the middle or late 1980s when I'd been along for a few consecutive concerts, is that while I was okay, visitors were sometimes a problem. On a big concert tour, moving from venue to venue, there are routines of setting up, meeting emergencies, running sound checks, and generally making sure that everyone is on the ball in readiness for the concert, and any guest must take care not to be a distraction. This is not really difficult – keep out of the way, and take care not to ask questions that can wait. My experience as a journalist helps: just shut up and watch.

In most concert situations, when it's over Neil might disappear to a room backstage, first to be alone for a time, then to gradually unwind and perhaps discuss with other band members or backstage personnel whether this or that worked or didn't work, and why. I have been admitted to such post-mortems and once in a while even contributed.

For instance, on Neil's tour with the International Harvesters I told him during one backroom post-mortem that one of his songs that hadn't been included in the program – "Powderfinger," one of my favourites – would have fitted right in. He immediately called to some of the band members, "Hey, we could have used 'Powderfinger' in that song list." Then he went ahead and summarized the song for those in the band who didn't know it, and later in the tour it made it into the lineup. But in those situations I usually kept quiet and listened, rarely really understanding the technical level of their discussions.

Which brings me to a review in the 13 August 1994 *New Musical Express*, written by Gavin Martin about the Neil Young and Crazy Horse album, *Sleeps With Angels*. This review floated back and forth over Neil's career and the influences that Gavin Martin found reflected in the new album.

There's little that's reassuring or familiar about the Horse sound that Young, Billy Talbot, Poncho Sampedro and Ralph Molina have created here. The scouring attack that they've been perfecting since 1969's *Everybody Knows This Is Nowhere* . . . is hovering in the background but it's been displaced by odd instrumentation (flutes, accordion, vibes, bass marimbas), minimalist settings and ambient atmospheres. From this environment came beautifully frayed, elliptic and sadly meditative melodies. Soaring, diving and swooping at potent points from all periods in his career, *Sleeps With Angels* is a landmark Young album fusing many of the themes that have long preoccupied him – the cruel carnival of the fame game, the fate of the frontier spirit, apocalyptic endings and their after effect, the blight and macabre fallout from the drug culture, the enduring but redemptive power of love.

Enough ghosts haunt this record to make it seem like requiem, a valediction for American dreams turned to dust . . . and the ghost of Kurt Cobain, the subject at the centre of the title track. . . . It's fitting that Young – a driven and mercurial performer and a responsive and diligent documenter of the subculture that sired Cobain – should have been stricken by Cobain's death. The Nirvana man's suicide note quoted Young's infamous lines from 'Out of the Blue,' 'it's better to burn out than to fade away.'. . .

At the bottom of my photocopy of the review (only partially reproduced here), I made a note, more or less to myself: "I don't understand much of this." And later, another note to myself: "Everybody knows more about Neil than I do."

There's a lot of love floating around in our family. The original 1984 edition of *Neil and Me*, stands as a heartfelt record of one part of our lives. Others have written, will write, or are writing, books updating Neil's life. I happily leave them to it. For myself, I like the idea that where Neil is concerned we are father and son, not author and subject.

All the same, some things deserve to be on the record.

There are two distinct areas of Neil's and my relationship that belong under the general heading of keeping in touch. One goes back to the 1960s, when keeping in touch was minimal, but had its own importance, the other dates to the more recent past, which I will get to later.

When Neil made his first appearance at the Riverboat coffee house in Toronto, family friends of around his age tended to be rather hostile to me, as if frankly surprised that I cared enough about what he was doing to show up, which also happened at a later Toronto concert in the much larger and more prestigious Massey Hall.

A rather funny incident connected to that Massey Hall concert went back in time to before Neil's move to the United States. He'd been playing with the Mynah Birds, among whose faithful followers was a young woman whose husband was John Craig Eaton, a member of the Eaton family, as in the chain of Canadian department stores carrying that name. The Mynah Birds, chronically broke but always in need of more and better instruments and other musical supplies, made use of this Eaton connection by opening a line of credit, a charge account, with Eaton's in Toronto.

I first heard about this when the charge account was a few years old and Neil was in Toronto for the Massey Hall show, his first major solo concert there. I was writing a daily column for the *Globe and Mail* at the time, and occasionally exchanged greetings with John Craig Eaton at Maple Leaf Gardens, where he was one of a group of well-off young directors of Toronto's National Hockey League team, the Maple Leafs. There had been a lot of publicity for Neil's Toronto appearance and when I had a telephone call from Eaton, my first thought was that it must be connected to the concert.

It was, but not in the way I had anticipated.

Eaton said he was embarrassed to be making this call but his partners in the Eaton family business insisted that he must make every effort to settle what they felt Neil owed the store from way back in the Mynah Birds days. "We've tried every means we can think of to collect but nothing works. The reason I'm calling is to see if you use your influence with Neil and get this cleared up."

This was all news to me. How this charge account ever came into being, and under whose name, I don't know for sure. But after the Mynah Birds went kaput and scattered, leaving Neil and Bruce Palmer out of money and out of work, what was left (largely unpaid-for) was sold to help finance buying the 1953 black Pontiac hearse in which Neil, Bruce, and a few volunteers headed south to seek fame and fortune. Now, with Neil having become a bankable performer, Eaton was being pressed by his partners to collect what was owed.

"So what are you going to do?"

"We've thought about attaching the gate for his Massey Hall concert."

"But there were at least four or five people from time to time with the Mynah Birds!" I protested. "How come you're chasing Neil for the whole load?"

The answer was quite clear. "We put the account in Neil's name because, well . . . I knew them all, and he seemed the most responsible – in fact, the only one of them that our firm ever would have given credit to."

Somewhere in there was an unspoken suggestion that I might like to pay up, and protect the good name of the Youngs.

What I thought was, succinctly, "Not me, kid." What I said out loud was that if Eaton's had called me before opening the account and I had said okay, I would guarantee it, that would be one thing. Otherwise, count me out.

I don't know how the matter eventually was settled, but it was done without a sheriff and posse. If I mentioned the matter to Neil at all, which I doubt, I treated it as being none of my business. The only subsequent mention was in a note to me in which Neil plainly indicated that the whole matter had pissed him off, "but Johnny Eaton didn't lose any money."

But that was long ago and far away. Neil and I got on with our lives, seeing one another every chance we had. After my two divorces, my *Globe and Mail* colleague Margaret Hogan and I were married in Omemee in 1980. We were invited at various times to spend Christmas with Neil, Pegi, Zeke, Ben, Amber, and others of Pegi's family in California. But by then we had a lot of family within driving distance of our own big Christmases at the farm when Margaret and I would cut Christmas trees off our own property and the young fry would slide or roll, doing a lot of shrieking, down the hill behind the house. Other invitations, such as to spend Thanksgiving with Neil and Pegi and their kids, we accepted , and in these and other ways we stayed in touch whenever we had a chance.

Neil flew to Winnipeg to be there for my induction into the Manitoba Hockey Hall of Fame in 1992, along with others famous as players in the game that I only wrote about. The all-time great Bobby Hull was also one of the inductees that night. He got a laugh in his acceptance speech when he said that there were two of us on hand that night who had more or less lost some of our identity.

"I used to be Bobby Hull," he said, "but now I'm Brett Hull's father. And I look out there [pointing to me] and see the one who used to be Scott Young – the one who's laughing. I mean Neil Young's father."

I went to Thunder Bay in 1992 when Neil was honoured with a doctorate in music by Lakehead University. He stood there in his working clothes and big boots (he'd flown in from Detroit) and spoke tellingly of the importance of the degrees that young people there were celebrating – and of the degrees he'd never had. He also came to Omemee in 1993 with many others in our family for the official opening of the new Scott Young Public School, an honour the community had bestowed on me.

Somehow in there, harking back to when, as an early teenager, he sometimes came with me to Leaf games, he had become a supporter and season-ticket holder for the newly formed San Jose Sharks of the NHL. Once when the Sharks were in the Stanley Cup playoffs with the Leafs he flew to Toronto and we sat in the season-ticket seats I'd had forever, and when the Sharks scored a goal he sprang into the air, waving his fists and cheering, causing some Toronto fans (who possibly loved his music) to roar, "Sit down, you jerk!"

Sometimes when he was driving a noisy carload to a Sharks game he would phone from his car and we'd talk hockey. For the Sharks games he didn't have one of those celebrity boxes so common in sports venues now, but had arranged to have one section near his seats to be made wheelchair accessible for, among others, his son Ben and some of Ben's classmates from Bridge School for severely handicapped children, which Neil and Pegi had started and helped to develop.

In Ottawa, when Neil and other Canadian artists were presented in 1994 with Governor General's Awards for excellence in the performing arts, we were there along with other family members. (Am I starting to sound too proud? But what can I do?) One more: in Toronto for the NHL's 1995 Awards Neil and I were chosen to present the Hart Trophy, for the league's most valuable player, to Eric Lindros.

So now we can sober up: later that year when I was awaiting surgery for colon cancer, Neil and his brother, Bob, wanted to come, but I am not one for bedside vigils and told them, "Please don't."

When Rassy was laid low by her final illness late in 1990 (I was living in Ireland at the time) for months Neil spent much of his time near where she lived in the New Smyrna Beach house that he had pro‑vided for her in Florida many years earlier. When there were things or people that made her feel apprehensive or uncomfortable, for whatever reason, Neil kept them at a distance. When she died on the day before her seventy‑third birthday, he was the one who made funeral arrange‑ments and kept us all informed through phone calls and faxes.

Now to shift gears rather drastically from that sad time for all our family: I'm not really famous for doing things on the spur of the moment, but there are exceptions. When I learned that Neil's 1996 summer tour of Europe with Crazy Horse (Billy Talbot, Ralph Molina, and Poncho Sampedro) would wind up in Scotland and Ireland, and might even add a few notes to this book, that was enough. I called Neil to let him know I would be there, checked the state of my Visa card, called the travel agent and found that to catch his last two concerts in Europe I could fly direct Toronto to Glasgow for one, then proceed to Dublin somehow or other (I hadn't checked it out) for the other. On a bargain charter such as mine I had to book for a certain minimum length of travel time, in this case nearly two weeks. That was a huge added attraction for me – a chance to visit our in‑law relatives in Ireland, the Finnegans. When Margaret's daughter Erin had married ex‑Dubliner Niall Finnegan, nineteen Finnegans had come to Toronto for the wedding, and we all stayed close friends during subsequent years when we lived in Howth Village, a suburb of Dublin on the Irish Sea.

When I told Neil my plans, I asked, "How are you getting from Glasgow to Dublin?"

"Charter. We'll be all packed up and checked out of our hotel before the Glasgow concert, and when it's over we just go. Straight to the airport."

"Does the charter have room for me?" I asked.

"Sure!"

So I flew from Toronto to Glasgow feeling that I had touched all bases. Or at least a few of them.

I hadn't discussed hotel accommodation with anyone, and I'd be in Glasgow a full day before Neil and the band got in from a concert in England. So I had booked a room in a club that has a reciprocal arrange‑ment with a club I belong to in Toronto, the Royal Canadian Military Institute. However, when I got through customs and immigration in

Glasgow I could see a young man holding a placard reading SCOTT YOUNG. When I identified myself he told me I was booked into the Glasgow Hilton, where Neil, the band, and others working on the tour would stay when they got to Glasgow the following day. He had a car waiting, and when we were en route to the hotel he asked if I'd ever been to Glasgow before.

"You mean apart from in World War Two?"

He looked at me and grinned. "Yes."

I said I really had been there during that war, but not since. Why did he ask?

"You know, Neil has played concerts here before. The first time, I remember, I happened to be down in Central Station one day and I was sure I saw him sitting on the floor and playing his guitar and singing, with his hat or a dish or something on the floor beside him, with these huge crowds pouring off the trains and sometimes – you know the way they do – just dropping a coin or two for him."

I think I was gaping at least a little. Often when I see and hear musicians working in subways or street corners or around liquor stores, I wonder how many of them have dreams of great public success. Sometimes I throw some coins into a hat and they say thanks, or not, and I say, "Good luck" or "You sound good," or whatever. Usually when I do that I think of Neil, and of the long, long string of hopes or dreams that must be there in many street musicians well beyond the sound of coins clinking into their hats.

"Anyway," my driver said, "do you know if I could have been right that it was him? I've seen him often, you know, every time he's been to Glasgow."

"I really don't know," I said. "I never heard that one before."

"The last time he was here," the driver went on," Pegi, his wife, was with him and I drove her quite a bit, and once I asked her if he would do a thing like that and she laughed and she said she didn't know." He looked back at me. "Maybe you could ask him."

I remember this all very clearly now, but on that morning when it was happening I was very, very tired. I had been up early on the morning I left Canada for the overnight flight, and had not slept for twenty-four hours. (Someone might wish to interject here also that maybe a few years ago, when I was only seventy-five, that conversation about Neil playing for loose change in Central Station never would have left my mind until I had the answer.) After I got to bed that day I slept for about twenty hours and forgot about that driver and his question. At one time in my life as a writer and reporter I used to travel on the assumption that if I saw or heard anything that was truly interesting, I didn't even have to make notes – the matter would fight its way to my agenda sooner or later. This time that didn't happen. The next day, when Neil and his group arrived and we made plans to dine together and proceed to the concert venue, the matter of Neil and Central Station never crossed my mind.

By then, my Dublin-bound bags were downstairs with those of all the others, stowed in the van that would take us to the airport after the concert. For Neil and the band, after the last encore there was a swift change to dry clothes, cars waiting, a drive to the airport, out on the tarmac, unload, climb aboard the chartered jet to be met by the pilot and a young woman bearing cold pop and good sandwiches. Take off. It's not a long flight from Glasgow to Dublin. By not long after one in the morning Neil and I were sitting in the lounge of Dublin's Berkeley Court Hotel, having a beer. In Ireland's hotels, if you're registered, the bar doesn't close.

A couple of strays recognized Neil and we chatted awhile, then I told Neil that in the morning I was going to Howth, where Margaret and I lived for two years or so in the house we'd bought there, before the lure of home country and grandchildren, not necessarily in that order, brought us back. Howth is a thousand year-old fishing port on the Irish Sea and would be my favourite place to live, if we ever left Canada again.

I told Neil, while we sipped our beer, "On Sundays when we lived here we always went to a pub called the Pier House on Howth Harbour, a few minutes from our place. Great Irish music," I said. "If you're up to it when you wake up the driver could get you there. I think you'd enjoy it."

Before we went to our rooms I wrote it down for him: "Howth, Pier House."

"If I don't make it, you'll know I slept in," he said.

When I got downstairs to head for Howth the next morning Billy Talbot, an early riser, was in the lobby. I told him what I had in mind: a walk around Howth Harbour, an inspection tour of some of my former haunts before the pubs opened at twelve-thirty, which we did. When we stepped into the Pier House a few minutes later the band was starting up. I waved to my friend Eric Fleming, the band's leader, sitting in his usual corner spot against one wall while he played – guitar or banjo, fiddle, mandolin, whatever fitted – and sang.

People were beginning to gather. Eric waved and moved over on the padded bench to make room for me and Billy while Eric's band members I knew from many sessions in the past smiled and nodded. "I thought you might be here," Eric said.

I told him I'd left a note for Neil but didn't know if he'd make it. Our part of the pub was jammed when, maybe half an hour later, Eric said, "There he is now," and I looked up to see Neil and Elliot Roberts in the crowd. Eric moved again to make room for Neil and the session sent on uninterrupted. After another break, while Eric and Neil shook hands and Eric brought us some pints of Guinness, the session went on much longer than usual.

Near the end one of our Howth friends, May Crawford, organizer of guest tickets for the crowd of our Howth familiars who would be at the concert the next night, came in. She had just been walking by and saw the audience and came in to have a look.

Later, after a considerably extended closing time, near four o'clock, Neil and Billy Talbot and I headed uphill away from the harbour for a long walk along the cliffs behind Howth. Downhill was the sea. Where we walked we'd occasionally encounter something new to me and, I found out, not locally popular – barbed wire put up by people who had bought some of what used to be open land. But unchanged was the gorse and heather, a few ruins here and there, the sight of the sea, and of a few hardy souls out for Sunday walks as we were.

Back in Howth later in the afternoon we connected with the driver and car that had brought Neil and Elliot and had been left for us. We found a place for a good meal near the harbour while the car waited and later returned us to the hotel.

A good day in Howth. Like old times.

A day or so later, after the Dublin concert, the *Dublin Herald* covered Neil's visit to Howth under the headline, NEIL'S TRADI-TIONAL DAY BE THE SEA.

The legendary American [sic] rock star, who packed Dublin's Point Theatre last night with his usual quota of devotees . . . joined his father Scott Young for the Sunday morning session in the Pier House pub in Howth Village. Neil Young's surprise Howth visit was prompted by the long distance correspondence between Eric Fleming and the rock star's novelist father, Scott Young.

"Scott lived in Howth a few years ago when he was researching and writing a book and he used to come in here to listen to our Sunday sessions," Eric told me last night. "Scott told me he would return to Dublin and Howth some day. So two years later he walks into the Pier House with members of his son's backing band, Crazy Horse. He told me Neil would be in later and, sure enough, he arrived and got into the full session for an hour and a half. They had a great time. It was like a dream come true."

So now you know where to go on a Sunday if you're in Howth.

The next day it was back to business for the band – an afternoon sound check for that night's concert. What is a sound check? It is basically what is sounds like, but apart from that my notes are not helpful. The Crazy Horse musicians and Neil and other members of the crew were there, all busy with various things to fine-tune the sounds they wanted for that night's concert.

Fragments, perhaps not decipherable:

Voice of Neil: "I just need a little bit of the keyboard and a little bit of the voice."

Then Neil, on the organ: "Is it coming out? . . . The monitor is louder than the organ . . . Now take us down just a little bit . . . Now lets get the vocals. . . ." And in a few seconds, "Now a few more . . . That's real funny sound."

Neil is at the organ. Calls: "Now, will that volume be the same? That's pretty good sound." At that point Crazy Horse appeared with some suggestions. Ralph Molina calls: "All hands back on stage, trying out sounds." And a little later: "That's good!"

And we left go back to the hotel, I, for one, none the wiser. We had dinner. Everyone was packed and ready. Luggage was being taken down to the van for the quick take-off. And it was when we were having dinner that night, just the few of us, that I suddenly remembered the big question.

"Hey, Neil," I said. "The driver who brought me from the airport yesterday told me that one time you were here before, he was sure he saw you at Central Station, sitting on the floor and playing your guitar and singing while people dropped coins into whatever you had with you."

"Yeah?" he said.

"Did that really happen?"

He seemed to think it over, for a few seconds, then looked around the table, everybody all ears.

"Yes, I did that once," he said.

There was laughter and a few unclassifiable sounds of belief or disbelief as I asked, "How did you make out?"

"Pretty good," he said. "I took in about a pound, maybe a little more."

More laughter, exclamations, and so on.

I asked, "Why did you do that?"

Again, a thoughtful few seconds. "I just wanted to know how it felt."

He told me later that the incident had been filmed by the crew that's always in attendance, mostly unseen.

"We film everything, for my archives," he said. "But it's never been shown."

The concert a few hours later in Dublin had some of the same qualities as earlier concerts on the tour – the real rock 'n' roll fans got their kicks, but maybe the fans of his early folkie days could have used a little more of the sweeter side of Neil Young. Still, everyone said it was a great crowd, and great music deserves a great crowd.

When the band came off the stage at the end, I patted Neil on the shoulder. His clothes were soaking wet. He plays that way, all out. But right then he had something else on his mind, besides that the tour was now over, home and family and his new tour bus waiting.

"Are the guests still around?"

I said yes.

"As soon as I get some dry clothes on, I'll be there."

At the Point Theatre in Dublin, a onetime harbour warehouse, there is a good bar well back of the stage area for concert guests – a great idea – this night including several dozens of our friends from Howth and Shane and Anne and Kieran and others among our Finnegan relatives sitting at tables having a drink or two. In a few minutes Neil walked in, dry, ready for conversation and picture-taking, questions, an easy atmosphere. He stayed on for an hour or so before we broke for the airport, that part of the tour over, with Neil and me hugging our goodbyes before he headed for the charter that would take him to Heathrow for a flight the next day to Florida, where he wanted to check on the new tour bus he was having built there; then he'd move home to California, while I had a free week or so around Dublin.

"What are you going to do in Dublin?" he asked.

"Check out of the hotel," I said. "Getting photos processed, moving in to stay with the senior Finnegans, Kathleen and Ned, driving across Ireland to Galway for a few days of Festival Week there with Kieran and Anne Finnegan and their two daughters and one son. I'm going to have a great time. . . ."

And so I did, staying at the home of two of Anne and Kieran's friends. It was race week in Galway, and Arts Festival Week, streets and pubs jammed, music playing on every corner, and after a couple of days we headed back across to Dublin, with one leisurely stop at a place I'd always wanted to see, the ancient religious site at Clonmacnois.

A week later at Ned and Kathleen's I was planning how I'd get to the airport (taxi to airport bus terminal and on from there) when Ned Finnegan waved all that away. "I'm driving you to the airport," he said, and did, and soon I was flying home. By that time I knew Neil was resting up for the next dates in his long tour – mainly concerts across the United States but with one in Canada at Barrie, Ontario, before returning to the main U.S. and Canada part of the tour, during which he and Elliot and driver Joe McKenna made the long haul from a concert in Columbus, Ohio, through Labour Day weekend traffic, and parked the two tour buses (Neil's new one and Elliot's road headquarters) beside the fire hall in Omemee. Neil signed autographs and stood for group photos with the Omemee kids who had heard he was there, then he and Elliot and Joe came out to the farm to join us and my son Bob for lasagna, wine, and a beer or two. (Joe, as full-time driver, drinks only water.) For a few hours around our big old table at the farm, built from our own maple and ash, we had a lot of laughs, then they had to move on to the next concert, go on with the North American phase of his 1996 tour. There are so many farewells in a tour that they tend to be kept short, even perfunctory, although with warmth and hugs.

Our farewells that night, back at the buses, were mainly along the lines of, "Until the next time," or, "À la prochaine."

Discography

Neil Young (released November 1968): The Emperor of Wyoming; The Loner; If I Could Have Her Tonight; I've Been Waiting for You; The Old Laughing Lady; String Quartet from Whiskey Boot Hill; Here We Are in the Years; What Did You Do to My Life; I've Loved Her So Long; The Last Trip to Tulsa.

Everybody Knows This Is Nowhere (May 1969): Cinnamon Girl; Everybody Knows This Is Nowhere; Round & Round (It Won't Long); Down by the River; The Losing End (When You're On); Running Dry (Requiem for the Rockets); Cowgirl in the Sand.

After The Gold Rush (September 1970): Tell Me Why; After the Gold Rush; Only Love Can Break Your Heart; Southern Man; Till the Morning Comes; Oh, Lonesome Me; Don't Let It Bring You Down; Birds; When You Dance I Can Really Love; I Believe in You; Cripple Creek Ferry.

Harvest (February 1972): Heart of Gold; Harvest; Old Man; There's a World; Alabama; The Needle and the Damage Done; Words; Are You Ready for the Country; A Man Needs a Maid; Out on the Weekend.

Journey Through The Past (soundtrack; November 1972): For What It's Worth; Mr. Soul; Rock & Roll Woman; Find the Cost of Freedom; Ohio; Southern Man; Are You Ready for the Country; Let Me Call You Sweetheart; Alabama; Words; God Bless America; Relativity Invitation; Handel's *Messiah*; King of Kings; Soldier; Let's Go Away for a While.

Time Fades Away (August 1973): Time Fades Away; Journey Through the Past; Yonder Stands the Sinner; L.A.; Love in Mind; Don't Be Denied; The Bridge; Last Dance.

On The Beach (July 1974): Walk On; See the Sky About to Rain; Revolution Blues; For the Turnstiles; Vampire Blues; On the Beach; Motion Pictures; Ambulance Blues.

Tonight's The Night (June 1975): Tonight's the Night; Speakin' Out; World on a String; Borrowed Tune; Come On Baby Let's Go Downtown; Mellow My Mind; Roll Another Number (For the Road); Albuquerque; New Mama; Lookout Joe; Tired Eyes; Tonight's the Night – Part II

Zuma (November 1975): Don't Cry No Tears; Danger Bird; Pardon My Heart; Lookin' For a Love; Barstool Blues; Stupid Girl; Drive Back; Cortez the Killer; Through My Sails.

American Stars 'N Bars (May 1977): The Old Country Waltz; Saddle Up the Palomino; Hey Babe; Hold Back the Tears; Bite the Bullet; Star of Bethlehem; Will to Love; Like a Hurricane; Homegrown.

Decade (October 1977): Down to the Wire; Burned; Mr. Soul; Broken Arrow; Expecting to Fly; Sugar Mountain; I Am a Child; The Loner; The Old Laughing Lady; Cinnamon Girl; Down by the River; Cowgirl in the Sand; I Believe in You; After the Gold Rush; Southern Man; Helpless; Ohio; Soldier; Old Man; A Man Needs a Maid; Harvest;

Heart of Gold; Star of Bethlehem; The Needle and the Damage Done; Tonight's the Night; Tired Eyes; Walk On; For the Turnstiles; Winterlong; Deep Forbidden Lake; Like a Hurricane; Love Is a Rose; Cortez the Killer; Campaigner; Long May You Run.

Comes A Time (November 1978): Goin' Back; Comes a Time; Look Out for My Love; Lotta Love; Peace of Mind; Human Highway; Already One; Field of Opportunity; Motorcycle Mama; Four Strong Winds.

Rust Never Sleeps (May 1979): My My, Hey Hey (Out of the Blue); Thrasher; Ride My Llama; Pocahontas; Sail Away; Powderfinger; Welfare Mothers; Sedan Delivery; Hey Hey, My My (Into the Black).

Live Rust (October 1979): Sugar Mountain; I Am a Child; Comes a Time; After the Gold Rush; My My, Hey Hey (Out of the Blue); When You Dance I Can Really Love; The Loner; The Needle and the Damage Done; Lotta Love; Sedan Delivery; Powderfinger; Cortez the Killer; Cinnamon Girl; Like a Hurricane; Hey Hey, My My (Into the Black); Tonight's the Night.

Hawks & Doves (October 1980): Little Wing; The Old Homestead; Lost in Space; Captain Kennedy; Stayin' Power; Coastline; Union Man; Comin' Apart at Every Nail; Hawks & Doves.

Re-ac-tor (October 1981): Opera Star; Surfer Joe and Moe the Sleaze; T-Bone; Get Back On It; Southern Pacific; Motor City; Rapid Transit; Shots.

Trans (November 1982): Little Thing Called Love; Computer Age; We R In Control; Transformer Man; Computer Cowboy (aka Syscrusher); Hold on to Your Love; Sample and Hold; Mr. Soul; Like an Inca.

Everybody's Rockin' (June 1983): Betty Lou's Got a New Pair of Shoes; Rainin' in My Heart; Payola Blues; Wonderin'; Kinda Fonda Wanda; Jellyroll Man; Bright Lights, Big City; Mystery Train; Everybody's Rockin'.

In addition, there's Neil's work with others: three albums with Buffalo Springfield; three with Crosby, Stills, Nash and Young; one album shared with Stephen Stills; approximately 104 two-song singles; a 1984 single which is a duet with Willie Nelson; one three-song EP; between eighty and ninety bootleg albums compiled and marketed openly in London and many other large cities; and an estimated ninety album-length tapes of material recorded surreptitiously at concerts for compilation into albums circulated on the bootleg market.

━ ━

Since *Neil and Me* was first published in 1984, the numbers of collaborations, singles, EPs, limited editions – and bootlegs – have only increased. Aside from the official solo releases listed below, also of note are Neil's excursions into movie soundtracks. He wrote and recorded the song "Philadelphia" for the 1993 film of the same name starring Tom Hanks – and was honoured with an Oscar nomination. More recently, he composed and performed the soundtrack for Jim Jarmusch's *Dead Man* (1996) starring Johnny Depp.

Old Ways (August 1985): The Wayward Wind; Get Back to the Country; Are There Any More Real Cowboys?; Once an Angel; Misfits; California Sunset; Old Ways; My Boy; Bound for Glory; Where Is the Highway Tonight?

Landing On Water (July 1986): Weight of the World; Violent Side; Hippie Dream; Bad News Beat; Touch the Night; People on the Street; Hard Luck Stories; I Got a Problem; Pressure; Drifter.

Life (July 1987): Mideast Vacation; Long Walk Home; Around the World; Inca Queen; Too Lonely; Prisoners of Rock 'n' Roll; Cryin' Eyes; When Your Lonely Hearts Break; We Never Danced.

This Note's For You (April 1988): Ten Men Workin'; This Note's for You; Coupe de Ville; Life in the City; Twilight; Married Man; Sunny Inside; Can't Believe Your Lyin'; Hey Hey; One Thing.

Freedom (October 1989): Rockin' in the Free World; Crime in the City (Sixty to Zero Part I); Don't Cry; Hangin' on a Limb; Eldorado;

The Ways of Love; Someday; On Broadway; Wrecking Ball; No More; Too Far Gone; Rockin' in the Free World.

Ragged Glory (October 1990): Country Home; White Line; F*!#in' Up; Over and Over; Love to Burn; Farmer John; Mansion on the Hill; Days That Used to Be; Love and Only Love; Mother Earth (Natural Anthem).

Weld (October 1991): Hey Hey, My My (Into the Black); Crime in the City; Blowin' in the Wind; Welfare Mothers; Love to Burn; Cinnamon Girl; Mansion on the Hill; F*!#in' Up; Cortez the Killer; Powderfinger; Love and Only Love; Rockin' in the Free World; Like a Hurricane; Farmer John; Tonight's the Night; Roll Another Number.

Arc (November 1991)

Harvest Moon (October 1992): Unknown Legend; From Hank to Hendrix; You and Me; Harvest Moon; War of Man; One of These Days; Such a Woman; Old King; Dreamin' Man; Natural Beauty.

Lucky Thirteen (January 1993): Sample and Hold; Transformer Man; Depression Blues; Get Gone; Don't Take Your Love Away from Me; Once an Angel; Where Is the Highway Tonight?; Hippie Dream; Pressure; Around the World; Mideast Vacation; Ain't It the Truth; This Note's for You.

Unplugged (June 1993): The Old Laughing Lady; Mr. Soul; World on a String; Pocahontas; Stringman; Like a Hurricane; The Needle and the Damage Done; Helpless; Harvest Moon; Transformer Man; Unknown Legend; Look Out for My Love; Long May You Run; From Hank to Hendrix.

Sleeps With Angels (August 1994): My Heart; Prime of Life; Driveby; Sleeps With Angels; Western Hero; Change Your Mind; Blue Eden; Safeway Cart; Train of Love; Trans Am; Piece of Crap; A Dream That Can Last.

Mirrorball (June 1995): Song X; Act of Love; I'm the Ocean; Big Green Country; Truth Be Known; Downtown; What Happened

Yesterday; Peace and Love; Throw Your Hatred Down; Scenery; Fallen Angel.

Broken Arrow (June 1996): Big Time; Loose Change; Slip Away; Changing Highways; Scattered (Let's Think About Livin'); This Town; Music Arcade; Baby What You Want Me to Do.

Musical Family Tree

Neil and his high-school friend Ken Koblun were mainstays of several Winnipeg teenaged groups (1962–64), including **The Jades**, **The Esquires**, and **Stardust**, before putting together **The Squires**, rated by Winnipeg rock radio stations in the top three among a hundred or so groups competing for high school and community club dance gigs in 1963 and 1964. The Squires played out-of-town dates in such Manitoba localities as Selkirk, Churchill, and Portage la Prairie before getting into the $350-a-week (for the whole band) range in Fort William, Ontario (now part of Thunder Bay). In the summer of 1965 Neil landed in Toronto and, after a few hungry months, made his first real Toronto connection with a group called

The Mynah Birds (October '65 to February '66), led by Bruce Palmer and including Ricky James Matthews (later to become famous as Rick James). With Neil playing lead on a twelve-string guitar, they were recording for Motown in Detroit when Ricky was arrested for having taken a long unauthorized vacation from the United States Navy. His incarceration on those grounds broke up the band, causing Bruce and Neil to hightail it for Los Angeles, where they soon were among the founding fathers of

Buffalo Springfield (March '66 to May '68), the originals being Neil, Bruce, Stephen Stills, Richie Furay, and Dewey Martin. Springfield was an immediate west coast hit, but the members (in their late teens and early twenties) didn't know how to handle the fame, the women, the travel, and their own interpersonal rivalries, so after two hectic years (which including fill-in playing by Jim Fielder, Ken Koblun, and Jim Messina, because Bruce was busted a couple of times) Springfield split. Neil made one album of his own work before hooking up with three musicians with whom he played as

Neil Young and Crazy Horse (February '69 to the present, off and on). His first Crazy Horse musicians were Danny Whitten (guitar), Billy Talbot (bass), and Ralph Molina (drums). Their first album was *Everybody Knows This Is Nowhere*, released just before Stephen Stills, by then in a trio with David Crosby and Graham Nash, knocked on Neil's door and asked him to join up, which he did, that group then becoming

Crosby, Stills, Nash and Young (June '69 now and then to February '75 and maybe not finished yet). Their second gig ever was Woodstock, and over the next year they became the biggest super-group of their time, even though Neil continued to tour and record separately with Crazy Horse. Whitten's deepening involvement with heroin caused Neil to split from Crazy Horse for a while, but in late 1972, Whitten overdosed and died after not making the grade in a tryout to join a new group Neil called

The Stray Gators (late '71 to May '73), with Ben Keith on steel guitar, Kenny Buttrey on drums (later replaced by Johnny Barbata), Tim Drummond on bass, Jack Nitzsche on piano and slide guitar. Their financially record-breaking *Time Fades Away* tour produced a live album by the same name before Neil, feeling that he was becoming middle-of-the-road and wishing to head for the ditch, founded

The Santa Monica Flyers, with Talbot, Molina, Keith, Drummond, and Nils Lofgren (guitar, keyboards, etc.). Their music was so starkly despairing that the album *Tonight's The Night* wasn't released for two years, by which time Neil had reconstituted

Crazy Horse, with Danny Whitten gone but not forgotten, and Frank Sampedro joining Talbot and Molina. They played together off and on for several albums and tours over the next few years before Neil put together his

Trans Band to record and tour. This group included Lofgren, Keith, Bruce Palmer (who'd been doing little over the years except playing the sitar), Ralph Molina, and Joe Lala. On the *Trans* album but not on the tour, were Talbot and Sampedro. *Trans* was Neil's synthesized and vocoded lunge into the 1980s, but he instantly evened things up by rolling back the clock for a 1950s rockabilly group called

The Shocking Pinks, with 1950s-style music and instrument played by Keith (sax), Drummond (string bass), and snare-drummer Karl Himmel, plus a backup doo-wah singing group called **The Redwood Boys**: Larry Byrom, Rick Palombi, and Anthony Crawford. Byrom also played piano, and a Nashville lawyer named Craig Hayes played sax. Actor Newell Alexander filled various roles, including that of dance-party host (à la 1950s). The *Everybody's Rockin'* album was the labour of this temporary crew; Neil has since changed it into a more country-oriented aggregation called

The International Harvesters, with twin fiddles by Anthony Crawford and Rufus Thibodeau, Keith and Drummond on pedal steel and bass respectively, Himmel on drums, and Spooner Oldham on keyboards. They wowed 'em in Los Angeles and Austin, Texas, in the summer of 1984 before joining the likes of Willie Nelson, Waylon Jennings, and Hank Williams, Jr., to play country music on an extensive tour of the United States and Canada.

In addition to these musicians, dozens of others appear on Neil's albums – some making single guest appearances on stage or in the studio, others coming in often when Neil felt their particular talents would fit a certain song or mood.

Since the original publication of *Neil and Me* in 1984, Neil has continued to perform and record with a wide array of musicians as his mood and the mood of his songs dictate.

The massive Live Aid famine relief benefit concert in 1985 saw him perform both solo, and with old cohorts **Crosby, Stills and Nash**. Three years later they recorded the album *American Dream* together. In 1986, he teamed up with guitarist/producer Danny Kortchmar and percussionist Steve Jordan for the synthesizer-flavoured *Landing On Water*.

He has frequently renewed his long association with **Crazy Horse** (Ralph Molina, Poncho Sampedro, and Billy Talbot): *Life* (1987), *Ragged Glory* (1990), the live albums *Arc/Weld* (1991), *Sleeps With Angels* (1994), and, most recently, *Broken Arrow* (1996).

Shifting gears again, Neil formed a blues-style band, **The Blue-notes**, for 1988's *This Note's For You*. The musicians included Poncho Sampedro and Ben Keith, as well as a distinctly bluesy horn section. This same collection of musicians, as well as a few more (including Linda Ronstadt) joined Neil to record *Freedom* (1989).

Following an album and tour with Crazy Horse, Neil's music became distinctly mellower as he recorded *Harvest Moon* (1992). He recruited **The Stray Gators** to recapture the right mood to echo the original *Harvest*, with Spooner Oldham taking over on piano, and Neil's half-sister Astrid helping with background vocals.

In 1993, after meeting them at the Bob Dylan Thirtieth Anniversary concert (which Neil dubbed "Bobfest"), Neil toured with Memphis soul legends **Booker T. and the MGs** (Booker T. Jones, Steve Cropper, Duck Dunn, and Jim Keltner) as his backing band. They did not release any studio recordings – but Neil did record with another band on the same tour bill. New superstar band **Pearl Jam** (Eddie Vedder, Stone Gossard, Jeff Ament, Mike McCready, and Jack Irons), who had already openly professed their admiration for Neil, recorded sessions with him that would be released as *Mirrorball* (1995).

In 1996, Neil hooked up once again with **Crazy Horse**, not only for the album *Broken Arrow*, but also for the mammoth European and North American tour that followed – from June 20 in Zurich, Switzerland, to November 10 in Buffalo, New York.